Praise for *Change Your Space, Change Your Culture*

"'We're leaving behind a complicated world that operated like a machine, to a much more complex world that operates more like an ecosystem,' he states, in a nutshell, the big idea behind workplaces that work in a hyperconnected world."

—Susan S. Szenasy
Publisher and Editor-in-Chief

"*Change Your Space* clearly articulates the power of technology as an influential business tool inside the workspace. It illustrates the importance of helping employees connect and collaborate to improve their productivity. Technology is rapidly evolving, affecting the way people think and work in their office environment. The key points that Mr. Miller and his coauthors present are among the leading concepts for the future of the workplace."

—Lew Horne
President of CBRE, Greater Los Angeles–Orange County

"This book is an excellent treatise on a topic that has been long underserved. Every CEO should be personally involved in the design of the work environment, and this is the book to read if you want to understand why that's important, what you should care about and how to proceed."

—Dave Gray
author of *The Connected Company*

"*Change Your Space* will transform the way you think about workspace. An insipid workspace is worse than a lost opportunity; it is a lodestone in a world where companies must innovate to survive. This book offers actionable insights and real world examples to demonstrate how and why your workspace is critical for forming, shaping, and retaining the sort of team and culture required for success. I found it so compelling that I'm planning to incorporate the book into my Building Innovation Teams and Cultures MBA course at Kellogg."

—Joe Dwyer
Partner at Founder Equity and Digital Intent; and teacher of
innovation at Northwestern University Kellogg School of Management

"Miller and his fellow research team are great investigative reporters. The goal of their investigation is to find out why 70 percent of today's workforce feel disengaged and why we are locked in an antiquated 'industrial era' culture that has little to do with today's increasingly 'highly networked, team-based, and transparent' reality. The authors' modus operandi for accomplishing this task is to study more than 20 companies that have achieved a degree of innovation, collaboration, engagement, agility, and sustainability. Although there is no single road map for achieving this new culture, the book provides numerous insights into creating an innovative culture that reflects the emerging nature of work and the workplace.

—Eric Teicholz
IFMA Fellow, Director, Board of Directors

"*Change Your Space* is a profound book that any leader interested in employee engagement and innovation should read. Given my career in commercial real estate, it was refreshing to see a research-based analysis of how to use office space as a catalyst for improving a company's culture. Our industry has been very slow to adapt and change, but I believe that is about to change. *Change Your Space* makes it clear that every company can improve their work place environments and achieve stunning results. Any company that does not change will increasingly be left behind in the ever more competitive race to attract and retain talent."

—Richard Kincaid
former President and Chief Executive
Officer of Equity Office Properties Trust

"Everything has or is changing: phones, computers, TVs, cars, music, communication. Office space has not changed for many decades and needs to be rethought for a new age. *Change Your Space* leads the way in reimagining why and how our offices need to change."

—Pat Sullivan
cofounder of ACT! Software and CEO of Contata

"Having taken a small startup venture to a NYSE listed company in five years, we faced constant change in applying our disruptive methods to a legacy industry. This book gets at the underlying connections of behavior, culture, and workplace and their impact on execution in the face of broad changes now happening across the economy."

—Doug Brien and Gary Beasley
Co-CEOs, Starwood Waypoint Residential Trust.

"*Change Your Space* uncovers the next dimension of the triple bottom line—where success is inherently rooted in a culture of rich engagement in the workplace. While this requires a somewhat complex formula, the brain trust behind this book has outlined a very clear business case for environments that foster collaboration and innovation. As society continues to evolve at lightning speed, healthy, vibrant work environments are within reach—thanks to this forward-thinking, thought-provoking, must-read book."

—Barbie Wentworth
President and CEO of MB Advertising

"As a two-time CEO of dynamic, fast-growth, tech companies I never underestimated the importance of physical space in energizing the people and driving culture; Rex's team gets it. This book is a must-read for leaders who want to compete in the new business climate and get their employees out of cubicle purgatory."

—Bob Vanech
founding Board Member of the 2020
Los Angeles World's Fair

"I am a proponent of matching the workplace to the culture to sustain innovation and creativity. Hill & Wilkinson has created a new position for a Culture Manager to assure that our corporate actions align with our culture. Case4Space is right on target with their thoughts about the importance of culture."

—Greg Wilkinson
Co-Chairman of Hill & Wilkinson

"Rex Miller and his collaborators have created an important book that has the boldness to propose that workspace can be used as an agent of change. *Change Your Space, Change Your Culture* is a thought-provoking publication that should be read by not just designers and architects, but anyone involved in leading organizations."

—Michael Schley
CEO and Founder, FM:Systems, Chair, Workplace Strategy Summit

"As business leaders we have the unique opportunity and duty to positively affect today's working culture. It is literally changing before our eyes. *Change Your Space* provides live examples and a road map for transforming static culture and becoming the innovative organizations our people will love to work in."

—Patrick Sean Kelley
Chief Creative Officer *MARTZPARSONS*

"This is a fascinating exploration of the multiple ways our work environments are hindering or helping us get things done. Rex Miller has done a remarkable job of chronicling the significant changes afoot in our culture and their impact on consciousness—a terrific treaty on the power that *form* has on *function*."

—David Allen
author of *Getting Things Done*

Change Your Space, Change Your Culture

How Engaging Workspaces Lead to Transformation and Growth

Rex Miller
Mabel Casey
Mark Konchar

WILEY

CONTENTS

FOREWORD

A lbert Einstein once defined insanity as doing the same thing over and over again and expecting different results. I'm guessing he would not have looked fondly at the progress we've made in workplace design over the last 15 years. When I first met Rex, he recognized the disconnect between what employers and employees were asking for and what the industry was delivering in workplace design. He also knew that to move the conversation forward, he needed to tap into new sources of information, test new paradigms, and take nothing for granted. Case4Space has done just that; it's a critical look at the value of space in our enterprises—the need for more than the status quo.

At Google, we design our workplace to build community, to increase velocity, and to inspire and motivate, while eliminating friction and focusing on employee health. There isn't a one-size-fits-all solution. It starts with our users and listening to our employees. It's about creating a workplace that supports their needs and our company's culture. Case4Space is the perfect reminder that just as our business is constantly evolving, so must our physical environment remain a strategic advantage. We must use spaces differently, try new things, be flexible, adapt . . . and keep listening.

Rex Miller, Mabel Casey, and Mark Konchar along with the Case4Space team have put us all on notice—we can't continue to do the same things and expect different results. I'm excited to see where the conversation leads us as more people read this pioneering book.

—David Radcliffe
Vice President, Real Estate and Workplace Services, Google

FOREWORD

Human capital is every organization's greatest asset in today's knowledge economy. How we inspire, encourage, and motivate our people can make the difference between success and failure in a quickly changing and forward-thinking world. As business leaders, we are increasingly asking our people to think big, to be creative and innovative. All too often we are asking them to do this in workspaces that don't support that mindset. *Change Your Space* sets the stage for our collective evolution in better supporting our people with the environments they need to operate, and thrive, in today's business landscape.

At Balfour Beatty, we build vital structures for our clients. To do this successfully, we must have a thorough understanding of their broader business goals. They see us as not just builders but as relentless allies for their business. As a result, our clients have often come to us to have conversations about extracting more value out of their real estate portfolios. In recent years, however, we have seen our most innovation-focused, strategic clients evolving the dialogue to focus on unlocking the capabilities of their people.

Unlocking that potential requires a new process and a new way of thinking, because creating an engaging workplace requires an engaging process where owners tap the talent working within their organizations as much as they do the talent of the project teams building their new workspaces.

This subject is also very relevant for us here at Balfour Beatty since we are making a cultural shift ourselves. We are evolving our learning organization through enabling greater connection to ideas and innovations across teams, functions, divisions, and geographies. This shift takes a new type of environment, and several of our offices have made the *Change Your Space* leap. Our employees on those teams responded the way we anticipated—with minds more open, more engaged, more inspired, and increasingly collaborative with one another and our clients.

This read is essential for executive chiefs, human resources leaders, designers, brokers, facility managers, builders, project managers, and anyone who has a role in creating the spaces we work in today and for tomorrow.

Join us. It's a great opportunity to unlock hidden value in your organization, right within your own walls.

—Mark Layman
CEO Balfour Beatty Construction Services U.S.

FOREWORD

Throughout my three generations of experience providing customers with effective office interiors, I have recognized in an intuitive way that the environments we provide for our workers are powerful culture-shaping tools. You simply can't expect to maintain a productive, pleasant, and efficient workplace if your workers can't wait to get away from their place of business. Simply stated, spaces help to create culture. Good workspaces, designed with the needs of employees in mind, support a positive culture.

That's why we've always sought to provide our own members with interior solutions that fully support their best work. At the same time, we've tried to bring the power of science to bear in providing the best work spaces to our customers. We study how people work, and what makes them successful. We embrace a passion for partnering with our customers to investigate and solve their workplace challenges and fulfill their vision for success.

It is gratifying, then, to see our intuitive and research-backed theory of developing effective interior environments borne out once again in Rex Miller's powerful new book *Change Your Space, Change Your Culture*. Rex's work is based on a thorough study of more than a dozen organizations that have energized and engaged their employees through the effective use of space. As he points out in his book, failure to give employees an environment that inspires collaboration and teamwork can result in a downward spiral of disengagement and failure.

It's time to shift the conversation and deepen the connection between work environments and business needs. But doing so requires the creative development of spaces that engage the work styles of a diverse universe of employees of all backgrounds and every age.

Change Your Space builds on the power first cultivated in what was called the *Mindshift* initiative—a consortium of thought leaders whose work resulted in a volume titled *The Commercial Real Estate Revolution*. *Mindshift* was dedicated to making the workplace a strategic tool that can positively influence an organization's culture. I have experienced the power of this strategy during the renovation of our own corporate headquarters in 2008. By applying what we learned from our research, we created an engaging space that enables our people to work more productively.

We're convinced that space is a catalyst that can change behaviors and transform businesses for the better. If you recognize this truth, I urge you to read this book and put it to work for you. As leaders in the rapidly changing and competitive twenty-first century, one of our greatest opportunities for success lies in creating inspiring spaces that enrich your employees and benefit your organization. *Change Your Space, Change Your Culture* can give you the foundation to do that.

—Matthew R. Haworth
Chairman of Haworth, Inc.

The From/To Formula

I s there a case for space as a tool to produce a culture of innovation in our workplaces? That question drove this book.

And here's the spoiler: "Yes." But you really need to watch the whole movie.

Yes, you can change your company culture. But those who want to fully utilize that tool must make a commitment to the effort. That's because innovation is always disruptive. Some companies are in better condition for that bull ride into innovation than others, but most companies can make the leap. This book shares some surprisingly simple lessons about what these consistently innovative companies do differently, and how you can do it, too.

It all starts with the From/To Formula. Think of it as this progression:

1. Innovation begins with a departure. Regardless of how we feel or what it costs, a changing world demands that we leave the comfort of our current conditions. We can do it kicking and screaming or we can go with confidence and curiosity.
2. The other side of innovation will be radically different. It will require new tools, new values, new behaviors, and . . . new people.
3. Culture is the challenge. The old culture that once brought success will hold on and resist attempts at change.

4. A new culture will form only if the invisible bonds of the old habits are disrupted and an environment that supports desired new behaviors and values erected.
5. Space is the catalyst to disrupt and transform culture.

I have to admit that we were surprised and encouraged to find that many leaders really do care about that formula. They are pressing in to understand the relationship between culture and engagement. And we also found an emerging shift. Despite the history of consultants acting on behalf of the owner and filtering them out of the process, a new breed of consultants is emerging. They have embraced design thinking. This approach to design leads to a social and engaging space solution that is exciting and liberating. It invites all the stakeholders, including those who will work in the space, to participate in its design. Perhaps the true test of success for space design is if it feels like "home" to those who work there.

Change Your Space provides a straightforward and clear strategy for transforming your company. The strategy is simple and clear, but the work is profoundly penetrating. That's why our approach invites leaders to engage in the change process at a deep level. The days of handing off the thinking and the work to experts and committees are over.

Changing the design of the workplace gets to the heart of all of the issues that make work complicated, distracting, and energy draining. That's why it forces leaders to think about and reimagine strategy, structure, and process. Changing space brings managers and leaders back in touch with how the work really gets done and back in touch with the people and the hidden culture that embodies the real drivers behind behavior and performance.

This book makes the case for a new level of engagement from leaders; a new relationship with consultants; and a new process for developing, procuring, and implementing projects. We know that a healthy culture *is the key* to engagement, innovation, resiliency, and growth. I believe readers will find the vital connection between culture and environment. They will see how environment can be used to reveal, refine, or reset culture.

This book will also speak to designers who have a desire to create highly engaged workplaces. I think you will find the tools for launching a new kind of conversation with your associates and clients.

Furthermore, this book will bring contractors and manufacturers together. From that, you can share and collaborate with your deep knowledge of what works and what doesn't.

We also invite the commercial brokerage community into the same conversation. I think you will find ways to help guide companies beyond the simple focus on "the deal." What if you could lead the parties into unlocking engagement and improving culture?

Finally, we want owners to feel comfortable again leading the crucial conversation about space and culture and resisting the pressure from experts to buy their latest ideas, services, or formulas.

We think everyone who has a stake in the workplace of today and questions about tomorrow will find this conversation exciting and practical. After all, it's the same conversation that we already have in our offices and over drinks at conferences. It's the same conversation we have as we walk out of presentations and utter our real sentiments about the same old and weary stories we just heard. And it's the conversation we already have when we allow our hearts to dream about what a great workplace could be.

Why This Book Is Different

Unlike previous books on these topics, the diversity of the Case4–Space leaders and our fifteen months of fieldwork, summits, research, and workshops gave us a depth and committed involvement that just might be worth your attention. The writing of the book was also unique. This was not a consulting practice using in-house case studies. This was not a compilation of subject matter experts covering a range of topics without a central narrative. This was more like a large investigative journalism project; over 30 "journalists" seeking answers to vexing questions.

This may be the first business book where this number of participants also became cocreators. We were enabled by new technology,
like Haworth's Bluescape, which allowed us to collect massive
amounts of information and visually organize it on larger-than-life
displays. We also designed a deeper level of personal engagement by
having smaller teams tackle different issues. This also made writing the
final manuscript more challenging. I remember my father sharing his
first experience with Japanese auto manufacturing in the 1970s. He
said the only bottleneck in the process was at the end of the day when
all of the workers walked around the finished cars to make sure the
preceding teams had maintained high quality. I know what he meant.
Many of the Case4Space members walked around each chapter to
make sure it met their quality standards.

The coalition that contributed to this book includes Haworth,
Balfour Beatty, Google, Cousins Properties, FOX Architects, the
U.S. General Services Administration (GSA), Autodesk, BHDP,
HDR, Jacobs Engineering Group, Building*i*, Idibri, the
ReAlignment Group, CoreNet, Scan, Parabola, Steven Elliott,
Renovus Collaborative, Darwin Branded Environments, SmartBIM
Solutions Group, Celeste Tell at the Bill & Melinda Gates Founda-
tion, the University of Denver, NICHE Creative, graphic facilitator
Michael Lagocki, and WH[Y] Mantra. Supporting our research
were organizations like W. L. Gore, IBM, Global Workplace
Analytics, Universal Health Services, Advocate Health, NetWave
Sensors, Red Hat, General Dynamics, Dean Stanberry from Jones
Lange LaSalle, David Dillard from D2 Architecture, CBRE, Randy
Thompson from Cushman & Wakefield, Bob Johansen from the
Institute for the Future and author of the book *Leaders Make the
Future*, military expert Richard Hayes (and coauthor of *Power to the
Edge*), Dave Gray (author of *The Connected Company*), Jack Hess
(Executive Director for the Institute for Coalition Building), Will
Miller (son of Cummins patriarch J. Irwin Miller), and Cummins Inc.

I thank all of you fellow travelers for your hard work and your
belief that we can all do better.

PART I

Why the Workplace Stopped Working

CHAPTER 1

Are You Ready to Sail the North Atlantic?

History becomes an astonishing succession of new media toppling old empires by repatterning perceptions of time and space.
—Michael Schrage, *No More Teams*[1]

On December 17, 2010, Mohamed Bouazizi, a Tunisian merchant, set himself on fire on the street where he once sold his goods. But this was not simply a personal tragedy or isolated political statement, mourned by a small circle of family, friends, or followers. Bouazizi's act was the spark that ignited a massive protest, the "Arab Spring," because social media had changed the rules.[2] In this case, the elements for social change included a spark (a dramatic suicide), a leveling catalyst (social media), a stage (the public square), and a unifying vision (the overthrow of oppression). Institutional leaders everywhere were put on notice that their constituents had a new voice and new power.

We are witnesses to an astonishing succession of crumbling empires. Social media has changed the way we can and do organize for action. It has removed traditional barriers to participation and makes it almost effortless to connect, rally, and act. Social media also connects once fragmented and faint voices into a unified chorus that has the power to topple institutions.

Until a few years ago institutional acts of injustice (or idiocy) happened behind a curtain, and therefore without serious consequence. Those trying to right a wrong, or make any kind of statement, had to overcome great hurdles of recruiting and coordination. That is changing fast.

A New Era of Engagement

Three years after Bouazizi's protest, four governments had been overthrown and another six had confronted major uprisings.[3] The Arab Spring and the many succeeding protests signaled a dramatic shift. Institutional power is no match for the politics of engagement and the tools of social media. This organizing efficiency and speed have placed new power in the hands of constituents, customers, and employees. Social media creates the context for a new era of social engagement. That brings a new social framework, new politics, and a new leadership with engagement at its core. Any leader who doesn't understand this profound shift and its ripple effect may have to reverse decisions, resign under pressure, or see a mob of angry people at the front door. Think of the recent series of political and corporate leaders who have had to resign because they didn't understand this new phenomenon.

The ability to easily organize and make a difference has spawned a revolution within the workplace, too. It is transforming collective enterprise with the same revolutionary power that Henry Ford's innovations brought to mass production. Here is a big difference about this new era of engagement: Organizing collective enterprises no longer requires capital, management resources, or rigid hierarchies to launch and coordinate. It does require tapping into a common cause, operating transparently, providing people a voice, and allowing them to participate and add value.

The new technologies of collaboration, with their global scale and speed of communication, bring unpredictable reactions, innovations, competitive threats, and new markets of opportunities. But the social or institutional framework that will predictably harness, regulate, or provide a moral ethos around these new capabilities is still being formed. That's why the outcomes are not always positive. In fact, right now, outcomes are not even the point. The Arab Spring is a great example; it was highly engaged in ridding the system of what was hated, but lacked a common vision of a better future. There was no cohesion or common engagement. The questions of why and to what end were missing.

Many of the norms and values from the industrial era, and the behaviors then allowed, are now out of sync with these new capabilities. The new collaborative technologies have a built-in ethos that is social and engaging. The old structures of command and control are hostile to anything social and engaging. The collisions between the two forces have a disrupting effect on organizational structures but a liberating power for those willing to embrace them.

"Oh, My God!"

Case4Space is a committed group of thought leaders who came together because we saw some outrageous realities:

- More than 70 percent of the workforce either hates their job or are just going through the motions.
- Half of all office space is wasted.
- The number of people who suffer chronic disorders—caused or exacerbated by the workplace—is alarming, scandalous, and exorbitantly expensive.

When our research connected these dots, we uttered a collective visceral groan—"Oh, my God!" That OMG moment rapidly went from "No way" to "No wonder." Could a small group of leaders really change a stagnant and stuck conversation about the possibilities of an engaging workplace? We knew enough about the new technologies of engagement to see that the flow of history was rapidly moving in our direction.

We used the social media tools of revolution to coordinate Case4Space. They afforded us great power for expanding our reach while lowering the cost and time commitments for busy and diverse leaders spread across the country. Our mission was simple: Topple institutionalized disengagement and, thereby, liberate people to discover their best ways to work. We were also learning these new ways to work and challenge ourselves. We will get into more detail about this later in the book.

Real and deep engagement is crucial to the success of any enterprise; companies must have it. However, their environments, on the whole, are not social and engaging. Ask one question: Would a Millennial (anyone born between 1980 and 2000) look forward to working here? Companies that have made the shift to an agile and collaborative environment shared common stories with us of people who had worked in the same office and on the same floor for years and yet had never met. One manager told us that a month after working in the new space, she thought the office staff had gotten 20 years younger. She hadn't noticed before because executives were segregated on a different floor and only those invited went there.

The walls are coming down.

Try this exercise. Take a group of people into a large, open room with tackable wall surfaces or whiteboards. Give them large sheets of paper, sticky notes, markers, and tape. Ask them to create a concept for a work environment (don't say "office") using the following words: *high-energy, collaborative, healthy, productive, engaging, innovative, interactive, high-tech,* and *regenerating.* Then ask them to create a poster to describe what the experience is like in that environment. Ask: "Does this look or sound like your office? If not, you are not alone." Executives want these qualities in the workplace but are stuck in a very old view of what an office should look like. This book explores the negative effects of that view in Chapter 2 and then where that paradigm came from in Chapter 3.

We could have called this book *The Leadership of Engagement* because that is what we've seen happen to leaders who have changed their space to reflect the new realities of work. Trust me: That kind of change is much deeper and more transforming than creating a few conference rooms, improving the technology, and adding a Starbucks. However, that is exactly the kind of superficial response that is currently blanketing office buildings across the country.

It is easy to miss the truth. A street merchant's dramatic protest was at first merely the tip of an iceberg. Employee disengagement is also below the surface. Although the water has not risen to the executive floor, the iceberg has already pierced the hull of the company's vitality. The leadership of engagement begins by reconnecting to the physicality and the people of a company, not simply its spreadsheet. It all begins in the workplace.

The hierarchy and vertical thinking that enabled Henry Ford to transform business in his time inevitably became inefficient and dysfunctional in ours. Ford Motor Company's structure and thinking had to crumble in the context of speed, scale, interconnectedness, and complexity. But that kind of thinking and those archaic structures are still enshrined in many of our offices.

We found a common tool, hidden in plain sight—the workplace. Any company could use that space to release engagement throughout the company—and that would bring a new kind of leadership for meeting the new challenges.

This new media landscape has created conditions that every leader can navigate. It is summed up in the acronym VUCA: Volatile, Unpredictable, Complex, and Ambiguous.[4] For this reason, 1,600 CEOs of global companies list innovation as their top priority.[5] Innovation is not just nice to have as a corporate capability; it is vital to keep up and get ahead in a world in constant flux.

Change as the new constant is not a new thought. It surfaced in the late 1960s and then hit the best seller's list with Alvin Toffler's book *Future Shock* in 1970. But the whole idea took on new power for me when I was given a very compelling lesson in shipbuilding.

Is Your Ship Ready to Navigate the North Atlantic?

A few years ago, I spent several hours with a director of design and construction for one of the largest oil companies in the world. What he told me about building oil tankers completely challenged my paradigms of how to build an organization to operate in an era of turbulent change.

Building an oil tanker is, as you might suspect, a daunting and monumental task. Each tanker is designed according to its purpose and operating environment. North Atlantic tankers work in the most treacherous environment on earth. Remember the *Titanic*? Fifty-seven other ships have met similar ends.[6] I learned that oil tankers designed for the North Atlantic have to be able to withstand a direct hit from an iceberg at 7 knots. They have to be able to locate and attach to a floating mooring in the middle of a turbulent sea. Without dropping anchor, they must maintain a relatively stable position while being slammed by 50-foot waves so that their large hose does not get ripped from the mooring and start dumping oil into the sea.

North Atlantic oil tankers rely on satellite tracking systems to hold their position. They have tremendous stabilizers that keep them positioned, even with mountainous waves crashing over their sides. Multiple redundant systems act as safeguards and backups. These ships are one-third the size of a regular tanker but cost three times as much to build.

That image and story should speak to leaders and managers who are trying to lead organizations in hostile and turbulent environments. Most companies are still designed for the more placid and predictable waters. They are built for steadiness and consistency, not rapid change and agile maneuvering.

Today many businesses designed for the stable and certain times of, say, the 1950s, are trying to move a little faster, equipped only with a little more relevance and a dynamic vision statement. But they are still operating in environments for which they were not designed. We must now learn—and quickly—to build seaworthy vessels that can handle external turbulence with a cultural agility in conditions as challenging as the North Sea is to oil tankers.

What are the criteria for designing and building an organization that can handle the dangers of the "North Sea"? What would a workplace look like that not only facilitates but accelerates change? Let me tell you about one.

The Great Flood

The damage was great and extensive. As I walked through the lobby, plastic drop cloths divided workable areas from those too damaged for operation. I was disappointed at first. I had heard of the beauty of the new CBRE headquarters, that it was a showcase for their advanced workplace strategies. I was there to see, hear, and learn. Lew Horne, president of CBRE, Greater Los Angeles–Orange County, walked down the lobby stairs and apologized for the mess. He explained, "Four days ago a sprinkler pipe burst in testing and flooded several floors. It damaged 50 percent of the office."

Then I learned that the great flood did the damage on a Thursday night, but by Monday they were fully operational. I was there on Tuesday. I walked through the space with Lew, pushing around tarps hanging from the ceiling and walking around makeshift furniture configurations. The office was not only fully operational, but the people also showed no indications of having just been broadsided by an iceberg. They were buoyant and energized.

Lew told me that none of their files were lost. They had been scanned before the move and were stored in the cloud. Everyone now worked from a laptop. CBRE's new mobile and free address work strategy allowed their operations group to find temporary space for half of the office. Those who were assigned to the temporary space were notified over the weekend and came to work without any interruptions. The damage was in the millions of dollars, but a small group worked around the clock to get things under control. This flood justified the new workplace strategy, but more importantly showed what adaptability and resilience actually look like. Lew had not realized that the desire to create greater collaboration and their new, cool, free address environment would also become a key part of their business resilience. It is one thing to have contingency plans. It is quite another to design contingency into the infrastructure of the organization and into its culture.

Welcome to the North Sea

The challenges business leaders face today are more like the North Sea than the previous era of predictable oceans and friendly ports of call. This book has a simple mission: to enable leaders to build vessels that will navigate change and discover new worlds of potential. The new vessels have to begin by reengaging the crew. They must also deal with complexity, resilience, innovation, and change.

The most challenging piece will be to change the culture. Old habits die hard and organizations—by definition—are designed to remain organized! They don't like chaos. But we now operate in chaotic times and environments. We may love the Caribbean, but we are caught in the North Atlantic. This is the reality for the rest of our lives. So, the only questions are: Will we sink and die, or will we reengineer our vessels for our new environment?

Change Your Culture

Assuming that you answered that you have chosen to survive in your new waters, you must change the culture of your company. Peter Drucker said, "Culture eats strategy for breakfast!" Edgar Schein, MIT professor and organizational scholar, wrote that culture is "a pattern of shared basic assumptions that the group learned as it solved its problems of external adaptation and internal integration, that has worked well enough to be considered valid and, therefore, to be taught to new members as the correct way you perceive, think, and feel in relation to those problems."[7]

People in all companies and social groups live inside a set of "shared basic assumptions." Every company (or school, town, neighborhood, church, sports team, etc.) is characterized by a distinct culture. It can be clearly seen in the spaces that facilitate life and work, like homes, places of worship, stadiums, offices, parks, restaurants, and stores. Because of external challenges (like icebergs), every culture has to engage and adapt. Static cultures cannot handle new ideas or problems.

We at Case4Space have learned that when you change space, you change culture. The leaders we interviewed verified that. Old habits get disrupted, and old dogs actually learn to appreciate new tricks. But there is something more basic going on. The thinking required to create an engaging environment leads to an engaging process. The workplace becomes the catalyst, the stage, and the enhancer for new values to emerge and grow.

This book will walk you through each of these challenges using stories from those who have made this journey. The great flood is just one story, but it shows how the leadership of engagement prepared the CBRE office. The transformation they experienced was more than just a radical office makeover. The office also embodied the depth of thought about the different values and behaviors they would need for the future:

- Have they been able to improve engagement?
- Have they conquered complexity?
- Have they risen with resiliency?
- Have they reinvented themselves?
- Are they prepared for change?

It certainly looked to me as if CBRE could answer yes, based on stories from those who made that journey. The flood revealed the depth and breadth of their transformation.

CHAPTER 2

The $1 Trillion Black Hole

Culture is hard to measure and it can't fit in a spreadsheet. For that reason investors, particularly those with a value bent, often totally ignore it. That's a mistake . . .

—Warren Buffett

The number one resource of any company is *engagement*. Businesses must have people who volunteer, speak up, collaborate, go the extra mile, work late as needed, and challenge everyone around them to be better. We know from the Case4Space research that engaged employees take 10 times fewer sick days, make 37 percent more sales, and stay in their jobs five times longer than disengaged employees.[1]

Yet *disengagement* is baked into the traditional workplace. And we all know it. We joke about it and it resonates for us as a basis for humor on TV and in movies. The popular television series *The Office* ran for nine seasons on the premise that work is a soul-killing enterprise and that it requires daily insanity to survive.

Why are we so disengaged?

The people who work for or around you live in centrifuges. Their lives spin so fast—working two jobs to make ends meet, driving kids to sporting and school activities, caring for aging parents, and the like—that they are pinned to the outside wall of their existence. Because of the centrifugal force, they have no freedom, and cannot rise to creativity or initiative. Many have given up; they are zombies. And many of them really need the workplace. We all know those who see their job as a respite, an oasis. Think of the recent widower who just wants to bury himself in work. Or the cancer patient who needs to be productive and part of a team so she can get her mind beyond the war raging in her mind and body.

However, when those people stumble through the front door of the workplace, they get hit by what Jason Fried, author and founder of 37Signals (now Basecamp) calls the "time Cuisinart." Their working days are sliced and diced into little moments that replace the long strides of planning, quiet, and uninterrupted work, and the rhythms essential for effective collaboration. In short, their lives are fragmented. They cannot find meaning, satisfaction, or a sense of achievement in their work or in their lives. And that adds to the pervasive stress.

A Constant State of Stress

One episode of the television series *World's Deadliest* shows a herd of impalas grazing peacefully at night on an African savannah, but alert to potential danger. All is quiet and still. But then the camera slowly pans to reveal a stalking lion hidden in the high grass. Suddenly the closest impalas look up; their heads jerk from side to side and their tails begin swishing rapidly. Like a synchronized chorus, all of the others quickly do the same. When one suddenly bolts, they all run.

Fear is universal and trans-species. Threats trigger the release of adrenaline to provide maximum response to danger. But when adrenal glands stay open for long periods, the result is stress. Imagine: Humans don't do their best work when they're stressed out. Simon Sinek, best-selling author and TED presenter, makes the case that the stress of the workplace sets our adrenal system on overload. This degrades our health and has caused the rise of chronic diseases in our time.

Just as the story of the impalas and the lion reflects, when one person in an office senses a threat, his or her behavior triggers a ripple effect throughout the workspaces. That "noise in the system" comes from the tension in the atmosphere, whispered lunchroom conversations, cryptic e-mails and texts, and so forth. Noise drives managers crazy. Frantic and frustrated management denials that jobs are threatened actually have the reverse effect; they *increase* anxiety. The herd has a mind of its own.

American business loses a trillion dollars a year because we do not know that life is integrated.[2] Personal health, safety, marriage, family, commuting, finances, and other burdens and crises are integrally related to our ability to achieve and produce. We can gaze at a herd of impalas and clearly see that the "compartments" of their individual and collective lives harmonize. Anything that threatens their food, water, dwelling, offspring, or safety constitutes a lethal hazard to their whole existence and future.

By contrast, for decades we have been building the structures of our lives as silos, cubicles, bubbles, and other isolating pods. We've thus created cultures of disconnection. When we noticed the effects, we started having concerned conversations about lighting, ergonomics, buildings, budgets, and better designs. Of course, those are not the truly relevant topics and we're therefore not having the right conversations.

The Power of Layout

In most offices the layout says volumes about our lack of integration and cohesion. Management tightly controls the information flow—there is no dialogue. Managers look safe because their private offices and meetings with other managers suggest that they are a herd unto their own. Off in their isolated area, marketing scrutinizes management's messages and creates talking points to assure that everyone is on the same page. They really believe that a unified message is the antidote to corporate noise. They don't seem able to grasp that the noise cancels out their signal. The herd flinches at the pulses of danger.

That's why part of a leader's job is to provide a safe place for employees. A safe place is marked by relief, hope, focus, and achievement. By offering safety from the dangers of the external jungle, they help employees find a collective focus on the mission. Leaders who fail to understand this soon find that they have both an external jungle and an internal jungle to deal with. Their people feel on full alert all the time.

As the Case4Space team traveled around the country visiting companies, we looked for work environments that were safe places. We found them at Google, Cummins Inc.'s Commons Office Building, W. L. Gore, the Haworth headquarters, Balfour Beatty's Western and Eastern Region Offices, Cousins Properties's head-quarters, FOX Architects, Idibri, Autodesk, Red Hat, the Bill & Melinda Gates Foundation, the Los Angeles CBRE office, the GSA's 1800 F Street headquarters modernization project, and many more. These organizations practiced a highly engaged design process that translated into a noticeably engaged work culture. We, as outsiders, were very impressed with the positive energy and focus people there have for their work and with one another. After visits to more than 100 companies, including many still clinging to the past, these safe companies were so vivid and distinct that we felt like we were entering a foreign country.

Space as a Proxy for Culture

In our visits to these highly engaged companies, we began to understand that space is a proxy for culture. In other words, the spaces—the actual designed places for work, conferencing, exercise regimens, eating, walking, and the like—reflected the values of the company, and also shaped the patterns of behavior and interaction. Naturally, when you change the space, you disrupt those patterns. And that can set off fireworks. Why? Because every organization has an official culture and a shadow one. The official one is engraved and printed, but the shadow culture actually runs the place. Changing the space will always reveal "the way things are around here." Because it disrupts, unmasks, and threatens the real power center (the shadow culture), changing the space can produce resistance and defiance.

For example, many companies place mission and values statements on their websites, on prominent walls, and in print media. These statements usually carry ideas like integrity, service, teamwork, diversity, dignity, empowerment, and partnership. But the designed spaces may reveal a strong shadow culture of hierarchy, control, command, and fear. By moving the space into alignment with access, collaboration, and value to the company, the true culture will be exposed. Trust me; it will not give up without a fight.

The old patterns and attitudes of space design were once acceptable and perhaps necessary norms for the command and control enterprise. In that world it was important to know each person's position and station in the order of things. But in a network-based workplace, position is replaced by capability and station is overshadowed by one's value to the mission and to others. We no longer need a designated floor, corner, or row of offices to know where to get a decision—we all have smartphones.

> "For too long we have relied on relics of past practices as the foundation of our current processes. This is carried forward with myth and folklore and presented as fact. This must change. We must collectively discover new ways . . . and places to accomplish our work and begin an insurgency of innovation."
>
> —Chuck Hardy, Chief Workplace Officer at GSA Public Buildings Service

If your office reflects past attitudes about work, no matter how often your company hosts town hall meetings, provides improved team dynamic training, or offers employee engagement workshops, you can't overcome the habits of how you live. Winston Churchill said, "We shape our buildings, and afterwards our buildings shape us."[3] Think about it for a moment. Where did you go this week? How did that coffee shop, movie theater, convenience store, meeting room, office lobby, hotel, park, house of worship, fitness center, doctor's office, or airliner affect you? How did each place shape, enhance, or detract from your experience, attitude, energy, focus, or level of interaction? Space matters!

A Day in the Life

Matt Traub, former director of sales at Four Seasons Hotels and Resorts, understands that management must put themselves in the shoes of their stakeholders. He told me, "If an arriving guest had a frustrating day, found the parking lot confusing and difficult to park in, waited in a long line to check in, and then found the person at the reservation desk disinterested or bored, that guest's stay at the hotel will be the sum of these experiences." In the same way, leaders are beginning to go upstream in order to understand the jungle their employees face before they even arrive at the workplace. Google has learned how to push back some of the external jungle. They, like the hospitality industry, understand and embrace looking at work through the employee's experience. Many are now creating "day in the life" scenarios of what employees and guests experience before walking through the door.

Many people go to work with their lives in shreds. They are barely hanging on. Whoever you are and wherever you work, people around you seriously struggle with special-needs kids, long commutes, economic pressure, teenager and marriage problems, health challenges, single parenthood, aging and infirm parents, and so forth. Many people are stressed even before arriving at the workplace. What they need is a safe place that offers some relief, hope, meaning, and accomplishment. That is, of course, *if* you hope to get engaged and inspired at work. But when they transition from one jungle outside to another inside the office—with their bodily systems already compromised—they operate on a very raw edge of life.

I'm one of those that would simply say, "We're a business! We're not here to solve the world's social problems." This is a logical but untenable reaction. Look at the risk of that position. Can you succeed with a 70 percent disengagement level? Can you survive the toxic 20 percent within that large majority who actually harm your organization? Can you count on your personal assistant giving his best when he has to leave in an hour to drive his father to the kidney dialysis center? You can't avoid life outside the company walls. Yet at the same time you can have a significant positive impact that will influence and improve the life of the people that spend half of their waking day carrying out the mission of your organization.

The workplace—the actual space—creates the landscape for that safe zone! The nature of the "where" of work has an intrinsic relationship to the way people associate. It forms a basic platform holding and shaping the who, what, when, why, and how of work.[4] We have seen organizational cultures change, and dramatically, in several companies that see their facilities as an extension of how they value and care for their people.

The professional and social cost of our stress-driven work and home lives has washed onto the shores of business and is not going away. Wise leaders have already started to have completely different conversations around the ideas of risk management, human resources, facilities, and engagement.

How Much Is That in Dollars?

Clearly, employers no longer have the luxury of living with a clear demarcation between the workplace and home. The lines are forever blurred. More of what happens outside encroaches more deeply into the domain of the workplace. Providing a productive place where people can find temporary sanctuaries, connections, meaning, and accomplishment will quickly evolve from a perk to a prerequisite for corporate resilience and sustainability.

Ignoring these real-world problems is a very expensive mistake. The toxic bottom 20 percent of employees costs U.S. businesses $550 billion a year, stress drains another $300 billion,[5] chronic health conditions balloon to over $1 trillion,[6] and working in sick buildings adds another $60 billion.[7] That totals 13 percent of the U.S. Gross Domestic Product (GDP).

> "Space, place, environment, policy set the stage for achieving some sort of end state. So why expend effort, time, and resources on delivering a building or space that does not make people happier, more engaged, and more focused on the broader organizational goals?"
>
> —Mark Pleskow, principal at Jacobs

Those leaders who do not actively provide a safe and productive workplace, and do not cultivate high engagement, will face great losses through disengagement, technology drains, and health risks.

Engagement Is the Issue

At the beginning of this chapter, I wrote that engagement is the number one resource of any organization. Engagement is that optional effort that employees (or volunteers) add beyond just following instructions. It is that sense of alertness and care—giving a damn!—that makes them seek clarification, ask questions, offer an alternative, or go the extra mile. Those people add a personal voluntary touch with a customer. They choose to improve their skills and become a more valued resource. In short, they love their job and they bring their best game to the workplace every day.

For the past 15 years, numerous studies have revealed a disturbing statistic: Over 50 percent of people in the workplace would rather be somewhere else—"anywhere but here." And maybe that's a good idea—the same studies indicate that you would be better off paying another 20 percent of your workforce *to stay home* rather than to come to work and share their toxic effect.[8] These folks are CAVE dwellers—employees who are Consistently Against Virtually Everything (see Figure 2.1). You know exactly who these people are. If one of them calls your phone, you think twice before answering. If a CAVE dweller is in your path to the coffee area, you take the longer alternate route. If you have to interact with this person, you have already thought through two or three exit strategies. As incredible as it may seem, nearly 2 out of every 10 employees are CAVE dwellers and are draining the life out of every workplace!

Think about that. If you have 10 people on your team, 3 are enthusiastic and will go the extra mile. Five will do a decent job if you tell them what to do, how to do it, and then follow up to make sure they did it. Two will drive you nuts with the friction and distractions they create, and the maintenance they require. Spread this dynamic across a large company, and it is easy to understand just how damaging

Figure 2.1   C.A.V.E. Dweller

CAVE dwellers can be. A 100-person firm has 20 toxic employees. In a 10,000-employee company, 2,000 are tearing your business down. At what scale does this horror show grab your attention?

How about this? Of the 140 million employed workers in the United States[9] as of October 2013, 42 million are actively adding value, 70 million are just trying to stay out of the way, and 28 million are actively draining the economy at a rate estimated between $450 to $550 billion dollars a year![10] Peter Farrell, blogging for the *Harvard Business Review*, describes "presenteeism" (present at work, but mentally absent) as the 800-pound gorilla in the office place. The cost to business from the harm done by CAVE dwellers is roughly 3 percent of GDP.[11] That cost is equal to the size of several industries including commercial construction, entertainment, and twice the cost of public education.

The ratios are worse when we look outside the United States. Only 1 out of 10 international employees are invested, 6 are coasting, and 3 are actively working against their companies. Tragically, these numbers have not budged since 1997.

Chronic disengagement shows up in a wide range of other statistics. For instance, data from Gallup states that while 96 percent of engaged employees trust their companies, this drops to 46 percent with disengaged employees.[12] Imagine a third of your company questioning your motives with every new initiative, announcement, change, or attempt to promote the good things that takes place.

In many offices people can and do hide. They are invisible. You see them, but have no idea what they do. They effectively get paid to write their novel or edit their movie. Nielsen reports that 25 percent of employees watch pornography at work.[13] Scott Adams, creator of the cartoon *Dilbert*, has captured this below-the-radar work ethic. The ones that hide and are ignored are twice as disengaged as the ones that receive negative attention.[14] But they like it; they enjoy coming to work. In fact, 42 percent of companies report that these low performers actually report high levels of satisfaction![15]

The Dilbert effect plus CAVE dwellers are killing the command and control organization. In addition to the $550 billion drain each year, companies with low engagement suffer from a 32 percent decrease in operating income, an almost 4 percent decline in net income, and an 11 percent reduction in earnings. Up to 3 percent of a company's gross revenue is lost in turnover.

Technology Drains

"Does anyone here expect someone to sleep well if they're interrupted all night? I don't think anyone would say yes. Why do we expect people to work well if they're being interrupted all day at the office?"

—*Jason Fried*[16]

We've all been caught in a restaurant with our spouse, family, or friends and felt that inevitable buzz in our pocket. Instantly it jerks us away from our lives; soon we're tapping out a stream of texts or giving other responses to the urgent message. Too few have the kind of discipline to make the boundaries between work and life clear and protected. We seem "always on call."

Jason Fried is relentless when it comes to eliminating complexity and distractions. For example, he promotes "No Talk Thursdays," a sanctuary of quiet to allow people to do focused work. This is certainly not for everyone, but the underlying principle is! We must have the time and space to do our critical work.

Of course, technology is essential to life and work. But it can also outstrip our social protocols if we let it. Too often it can and has become the tail that wags the dog. We must build boundaries and norms in our workspaces so that technology serves rather than controls us.

That is why many companies, having adopted an open work environment, are finding the need to rebalance and provide more breakout rooms with doors or quiet zones for people who need focus time. I know that when I undertake a project, I need at least 2 hours of uninterrupted time to go from context, to thinking about what-ifs, to drafts or prototypes, and finally to synthesis. The general rule of thumb is that it requires 20 minutes after an interruption or a distraction to return to workflow when focused on a complex task.

I know that e-mail is an easy target, but it remains a serious technology drain. The incessant flow has created a condition that I call the "six-minute twitch." We check our mobile devices about 150 times a day, requiring an hour or more just to keep up with the data flow.[17] E-mail and mobile devices consume more than half of our attention. The distraction of the Internet tacks on another half hour a day on average per employee. That doesn't sound like much, but add it all up and 35 percent of employees are browsing and watching between 1 to 2 hours a day.[18] Obviously, when people are focused on e-mail and the Internet, they are not focused on work. So our information waterfall has washed attention right out of our places of work. That is why the workplace has become a key laboratory for business to begin defining how we can live and cope with ubiquitous technology.

Of course, space is a powerful tool in that defining process. It can help us avoid the tyranny of technology. Space can craft new habits and norms. For example, the more open office environments reduce the ability to hide, and they offer more engaging venues through the workspace. That space flexibility fits the work mode required at the time. Some organizations like CBRE, Google, and GSA are defining space by the *kind* of work: quiet zones, private room for focused work, small interactive spaces, larger coworking spaces, and so forth. CBRE's Los Angeles office went from 4 work venues in the old traditional space to 16 in their 2013 renovation. In addition to offering more choice, the new workspace is also shaping new, more productive behavior.

Health Risks

Beyond the technology concerns, today's companies have larger and more alarming worries related to the crisis of employee health. Health insurance companies are forcing policyholders to adopt preventive health and wellness programs. Without the conviction needed to move from "health programs" to a wellness culture, compliance efforts amount to little more than poking a finger in a cracked dam. When Simon Sinek says, "Our jobs are killing us," what do we not understand? His exhortation should trumpet a national call to action.

There is no separation of work and life when it comes to chronic health conditions. Ten percent of your workforce is taking antidepressants.[19] Fifty to 70 percent of primary care doctor visits are for stress. Simon Sinek claims that 83 percent of employees are stressed at work. Remember: Stress leaves that adrenal gland open all day. Harvard Medical School found that the high-pressure demands on senior leaders create a feeling of burnout among 96 percent! One-third describe it as extreme burnout.[20]

This problem is greatly compounded by obesity. Chances are you are overweight or obese, and your workplace is a major contributor. About 25 percent of the workforce is overweight, but more than 40 percent are obese (body mass index of 30 and above).[21] Obesity and sitting both lead to high blood pressure, diabetes, and heart disease. Megan Mcardle cites in an April 2010 *BloombergBusinessweek* article that the enzymes that help break down fat drop 90 percent when sitting.[22]

Thirty percent of Americans must manage high blood pressure.[23] Almost 1 out of 10 adults has diabetes, but half are pre-diabetic. Obesity is the cause of almost half of diabetes, 40 percent of certain cancers, and a quarter of coronary artery disease.[24]

And many people live with great pain. Pain is one of the gauges on the dashboard of life. It tells us that something is wrong under the hood. The real cause for pain is usually stress. Today, it is flashing red for too many people. I went too long with a torn rotator cuff limiting my activities, robbing me of sleep, and creating mental distraction. Finding relief can be vexing, time consuming, and soul deadening. Because pain is invisible, it is often misunderstood by those who don't experience anything similar. It's easy to discount the distraction and all of the workarounds a person with chronic pain must devise. No wonder pain can quickly lead to depression.

Simplifying the Challenge

Firms like Google are now looking upstream in the working routines of their employees (who, reflecting their strong culture, are called "Googlers"). Doing so leads to a different conversation among human resources, risk management, corporate real estate, and facilities. For example, the wellness movement is an important early indicator of companies shifting their risk paradigm. Personal health is forcing employers to dive deeper into the lives of their employees. This further blurs the traditional lines between employer and employee, and it is only just beginning. Once the wellness movement builds momentum, the next breakout firms will not simply manage the risk, but will seek to own it completely by moving from health programs to wellness cultures.

Google is redesigning its campus to spread out exercise spaces to create more reasons to walk and talk. The company is also redesigning the food displays in the micro-kitchens so that healthier foods are readily available. Google sees their workspaces as a powerful tool for addressing and cultivating a wellness culture.

Ever wonder how the problems of the workplace became so complicated and so big so fast? This complexity crisis has forced companies to add the ever-expanding "Chief" roles (CEO, COO, CFO, CIO, CMO, CTO, etc.) in an attempt to stay even with increasing demands. The focus makes sense on paper. However, these new roles within the context of all of the other functions simply add to the complexity, battles over role and turf, and competition for resources. All of that makes coordination exponentially more difficult.

Part of the answer is not to add more single-focus initiatives and roles, but rather to reduce and integrate. When leaders regain both a common touch and common sense, the effects can be transforming. One of the best vehicles for rebuilding a deep level of intimacy with the culture and flow of the organization is direct involvement in redesigning how the people in an organization will work and live together.

The new awareness around health and wellness will change the way leaders lead. If you have ever reached a point where your doctor warned you to change your lifestyle and adopt healthy habits "or else," you understand how it begins a cascade of new discoveries and an awareness that everything either contributes to or threatens your health. You may start by dieting, then monitoring your weight, then shifting from dieting to eating healthfully, adding exercise, becoming more aware of your sleep, managing stress, and seeking more work–life balance. We learn that health is inter-related, not compartmentalized. So what looks at first like a complex matrix of interventions soon turns into a life-rhythm, and habit then resolves its complexity.

As most of you know, in commercial real estate, the cost of building is known as "sunk costs"—those costs that can never be recovered. That mind-set has influenced the way we think about space. We see it as a cost always to be minimized, regardless of other factors.[25]

But what if we thought of it as compound interest? If we could see it as the way to shape culture, we might begin to understand that it grants a great return on investment. And it compounds the return! For example, as I shared in Chapter 1, a water pipe burst and flooded several floors of CBRE's new Los Angeles office. Yet incredibly, they were fully operational on Monday morning.

That happened because CBRE had moved beyond the sclerotic thinking of sunk costs. They designed their space as a flexible, open, and engaging workplace. Their files were digitized and stored in the cloud. All offices were "free address," meaning that working space was chosen according to the needs of the task rather than assigned by position, and everyone was well-trained in using their new digital tools. There were no file cabinets, desktop computer towers, or other relics from traditional office design. There was absolutely no loss of productivity. Client information remained intact and secure. Employees continued to operate and communicate effi-ciently. Had they been trapped in the old design, they would have been inoperative or handicapped for months.

That is the immeasurable beauty of receiving compound interest on an investment rather than viewing it as a sunk cost.

Summary

In this chapter we have considered the soul-killing world of work that many employees experience and the environments that reinforce it. And we also looked at the staggering cost—$1 trillion a year—of our stressed, fragmented, disengaged workplace. We seem to not know that life is integrated. Why else would disengagement be baked right into the traditional workplace?

> "There is a powerful business case for employee engagement. It is the only way to achieve high profit while meeting corporate mission goals and caring for your people."
>
> —Craig Janssen, managing director, Idibri

We also introduced several companies that positively changed their culture through a linked process of strategy and changing their space. They discovered the compound interest of making great investments in space design. Later, we will discuss exactly how to use space as a tool to reveal, understand, refine, or reset culture.

We all know that our organizations face new threats. Success is no longer a matter of speed and scale; it also requires navigating complexity and dealing with unpredictability. The next chapter addresses those conditions. We will examine why most companies have yet to understand the peril that is rapidly approaching them, and why they still follow obsolete business structures, practices, and thinking. Chapter 3 will resonate loudly with companies that feel they need a major reset but face legacy issues and entrenched cultures that make such changes almost impossible.

CHAPTER 3

Something Wicked This Way Comes

Efficiency versus effectiveness has always been at odds. For the last five hundred years, the numbers have favored efficiency. In an era of wicked problems, the balance has shifted. Sustainable results highly favor the effectiveness mind-set.

—Case4Space

Jim was clearly frustrated. Plans to build a new community center were spiraling out of control. Six months after the initial budget was presented, project costs had increased by 50 percent, and work was already months behind before final plans had been finished. Weekly project meetings delivered a predictable mantra. Each company reported the most recent changes, along with new cost estimates, and the numbers seemed always to go higher. Jim's team had reached a discouraging crossroads. They might have to pull the plug on the project, letting down a community with high hopes and in desperate need of its services. If it came to this, the decision would severely damage the years of trust they had built.

This common story is what happens when a complicated process confronts a complex problem. It was clear that continuing to send each company back to its office to find more savings had run its course. Fortunately Jim's team found a way to break through the complexity. Jim asked the team to set aside a full day for a different kind of meeting. Instead of each trade reporting their progress in the usual ritual, the session would become a joint design and budgeting session. Each trade's problem was now everyone's problem. The dynamic had changed from a focus on efficiency to an atmosphere of effectiveness.

Team members that had never understood how other trades estimated and planned their work now stood in front of one another to map their workflow on a large wall using sticky notes, markers, tape, and string. After several hours of simple mapping, questioning, coordinating, bargaining, and brainstorming, a path emerged that surprised everyone. The original budget, for the first time in months, was now within reach. They came in to the meeting more than 30 percent over budget and were walking out of the room leaving a map that met the original estimated cost. What eight months of the normal process could not reach was achieved in one day, in a room that tied everyone and everything together.

Construction is a complicated business, but what confronted Jim was the ugly face of complexity. What makes construction so complicated are the many different pieces to the puzzle and putting each piece in the right place in the right sequence. When projects are like puzzles, there is a clear logic to the process that has proven highly effective and continues to work well when problems arise. However, there is a clear dividing line when problems grow beyond puzzles into interwoven knots, sometimes Gordian knots.

Jim's problem is a small demonstration of what is now commonplace for leaders. There seemed to be a historical shift somewhere in the 1960s when the world went from complicated to complex. Many call this an age of "wicked problems." This chapter provides the context for understanding this historical shift and why companies designed to thrive in a complicated world continue to fall from being dominant to becoming statistics. This new era requires a new mind-set for leaders to know how to pivot easily from solving puzzles to untangling gnarly knots. The instincts, skills, and tools are on opposite poles.

There is no place where this collision between puzzles and knots plays out more clearly than the workplace. Simply put, our approach to solving puzzles is detached and disengaging. Untying knots is engaging, immersive, and, when pursued with others, transforming. Leaders who can solve the gnarly knots within their own "households" can easily scale these lessons to the marketplace. However, leaders who attempt to tackle the wicked problems of the marketplace but still approach their companies and cultures as puzzle pieces will also find themselves among the many unfortunate statistics.

Wicked Problems

Wicked problems are social or cultural issues that are difficult or impossible to resolve because of incomplete, contradictory, or changing requirements. But beyond that definition, it seems that many problems today have no known frameworks or formulations. They are complex, vague, vexing, and shifting; we are never sure when, how, or if we have solved them. Many of the problems we deal with today are, in that sense, wicked. And, like Gordian knots, they seem to require divine intervention to unravel!

Many business leaders understand that we have left the age of "solving problems." Today, problems must be navigated. To "solve" a problem means that you can walk away from it. To navigate a problem or dilemma means that we must find a path between competing pressures. See Figure 3.1.

Fast and Furious!

The road to complexity began when the world's rate of change suddenly accelerated. In 1970, Alvin Toffler's best-selling book, *Future Shock,* announced that in the new world, change would be constant. He was right. As businesses ran faster and faster, many resigned themselves to the Red Queen syndrome from *Alice in Wonderland:* "Now, *here,* you see, it takes all the running you can do, to keep in the same place." See Figure 3.2.

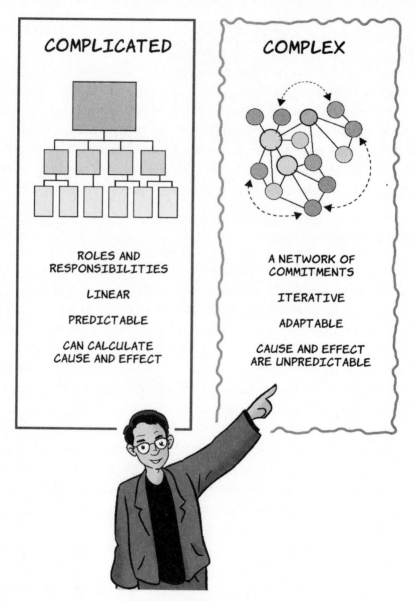

Figure 3.1   A Shift from Complicated to Complex

Figure 3.2   The Faster Your Go the Behinder You Get

The Internet's accelerated pace of communication beginning in the 1990s added a new dimension and new complexities for everyone. The speed and the interconnected nature of communication now create potential feedback loops with unintended consequences, unpredictability, and viral implications spreading everywhere, and at the speed of light. Toffler's diagnosis that keeping up would strip our gears is now a challenge of not only running fast but also staying vigilant, resilient, agile, and . . . alive. Many of us are living in both worlds.

From Gutenberg to Google

The revolution of the printing press is hard to put into perspective briefly. Putting books, magazines, and newspapers into the hands of the masses truly shifted the power curve away from an elite class of knowledge brokers. Knowledge became democratized. The invention also cleared a path to a new mind-set, a way of seeing the world through the practiced precision and progression of writing. The literate mind is distinct from the oral and tribal mind, and—we now understand—distinct from the digitally wired mind.

Gutenberg created a world of rational and stable (yet competitive) markets, predictable forecasting, and organizational continuity. Google represents a world of complex and volatile (viciously competitive), unpredictable and disruptive markets that reward fluid organizations. The transformation involves not just the tools to manage it but also an accompanying temperament.

The problems created during an era of specialization and standardized capabilities have reached a tipping point and can no longer be solved by the same thinking that created them. Problems that were never seen as connected have become so interwoven that attempting to determine where one element begins and ends is now impossible. The only path now is to dive deep into the challenges and deal with them as one, not many. Finding that unifying entry point can be elusive but only because it is usually simple and in plain sight. Jim was initially unable to find that entry point.

When I spoke with Jim about the problems of his project, it was clear from the tone of his voice how draining, frustrating, and hopeless the condition felt. Each discipline operated as a silo, representing a microcosm of the larger epic struggle. No wonder he was ready to capitulate. At one point he was resigned to accepting the higher cost as a blunt reality of a process where all of the knowledge and power were in the hands of the experts. It was the price to be paid for the higher cause of serving the community. But that higher price also brought hidden and unintended consequences. The project now had a tainted feel. Trust and enthusiasm toward the team turned to cynicism and a harder edge. That experience would certainly translate to future projects: "Fool me once, shame on you. Fool me twice, shame on me."

However, Jim was able to step across the complicated divide into the other side where complexity felt like magic. For Jim, the bridge appeared when he created a context for the team to look at the problem as a whole and approach it as one mind. Companies challenged by disengagement find that bridge by shifting focus from solving it to a more integrated mind-set addressing culture and the environments that shape it.

The Gutenberg Fallout

Do you realize that the *Fortune* 500 list was created in 1955, before the era of wicked problems? In 2014, only 65 of the original 500—once household names—still remain on the list.[1] Today, Booz Allen regards CEOs as an endangered species; the research predicts that they will, on average, stay at the helm less than six years.[2] The tenure of an employee is even less: The Bureau of Labor Statistics posts that employee turnover is four years.[3]

Steve Elliott, our equity capital expert in Case4Space, shared a growth dynamic that cities and loosely structured but highly networked companies experience call "superlinearity." It's essentially a virtuous loop of new life. He says, "It's amazing how successful cities are at leveraging both the superlinear, or network effects of social collaboration in combination with economies of scale." Today, the mean life of companies is 10 years. But cities survive great cataclysmic events, like terrorist attacks and even nuclear bombs. And "cities are the crucible of civilization," Steve notes. They are the major source of innovation and wealth creation. Currently they are growing exponentially. "Every week from now until 2050, one million new people are being added to our cities," Steve says.[4]

Traditional companies, on the other hand, experience what Steve explained as the 3/2 rule. When a new company with an innovative idea launches, they can expect a spurt of rapid growth and creativity, and a good bit of chaos. As more employees join, and structure is built to support the growing size, bureaucracy begins to drain productivity at a 3:2 ratio: For every three new employees, productivity drops by half.[5] Healthy and cohesive cultures will allow companies to decouple from command and control structures and experience city-like resilience. Highly aligned but loosely structured organizations exhibit the kind of DNA fit for volatile and unpredictable conditions.

The postmortem on stories of failed and struggling companies and brands like Blockbuster, BlackBerry, Nokia, the *Washington Post*, Kodak, Twinkies, American Airlines, the *Boston Globe*, Best Buy, Borders Group, and a long list of others is that each was slow to acknowledge the need and nature of the change necessary to cross the divide.

Steve Elliott raises a penetrating question: "Are these failure rates a sign of a weakness in our economic model or simply a thinning of the herd to make way for companies better suited for this new world?" We think the latter.

Will Huawei dethrone Cisco, WeChat erode Facebook, or KakaoTalk supplant Twitter for similar reasons? Has Apple peaked, and is there a second chapter of innovation for Microsoft? Will HP right itself or IBM regain its recently lost aura? At one time we would never have thought of asking questions like this about market leaders. In the 1970s, no one imagined that Toyota could ever overtake GM. Our paradigm wouldn't allow such a question. The 1970s marked the turning point in the narrative. What was once a rare and attention-getting headline has now become commonplace. Our new assumption is not whether a firm will fall, but when.

In Search of Innovation: The Holy Grail

IBM conducts an annual global survey to see what keeps them up at night. In the 2013 survey the answer was clear: How do we repeat the same miracle we pulled off last year? Innovation ranks at the top of the list and for good reason. Jack Welch understood and implemented an innovation mind-set as well as any leader in the past 30 years: "If the rate of change on the outside exceeds the rate of change on the inside, the end is near."

We found that leaders understand the need for innovation simply to stay even. However, it still looks like puzzle solving when closely examined. Companies have departments focused on innovation, programs for innovation, but what is vital and missed is that companies need innovative cultures first.

The IBM survey provides what Case4Space refers to as the "Ladder to Innovation." The study reports that innovation is tied to collaboration and collaboration is tied to engagement. But how do you produce engaged employees? The study stops short of answering this question. We think the first and essential rung is an engaging culture. The workplace becomes a vital barometer and tool for creating that culture. See Figure 3.3.

There seems to be a disconnect between the innovation goal that CEOs say is essential and their actual behavior. If we were to look at corporate decisions in general, we could quickly conclude that the drive to survive in the short term outweighs the desire to cultivate the right soil that produces innovation.

"Think about innovation—the very art and science of bringing a great idea into a community of practice. Think about the attitude required for improvement. At the same time think about the friction that impedes innovation. Innovation and waste are two sides of the same coin, and both are invisible unless you consciously look for it. The environments we create tend to reveal one or the other."

—Mark Konchar, chief of enterprise development at Balfour Beatty Construction

The pressure to focus on short-term results is understandable. The horizon of longevity used to go well beyond an executive's career. The life span of an S&P 500 firm in the 1950s was about

Figure 3.3   The Ladder of Innovation

50 years. That benchmark typically signaled a company that had built a strong and stable leadership position. By the 1990s, that life span had shrunk to about 20 years—still the span of a healthy career, but the 50 percent drop did signal a new era of heightened competition and a need to rethink the business. See Figure 3.4.

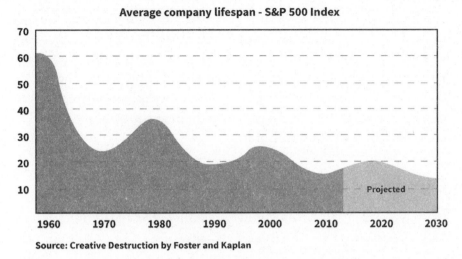

Source: Creative Destruction by Foster and Kaplan

Figure 3.4   Declining Life Span of S&P 500 Companies

Why the Strategies and Tools for Innovation Aren't Working

Reengineering[6] emerged as an early recognition that the old rules needed retooling. Leaders bought into reengineering in a big way. However, the various change models haven't worked. Several studies show that failure rates for change initiatives are in the 70 percent to 90 percent range and the S&P 500 survival rate has continued to drop.

By the late 1990s, a new focus emerged: employee engagement. The race to attract and retain talent fueled this interest. The first national and global surveys handed out a failing grade to corporate leaders with less than 30 percent engagement. The Gallup Organization began to monetize the high cost of disengagement and showed the competitive advantage of engagement. Numerous firms have brought their own spin on the theme—"Best Place to Work," "Trust Index," "Happiness Index," "Employee Satisfaction"—and many others created their own assessments and training. Almost 15 years after the first engagement surveys, there is no movement on the engagement needle. It still remains under 30 percent in the United States. Globally, the picture is far worse.

The magic doesn't seem to exist in either the strategy or the tools. That's because the wicked problems are complex, vague, and vexing. They don't respond to the old tools, models, and strategies. However, we have seen these strategies and tools work, and work well. The difference is between those who use these tools as levers to tune a machine and those who see them as patterns to be woven into the fabric of their cultures.

Culture Is the Constraint Leaders Overlook

In mid-April 2013, a global services firm convened more than 150 leaders for its annual officers' meeting. This meeting was designed to deliver a single message: Past success will no longer continue unless dramatic changes are embraced.

Jimmy Allen, co-head of Bain's Global Strategy practice, kicked off this three-day strategy meeting by sharing research from his co-authored book, *Repeatability*. Allen combines a high level of confidence and a large physical presence, backed by a rapid delivery of deep research and multiple case studies.

Allen announced that complexity is a prime killer of corporate innovation. Complexity leaves leaders disconnected from how their business really operates: spread too thin, running in too many directions, buried by fighting major and minor crises, tired, and burnt out. He now had our full attention. The breakout sessions that followed sounded like group therapy, where director after director confessed their weariness, finding themselves lost in the mire and frustrated at the bureaucratic hoops they needed to jump through and their inability to create traction.

Allen's short answer: Look within!

Bain's research found that most management teams fixate on outside conditions as their key challenges and constraints preventing success. By contrast, Allen was clear:

• External factors create the pressure but not the cause for failure.
• Changes in fortune make up only 15 percent of the problem.

- The obstacles are mind-sets: an unwillingness to accept reality and overconfidence from past success.
- Companies die because of inflexible and resistant cultures.

The IBM survey and Bain's research intersect at a similar point. The key to sustainable growth is innovation. IBM confirms it as a top-of-mind priority, and Bain offers a compelling business case, along with strong metrics to back up this source of superior performance. The temptation then is to focus on solving the challenges in innovation, collaboration, or engagement—separate from the culture and environment. This will be money poured down a hole. Unless the context changes, the story will remain the same—no matter what other interventions are tried.

Recalibrating Expectations

The ripple effect of the 2008 economic crash has already transformed the business of commercial real estate by raising awareness of the waste and inefficiencies that were always there. For example, the footprint for offices is shrinking. In 2012 the average space allotment per person was 200 square feet. In 2013, companies shifted to 150 square feet for two-thirds of their people and 100 square feet for another 20 percent.[7] The traditional 10- and five-year lease terms are under strong pressure to become shorter and more flexible. Managers have begun asking, "Who is really in the office and how much time are they here? When they are here, where do they spend most of their time? Do they even need an office? What is the new nature of work and how do we support it?" If owners and tenants realize that 50 percent of their office is underutilized and shift to "smaller and smarter" leases, a revolution will sweep through commercial real estate firms. That revolution will require new business models and new levels of sophistication.[8]

I don't know anyone who thinks business will go back to its pre-2008 ways. We are like pioneers crossing the Continental Divide. Today, however, it's called the digital divide.

Disruptive market shifts can take 10 years just to reach broad recognition and another 10 years before people begin to adopt and implement them.[9] If the Google revolution (creating a networked and complex world) launched in 1998 at the company's inception, 2008 was the 10-year wake-up call; by 2018 we will see a general understanding, diffusion, and broad implementation. That shift in the adoption and dominance of digital media coincides with a tech-savvy generation (called the Millennials) becoming the dominant force in the workplace.

Continuing to solve problems and define space with Gutenberg-era thinking reinforces the hierarchy, silos, and cumbersome bureaucracy that is antithetical to a complex world of wicked problems. At the same time, we can use the power of changing space to transform and leap from Gutenberg to Google.

The sobering effects of a near-global financial collapse has had the unintended positive effect of shaking leaders out of their Gutenberg stupor, not sure of what the alternative might be but certainly willing to consider plausible options. Stepping over and into the mind-set of an interconnected and complex Google world can be as simple as stepping into the interconnected and complex territory of your own backyard. To understand where the office in a wicked world is headed, let's take a brief look at how we got here.

A Brief History of the Office

Henry Ford defined a new era of business. He codified a new business model, process, and leadership style. Naturally, he created a new office environment to support his enterprise. The division of labor, command and control decision making, and station-to-station workflow was replicated in the office with the same precision and organization of work.

In 1943 Abraham Maslow wrote an academic article that introduced a new understanding for human motivation, *A Theory of Human Motivation,* based on a hierarchy of human needs. His theory would eventually find a natural home with emerging service related businesses.

Sears, Roebuck & Company in the 1950s represented a new divide for a new business era that would become defined as the service economy. Sears, like Amazon, was *the* aggregator of goods, the one-stop shop. Here again, a new business model, process, leadership style, and environment emerged.

Sears recognized that a business that deals primarily with people is much different from a business that makes things. So James C. Worthy, at the time Sears's vice president, surveyed over 100,000 employees and wrote a controversial and groundbreaking article in 1950 for the American Sociological Association. The article, "Organizational Structure and Employee Morale," identified two kinds of organizations, tall and flat. He saw that the command and control model that worked well for factories didn't work as well for large-scale service businesses.

In 1964, Douglas McGregor built on both Maslow and Worthy to provide the capstone for this divide; "Theory X" represented an older command and control management style, and "Theory Y" characterized an emerging philosophy of empowerment and incentives.

The legacy of Theory X is still alive, but not well. Professors who knew only Theory X principles and a manufacturing world-view trained the boomer leaders, who are now in their fifties and sixties. That's why we still have corner offices, privileged space, and a requirement that certain people "clock in." Practitioners of Theory X see hours worked as representing an essential level of dedication. Old habits die hard.

The cubicle era was born in 1968 with Herman Miller's Action Office. "AO" was originally designed to address the new importance of information as a driver for business. It was to become a tool to help adapt to the changing nature and flow of information and a new way to work. Cubicles are the most visible symbol of the new divide between a service economy and an information one. When first introduced, the intent was an open space with 5-foot-high dividers that offered a balance between privacy and visibility. The layouts flowed in a somewhat organic fashion with three- and four-sided enclosures. Hinged panel connectors softened the geometry of the space. Originally Herman Miller only offered three panel widths; 1, 2, and 4 feet. The reason for those panel widths was ultimate flexibility, or what Robert Propst, creator of AO, called "modular limited."

The success of the open plan created explosive growth. The movable mid-height panel divider was an idea whose time had come. The intent of a fluid and open office, however, soon morphed into optimizing space density. When personal computers entered the workplace, each computer needed access to electrical power. Fixed power outlets drilled into the floor, poles providing power out of the ceiling, and pre-wired panels chained together took away the ability to easily reconfigure workstations. Now fixed in place and optimized for density, offices became the equivalent of workplace stockyards and earned the well-deserved name of "cube farms."

As early as 1970, George Nelson, another Herman Miller designer, recognized the logical trajectory of a cubicle-dominated workplace: "One does not have to be an especially perceptive critic to realize that AO II is definitely not a system that produces an environment gratifying for people in general. But it is admirable for planners looking for ways of cramming in a maximum number of bodies, for 'employees' (as against individuals), for 'personnel,' corporate zombies, the walking dead, the silent majority. A large market."[10]

This brief history of the modern office reveals something important. A major shift to a new kind of business creates new paradigms and strategies, and they require new structures. New structures are enabled by new processes, and new processes demand new skills, and all of these become released or constrained by their environments.

All workplace designs and structures facilitate a particular kind of work and behavior. Today, the average office building is about

Figure 3.5 Eras Our Offices Reflect

60 years old. That means most of us still work in spaces with 1960s thinking. Most renovations to these spaces are the building equivalent of a comb-over. See Figure 3.5.

Similarly, everyone in the real estate world experienced a major reset of expectations after the 2008 financial meltdown. Many companies that downsized found themselves tied to space commitments they could not easily shed. About half the space they had been using was empty or underutilized. Until 2008 the problem remained hidden or low on the priority list, but the pain of paying for the unused real estate revealed a larger reality.

Suddenly it all became a very high priority. Companies examined their assets and personnel through a new lens. What and who is essential, where do we need flexibility, and how productive are our assets? Utilization rates for office space are the building equivalent of productivity for people. Discovering that office space, on average, is less than 50 percent utilized led us at Case4Space to some deeper questions. Is this 50 percent reflected in the larger system within which that office space and corporate real estate is nested? Owners are beginning to connect the dots, rework their strategies, and express new expectations. The story is just beginning to unfold.

Flexibility and the capacity to adapt are now crucial. But today, because of management's legacy mind-set, structure, and culture, most leaders have little clue of how to adapt. True leaders will try to build so that they never get blindsided on this wholesale level again. Creating an adaptive organization that can craft a new future is certainly possible, even with legacy organizations. It's simpler than we think and harder than we realize. It will demand discipline, engagement, and conviction.

We hear it all the time: "Why are we still getting such poor results after spending billions of dollars on training, providing new workspaces, and flexible work strategies? Why are consultants not improving the overall engagement numbers or success rates for innovation?" It's not necessarily because the advice is wrong or the training ineffective. What if all of this advice is designed to work for an era of relative stability but will also fail under unstable and unpredictable conditions? Or, what if your "ship"—designed for the balmy and placid Caribbean—is now moving through the frigid North Atlantic?

Changing the Culture

The 2011 movie *Moneyball* is the story of the Oakland A's of the 1990s, an underfunded but overachieving professional baseball team. Each year, their ability to find under-the-radar talent in their farm system kept them a perennial playoff team. After the 1991 postseason, the A's had their best chance to go deep into the playoffs. But they lost early. Then three of their top players became free agents, and richer teams like the Yankees and the

Red Sox picked them off. Every year the A's seemed to pull off another miracle, but this insult added to injury pushed their general manager, Billy Beane, over the top.

He recognized that their model was unsustainable. They could never get the continuity necessary to go deep into the playoffs if every year their best talent was picked off in a bidding war. At the same time, his scouts were locked into playing the same talent game that every other team played.

In a poignant locker room scene, Beane has a moment of clarity. He confronts the absurdity of their ritualized annual exercise to fill their roster gaps, then redefines the problem. To the scouts, the problem was simply trying to find the best players possible with the money they had to spend, hoping to find a few sleepers that others missed. The discussion around the table in this scene offers a clear reflection of just how convoluted the rationale gets when leaders are trying to solve the wrong problem.

Beane confronts his scouts by exposing their futility and forcing them to face reality: there are rich teams and poor teams . . . and then there were the A's. With the A's payroll, the deck was overwhelmingly stacked against them. To compete they would have to play by different rules. Beane found key inefficiencies in baseball's tradition of talent selection. To exploit those inefficiencies he would have to choose players that defied the logic, the appearance, and the tradition that baseball had operated on for generations.

The reality is that the game has changed for every corporate leader. Some have the good fortune of starting off in this new reality without legacy baggage. Some have transformed their thinking like Beane. Others will continue to play the game the way they always have and fall behind.

As Jason Jennings and Laurence Haughton told us, echoing the title of their book, "It's not the big that eat the small, it's the fast that eat the slow." A company cannot act fast or think fast if they live in a big and slow mind-set.

The *Moneyball* Approach to the Construction Industry

In the prior MindShift initiative, the team tackled the wicked problem of dysfunction and waste in the construction industry. In 2007, this $1.2 trillion–dollar industry was known for conflict, waste, and cost and schedule overruns. For decades the industry tried new delivery models, adopted advanced design and fabrication technology, and added new roles of oversight. And still, for more than 50 years, efficiency and effectiveness declined. We ran into a similar brick wall. Every promising strategy or tool ran its course without ever moving the needle.

Culture was the obstacle. Peter Drucker was right and we saw old culture trumping new strategy in action. Every day we encountered a dysfunctional legacy culture born out of a once-successful model of checks and balances. Over time, those distinct roles grew out of step with an industry that was becoming more complex. The new era required speed, greater sophistication, and low cost as new drivers. But the natural checks and balances eroded into distrust, with each party looking out for only their interest. That behavior was antithetical to a new reality of work requiring tight coordination and collaboration.

We experienced, like Jim earlier, our moment of stepping over the divide, moving away from being hopelessly stuck in our efficient approach to trying to solve a riddle. After a morning of frustrating debate to identify the root cause (often a person) for projects that go wrong (which is most of them), a curious and magical shift occurred. Tom Gerlach with Turner Construction said, "The companies in this room have some of the best people in the industry, we have happy clients who love our work . . . but . . . when a project begins to go sideways, we don't have any way of getting it back on course. It becomes a dogfight to the end."

Another person commented that "the system is designed to create distrust from the bidding process, to the contracts, to the third-party checkers, checking checkers . . ."

Finally the answer to the riddle was revealed in a question that led to a two-year quest: "I wonder what a trust-based system might look like?" We broke through the complicated mess that had bogged down our morning debate and had plagued our industry for decades. We were now pointed in a new, unexpected, and ultimately transforming journey. Getting across the divide is like an initiation. When you come across someone now trying to solve a Gordian knot like a puzzle, you can see the portal to the other side. What you are likely to encounter, however, is someone fixated on solving it as a puzzle. That is how finding those who are already on the other side of complex problems becomes so key to our own discovery process.

When the MindShift consortium searched for those doing things differently and getting great results, we found a difference in two key areas. First, these outlier teams had redefined the fundamental nature and context of construction. Construction was no longer a game performed in discrete phases of work handled by separate silos of expertise and then assembled in a predefined time sequence. The new nature of the work required a collective effort early in the project's conception and a social construct that would enable one-time adversaries to work transparently and together. Second, the transforming catalyst was not a new contract, delivery model, or technology—but a space, the Big Room. This colocation and integration space fostered the formation of a new social technology necessary to support open trust, transparency, and collaboration. Once that was in place, the new tools of 3D modeling, pull planning, visual thinking, shared risk-reward agreements, and other enablers produced improvements on an order-of-magnitude of scale.

If culture eats strategy for breakfast, then culture needs a physical setting, a home that reinforces its values.

Space as the Catalyst

We observed over and over that when space is changed, relation-ships shift, and culture gets revealed clearly. That process also helps us to see the shadow culture that reveals the real power centers. Once surfaced, a company's culture is accessible for refinement, realignment, or other shifting. Ask any designer or facility manager who has directed a relocation project; he or she will share, in far greater detail than any assessment, the true nature of an organization's culture. Such individuals see the informal entitlement structure, the power centers, the "sacred cows," the triggers for sensitive issues, the real principles versus the official ones, and the pain and loss that people undergo when getting dislodged and moved to a new place to work.

> "Space is a powerful tool—it brings together people, technology and ideas. It has the ability to communicate bold new concepts and define the culture of an organization."
>
> —Bob Fox, principal, FOX Architects

Using space as a means to shift culture requires far different skills from the typical design-and-move management. I will cover this difference later in the book, but it follows the earlier difference between the Gutenberg and Google mind-sets. I will describe this as a *PUSH* (hierarchy) approach, and how that thinking is being transformed by a new mind-set, the practice of a *PULL* (co-creation) approach. Design within a PUSH context creates the expert-driven "grand solution." Design at its best within a PULL context is social and engaging by nature. In Chapter 6 I will explore more fully the power of this key principle whether in design, reengineering, or engagement.

Safe-Fail Leadership for Managing Wicked Problems

Adapting gracefully is today's organizational version of the Holy Grail. Large-scale complicated initiatives, however, still follow the basic principles used by Henry Ford. Take something big, break it into small pieces, assemble the components, and you're done.

Over time the model evolved into what is called the waterfall[11] project method and critical path scheduling. Big and complicated projects, or ones with high stakes, put more emphasis on planning. The logic is clear. Planning is the time frame to think through all of the variables and design for contingencies. When something is overengineered or over-designed, it is the result of planning to cover *all* contingencies. This is also where considerable waste, complexity, and cost are added to a project. This paradigm is anything but graceful and adaptable.

Fail-safe thinking attempts to plan away any potential problems. But there is a problem; in a wicked world, by definition, one cannot know ahead of time how reality will respond to a solution. Using a grand strategy precipitates a grand crash and messy fallout.

Fail-safe thinking is being replaced by safe-fail thinking and safe-fail leadership. Digital-culture guru Clay Shirky offers Healthcare.gov as a high-profile example of a large, complicated project that had no room for failure; for that reason, it failed at its launch and failed spectacularly. Shirky's postmortem illustrates the difference between fail-safe and safe-fail.

This is more than a lesson in delivering large projects. It is a new model and mind-set leaders must master. According to Shirky, when a staff member with the department responsible for Healthcare.gov sent a clear warning, his superiors wrote back, "in effect, that failure is not an option, according to people who have spoken to him. Nor was rolling out the system in stages or on a smaller scale, as companies like Google typically do so that problems can be more easily and quietly fixed."[12]

When any solution is complex, failure is certainly an option! In fact, it is the norm and the only vehicle for understanding the behavior of the system. In the tech world, the front-loaded linear waterfall rollout of an idea is now replaced by an iterative "double-loop" learning approach. When a failure occurs within a fail-safe framework, it is fixed as if it were a one-off problem—a single loop.

In an iterative world, a failure is assumed to be systemic, not one-off, which leads to searching upstream for the cause.

Companies like Google, Facebook, Twitter, Amazon, Word-Press, and others with large-scale complex platforms take a safe-fail approach. Large systems don't start out large. There is no grand rollout. In his book, *The Lean Startup,* Eric Ries writes that the planning involves taking a hypothesis to a "minimum viable product" and then testing the idea as quickly and as inexpensively as possible.

WordPress, for example, will roll out a feature or upgrade to their blogging platform and then watch the traffic. They look for bugs and how well people like the feature. If errors are surfaced, they can be quickly fixed without affecting the entire site. If no one seems to be interested in the feature, it can be easily dropped. Projects start simple and then scale by expanding a network of related capabilities. App and website upgrades have become so invisible that we don't notice the new releases every 30 minutes. Designing safe-failures to root out system flaws is common for tech industries but counterintuitive for nontech companies and leaders.

In contrast to Healthcare.gov, the 1800F GSA renovation offers an example of engaged leadership and a safe-fail approach to transforming a 90-year-old building and a government culture living in a past era.

Success!

The General Service Administration is the agency that helps the U.S. government fulfill its basic functions. In that role, the GSA provides, among other services, office space for the federal government. The GSA's own headquarters, "1800F" (1800 F Street NW, in Washington, DC), faced a perfect storm of opportunity and high risk. 1800F was built in 1917 and last renovated in 1935. It was old, inefficient, and reinforced the image and behavior that the federal government is a hierarchical bureaucracy with entitlements and turf protection, ingrown and unresponsive to the public. It housed 2,200 employees with another 1,800 spread among three other buildings.

GSA faced its perfect storm with federal budget cuts, the Telework Enhancement Act of 2010, carbon-footprint reduction mandates, a declining building in need of major renovation, and the internal challenges of running a 4,000-person organization dedicated to operating in silos. Their business model was no longer sustainable and this combination of forces drove a need to change.

On the positive side of the perfect storm was the American Recovery and Reinvestment Act of 2009 (ARRA). The ARRA could provide much-needed funding, but the GSA's main assets were two leaders who saw this as an opportunity to model for the government what the future could look like.

Martha Johnson and Bob initiated the mission to change GSA, which Dan M. Tangherlini, administrator for GSA, followed through. The 1800F renovation became the primary stage and catalyst for a dramatic transformation. Their story is included in Chapter 10, "They Did It, You Can Too." The project was both a financial and culture-shift success. Unlike those behind Healthcare. gov, Martha and Bob took an engaged approach to create alignment with key leaders and influences.

GSA had launched several regional prototype projects that allowed them to learn and modify instead of attempting a grand launch without any real-world testing. They used their time in temporary space, while the building was under renovation, to test ideas. Their living-lab approach offered the ability to flex with the fluid and complex dynamics of this large organization and to learn while doing. The transparency of their living lab invited participation and allowed people to reimagine their new roles and work lives. There was no big build-up; the setbacks were incremental because the process was iterative. There was no sink or swim, on-off switch as with Healthcare.gov. Rather, there was an intentional effort to use the temporary transition space to break down departmental isolation and develop new kinds of behavior.

Healthcare.gov took an old culture with old practices into a new world and got clobbered. It viewed its mission as technological and political, and overlooked the culture needed to make it successful.

By contrast, 1800F redefined the new desired nature of GSA's work as a customer-service–centered organization. Once this was defined, they began adapting the old culture and practices to this new vision of work, using the opportunity of the renovation to model their future culture and then designing a facility to support it. In the old building, for instance, each person had a permanent office. In the new building, almost no person "owns" an office. This allowed them to increase the capacity of the building from 2,200 people to over 4,000. In doing so, they brought four organizations under one roof for the first time.

The new building has saved taxpayers over $100 million, reduced the organization's carbon footprint, and improved the engagement levels of employees with a marked improvement in the internal communication and coordination between organizations.

In a conversation with several of the key project leaders, they said this effort really became a conversation around organizational health. They recalled asking themselves, "What kind of work are we doing today? In the future? And what kind of organization will we need to be?"

This kind of values-based conversation doesn't often happen when it comes to designing space. It's powerful when it does.

Crossing the Divide

Dean Reed of DPR Construction has the persona of an easygoing sage, certainly not a revolutionary. Dan Gonzales, also with DPR, is clearly a bit mischievous and exhibits revolutionary passion. These two were some of the early pioneers for trust-based design and construction. I met both of them in 2007, 10 years after they had begun solving the riddle of keeping up with the dot-com era's demand for growth.

As I wrote in *The Commercial Real Estate Revolution*, "The dot. com boom (1995 to 2001) placed a premium on speed-to-market. The entrepreneurs launching these companies did not realize that their timelines were impossible. So what do people who have to fulfill impossible expectations do? They talk."[13] Dean, Dan, Martin Fischer, and Chris Raftery met regularly at Hobee's coffeehouse in Palo Alto.[14] The sessions created a context for the candid conversations that enabled them to untie this complex knot. Their association soon led to an insight that would find expression in the formation of the Virtual Builders Roundtable, which transformed the industry.

The riddle the industry faced at that time (and that most still chose to live with) was there are three components to a project: speed, quality, and schedule. You can only choose two. This is called the Triadic Trade-Off. Most leaders and all parents are familiar with these puzzles. You can have this . . . at the expense of that. What typically transpires, as it did for Jim at the opening of this chapter and as it does right now in conference rooms all across the world, is a game of musical chairs. We walk in circles around the three options with a full awareness that, when the music stops and the deadline appears, one of the key components will remain standing. Or, as in many of these contests, there will be two attempting to occupy the same chair with half a cheek on and half a cheek off—both losers.

What was discovered at Hobee's was an atmosphere for solving riddles. The solution was not a better process, although a better one emerged. It was not a new technology, although 3D modeling became the catalyst for a deeper form of collaboration. The answer to the riddle was found in the trust that a small cohort formed over pancakes.

This era of wicked problems presents many similar trade-offs. Most will be in the form of choosing one thing at the expense of profits or some other program:

- Improved sustainability
- Improved safety

- Higher engagement
- Better design
- Increased marketing
- Research and development

These, however, find resolution once you cross the divide. The common component is the full and equal engagement of the different parties in an environment of inquiry and discovery.

Roger Martin, former dean of the University of Toronto's Rotman School of Management, has developed an integrative practice for business. He's adopted the principles of design thinking from the d.school at Stanford and IDEO.

Roger Martin's critique of business is that we are still operating under that 500-year-old Gutenberg paradigm of efficiency. He makes the case that efficiency has to meet creativity at a crossroads he calls "abductive reasoning" or "integrative thinking": "There are big questions that could be addressed by business education, like integrative thinking, like integrating corporate social responsibility into the business world, like imagining the world is full of people that have emotions and biases, and integrating that into accounting, finance, and marketing. But we just avert our eyes; we don't want to think about these things because they are too complex."

The accountant deals with the rational. The artist works with intuition. They both look for pattern and meaning. For one, the sum of the parts is the whole. For the other, the whole is greater than the sum of its parts. Complexity has shifted the demand to better understand the processes and temperament of creativity, but this has to be more than lightning in a bottle. It has to be repeatable and scalable. These two elements are now non-intersecting pieces of the innovation puzzle. If you step back, the picture appears clear. They form two halves, and when integrated, function well. When isolated, they become warring camps.

"My greatest desire would be to move toward and land on common ground between the financial formula (hard metrics) and the 'human' formula (soft metrics)—this is the discussion that has been ongoing for more than a decade. We continue the dialogue but never reach consensus. The idea that it has to be one or the other will never work."

—Katherine Tracey, marketing coordinator at Cassidy Turley, and Millennial

The specialized and standardized world that served us well has become the monstrous impediment creating silos and conflict. And it's right where we need integration and a common mind to untie the Gordian knots and answer the unsolved riddles we face. These old frameworks are engrained in our thinking, our cultures, and our environments. The leaders we met who successfully led their organizations through this transition embarked on a journey to understand key technology drivers, embraced the wisdom of the crowd (stakeholders), and invited Millennials to participate and shape their future.

PART II

What You Must Know about the Workplace That's Coming

CHAPTER 4

What Every Leader Needs to Know about the Future

If you want to teach people a new way of thinking, don't bother trying to teach them. Instead, give them a tool, the use of which will lead to new ways of thinking.

—Richard Buckminster Fuller

If you would like to take a peek behind your company's curtain, Roland Openshaw can create a map of how your company really works. It is no secret that organization charts are fictional. No company operates as they are drawn. In a time when reporting lines were less blurred and cross-functional cooperation was rare, the organizational (org) chart provided logic for organizing work. Today, however, the org chart often just gets in the way of organizations encouraging cooperation and collaboration. Even though we give token allegiance to the chart, its vestigial power flexes the minute Sally from Marketing needs support from Bob in Sales to launch a new service. Then it comes alive, flexing its fading power over common sense.

Sally crosses boundaries easily, but Bob plays "by the book." This fiction turns to friction that kills opportunities in a playground/workplace version of "You're not the boss of me!" Sally has to climb her chain of command to reach the diplomatic or command bridge capable of exerting force on poor Bob to play nice for the greater good.

What if Sally's company better understood how the proverbial sausage really gets made? What if her company's mental model of work looked like a network of relationships rather than a pyramid of positions? What if they could see the invisible roads and rivers where cooperation flows? What if they could see the hubs and bridges, those people who operate as connectors between different

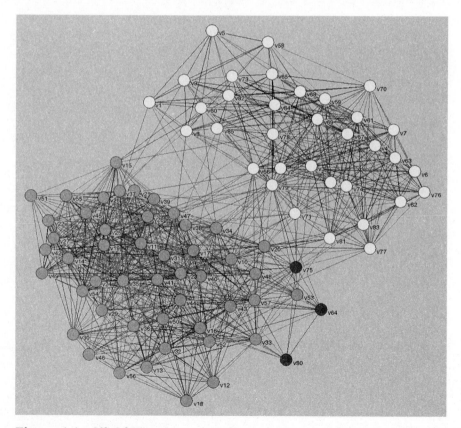

Figure 4.1   Silo'd Team

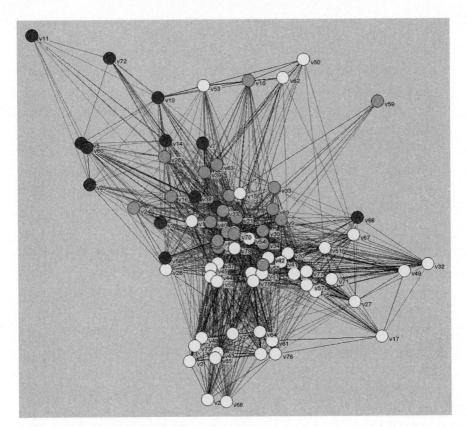

Figure 4.2   Healthy Team

internal tribes, villages, and cities? Sally might then know to go to Jamal, that bridge builder in Sales.

Roland uses a tool called Social Network Analysis (SNA) to map the communication patterns. As shown in Figures 4.1 and 4.2, the maps looks similar to the social media network maps you've seen that resemble complex spider webs or airline route maps. (For a full explanation of these maps, see Appendix B.)

Roland met with us at Case4Space and demonstrated how this analysis improved the success rate and innovation cycle for pharmaceutical research and development teams. The path for developing a drug is long, complicated, costly, and high risk. SNA released new communication flow among different teams and helped identify patterns in teams that consistently create break-throughs. Roland was then able to change the space to break barriers, build more bridges, and increase the frequency (density) and diversity of the communication.

Office furniture manufacturer Haworth has brought a similar "MRI" to corporate culture and its many subcultures. This deeper look helps to create environments tailored to a group's natural behavior patterns. It also helps companies align culture and strategy. Haworth's methodology models the team and organizational culture, looking at four ways groups tend to organize:

1. A human relationship model optimized for relational cohesion and cooperation.
2. An open systems model designed for flexibility to adapt and innovate.
3. A rational goal model built for goal setting, planning, and control in response to external demands.
4. A process model designed around internal procedures, stability, and controls.

Every group and company is a blend of these archetypes. By looking at the different traits, managers can develop a more evidence-based approach to playing to their strengths or making adjustments.

Construction firm, Balfour Beatty, also uses very creative and innovative tools to map and identify the latent talents of their employees.[1] Technology is rapidly leading us toward the soft side of organizational leadership. While we come to terms with an explosion of invisible tools, it is important to remain human.

In Part I, we looked at why and when the office quit working. Starting here in Part II, we will look at the office that is coming. First, you should know that the new office is a place of revolution—the deposing of the exhausted forms and structures born in the industrial age. That crumbling age is being replaced by a new workplace and new ways to organize, create, and collaborate. Connection, cooperation, innovation, wellness, and transparency mark the emerging culture. You've just seen a glimpse of some new tools, offered by Roland Openshaw, Haworth, and Balfour Beatty, for understanding this: a new and more dynamic office and its culture.

In this chapter, we will look at of some of the key technologies and ideas that reflect the revolution; they are changing the workplace, transforming work, and redefining businesses. Serious leaders are trying to discern the shapes and sounds of the future. These new technologies are critical tools for that new workplace, and therefore need to be understood and appreciated. They are:

1. The increasing mobility of work
2. Transparent organizations and markets
3. The networked intelligence of buildings
4. The rock-bottom cost of information
5. Mining the big data of the workplace
6. Your brain at work
7. From wellness to well-being
8. The intelligent workplace

The speed of these changes is faster than most leaders realize. All eight areas present powerful and disruptive opportunities, and they will converge within the next decade. That convergence sets the stage for a new kind of economy, organization, worker, and workplace.

"Change. More. Faster. That is the demand side of the workplace equation. On the supply side, we need to get beyond archaic notions of space as just a fixed capital asset. The imperative is to create space that is agile and adaptable to short-term organizational needs while at the same time less resource-intensive."

—Celeste Tell, workplace strategy manager for the Bill & Melinda Gates Foundation

We still have a steep learning curve and hurdles to climb. I mean, people and companies are still trying to figure out how to effectively use PowerPoint after almost 30 years. As of 2013, 30 percent of computers are still using Windows XP, released 13 years ago. Almost 50 percent are using Windows 7, now seven years old. CBRE chose a better way: They bought a complete upgrade in technology and added training and coaching. They wanted everyone to feel comfortable and confident in using the new tools.

The Increasing Mobility of Work

These days, almost everyone does work outside his or her office. I'm currently working at Starbucks. I've been coming here long enough that most of the staff knows my first name, and they regularly bring food and drink samples to me. When I make or receive phone calls, I can easily step outside—even take a short hike around the large retail complex—so that our conversation does not have to compete with Sinatra or Fleetwood Mac. While I take a hike, I can also use my Moves app to keep track of how far I have walked during my calls. Today it was 2.1 miles.

Part of the mobile-nomad work mind-set is making the most of that habitat where you happen to be working. I recently did some work out of the Roam Atlanta cowork facility. Daniel Homrich, who created a community culture for the space, walked me around to show me the many work venues I could choose from. It was clear that Roam Atlanta was conscious of the culture they want to achieve.

So even though the tools for working mobile are advanced, it is clear that the facilities supporting this kind of work are just beginning to form. Most workers today are adept at converting a travel-club lounge, Starbucks, Panera Bread, executive suite, or hotel lobby into relatively suitable workspace. Thankfully, real estate developers are recognizing this new level of mobility and creating more work-friendly spaces.

We all sometimes need a quieter and more suitable work environment than Starbucks. That level of workspace has been hard to find prior to the advent of coworking facilities. Now, Workspace as a Service (WaaS) is coming! And several new tools are emerging to help. For example, the LiquidSpace app will locate and show pictures of available offices that are nearby and for rent on an hourly or daily basis. We can view, reserve, and pay for a temporary office through the app. Companies or office buildings that hold empty offices (remember, about 50 percent), executive suites, and now hotels are listing their inventory on LiquidSpace. Some hotels are appearing on LiquidSpace and listing their lobby as available for free! Furthermore, some hotels are partnering with designers and furniture manufacturers to convert sleeping rooms to work-friendly space.

Haworth, one of our Case4Space partners, has implemented the club concept in partnership with developers in the Asia/Pacific region. Tailored to the tenants of the building, the space functions as a private club. Think of an Airport Traveler's Lounge with the support you might find at an Apple Genius Bar.

Transparent Organizations and Markets

"A powerful global conversation has begun. Through the Internet, people are discovering and inventing new ways to share relevant knowledge with blinding speed. As a direct result, markets are getting smarter—and getting smarter faster than most companies."

—*The Cluetrain Manifesto*[2]

Jim Clark, along with a few young engineers, created Netscape in 1994 as the world's first mass-market Web browser. He expanded the Internet from an exclusive techy tool into a consumer's engine of change. The public's relationship with merchants forever changed. This evolution in listening has gone through distinct phases:

• Hey, I'm trying to get through to you! Huh, I'm not listening.
• Listen and respond (quickly).

- Listen, learn, and improve.
- Listen and share with other consumers.
- Listen and connect others to share with each other.

Today, technology has reached a new stage. Merchants (and, yes, governments) are always listening and anticipating your intentions through apps, online use, data scrapers, or embedded devices. And we are not too sure that we understand or like it. But that is a subject for another time (and book).

This same progression is moving into the relationship between employer and employee. Perhaps 10 to 15 years behind the progression of the marketplace, it has nevertheless arrived. Companies who jumped to the front of the line in the marketplace, like Amazon, Netflix, Facebook, Google, and others, have attained dominant market positions. That is the promise for those who follow this progression and also jump to the front of the line by listening to their own companies.

The Fine Art of Listening

When one of CBRE's committees met to discuss the new "free address" work environment, Seth, a 30-something, mentioned that he was looking forward to their new boundary-less office because it would give him greater access to senior brokers and senior professionals. One of the senior brokers, not fully on board with giving up his office, asked Seth, "Why would that kind of change make a difference?"

Seth said that he was too intimidated to walk into that broker's office, so he never did.

Traditional organizations develop a certain unintentional institutional deafness toward the needs of their employees. Those needs too often get delegated to an invisible help desk.

For example, United Airlines was brought to its knees by the song "United Breaks Guitars." United Airlines broke Dave Carroll's $3,500 Taylor guitar. He and his band even saw baggage handlers tossing their instruments on the tarmac in Chicago. Dave could not get United to make amends. So Dave wrote the now famous country-Western novelty song. It had almost 14 million views as of May 2014. It also launched a Wikipedia entry, Carroll's speaking career, and now a book at www.unitedbreaksguitarsbook. com. After a few million hits, United applauded the video and paid for his guitar. In fact, a United spokesman addressed the need to make changes. Do ya think?

Employees can now give their opinions on their employers at eBossWatch, Glassdoor, RateMyBoss, and many other websites. Clearly, employers need to quickly improve their listening! They must also deploy all the tools available to gain deeper insight into and awareness of what is going on with their employees.

Amazon is "listening" even when we're not directly talking to them. In 2014 they announced a patent for "predictive delivery"; in the future they will ship what you want, before you order it! They will adjust our user interface to modify the kind of data gathered along with new algorithms to predict, ship, and bill the products we "want." Part of this feels like subtle conditioning to prepare us for deeper boundaries they will inevitably cross. Like the frog in the slowly heated pot of water, we won't notice or respond to its boiling point. Perhaps we need embarrassing reminders like Wiki-Leaks, regardless of the politics around it, as a reminder that good intentions can quickly get distorted by technology's own impulses.

The Networked Intelligence of Buildings

As a society, we are embedding billions of intelligent devices into our infrastructure. All of them collect data, perform functions, and, when connected to the Internet, can "talk" to one another. When all of these are connected and talking to one another, our world will transition from just being technology driven to being a Techno-verse. If Ray Kurzweil is correct in his predictions, we are approaching a point where machines will take on self-organizing behavior. Our environment will begin to respond to us and to the vast network in which it is embedded. This opens incredible opportunities and questions for the workplace.

John Chambers, CEO of Cisco Systems, told the Consumer Electronics Show in January 2014, "It isn't just about connecting a car or a refrigerator [to the Internet]; it's the combination together that changes the process. 2014 is the year everything will START to change."

The Rock-Bottom Cost of Information

The technologies of collaboration have two powerful effects for organizations. The first is to lower the management cost for organizing and coordinating work. Collaboration tools as simple as Google Docs or Meetup lower the threshold for action and engagement. These tools reduce the transaction cost of turning an idea into a revenue stream. What is taking place primarily outside of traditional institutions will become a normal means for companies to initiate and coordinate work.

Second, these tools increase the size of a group enterprise without raising management costs for organizing and coordinating the work. Examples of large-scale, low-cost enterprises include Wikipedia, Linux, and Foldit (more on that later).

Dave Gray, a colleague who wrote *The Connected Company*, talks about the built-in constraint for employees trying to collaborate in a territory-bound department. There is a strong diminishing return on employee effectiveness when they try to handle work that crosses department boundaries. Anyone who has had to seek cooperation from another department knows the time, hassle, delays, and sometimes the need for management help in overcoming those barriers. There is a natural limit to institutional size before losing effectiveness unless you leverage collaborative tools, limit the scale of business units, or take on a less-structured environment that is designed for self-organizing teams.

W. L. Gore scales the company, now over 16,000 employees, by limiting the scale of each business unit. Bill Gore discovered while working at DuPont that work groups got more work done and were more engaged than departments. He left DuPont in the 1950s to create a company that functioned like a work group. For that reason, its business units try to stay between 150 and 200 people in size to maintain a stronger sense of group identity and make it easier to coordinate and cooperate when everyone is on the same team.

Valve Software, WordPress, Basecamp, and Menlo Innovations have adopted a self-organizing team structure. Some call this "the bossless office." These companies are small, technology based, and have very open work environments. In the case of Valve, all of the desks have wheels; if someone feels disconnected from their current team, they can roll their desk to another team. The fluid work and resource flow requires an extremely flexible environment, a high level of transparency about what work is scheduled and who is working on it, and a different accountability structure. In other words, everyone's work is visible to everyone else, and everyone has a stake in the results. So the issue is not management "running a tight ship," but rather the whole team having a vested interest in the work.

For leaders looking to the future, adopting the tools of collaboration in the workplace offers an opportunity to reduce coordination costs and to lower the cost and risk of taking on new initiatives. These tools will also build new habits and mind-sets, leading to new ways to organize work in the workplace.

The work of Case4Space and its predecessor, The Commercial Real Estate Revolution, was possible because the tools of collaboration made it easy to recruit a team of leaders from multiple organizations, with a common interest to work within a bossless framework. We know it is possible to coordinate with a large, diverse, and distributed team when the tools of collaboration are supported by a new mind-set, structure, and environment.

Mining the Big Data of the Workplace

We will quickly move from smart buildings to smart workplaces as we better capture the building-use and occupant-experience data.

This conversation was too sensitive to consider a few years ago when we launched Case4Space, even with our Silicon Valley contingent. However, this is the path that data will travel. Past objections centered on the intrusiveness and cost. Surveys are inexpensive but not very accurate. Sensor technology is more accurate but expensive and raises privacy concerns. But smart-phones and apps are lowering the threshold of both intrusiveness and cost. The benefits will be transformative to employees, companies, and building owners if the insights gained can increase engagement (less than 30 percent) engagement, improve office utilization rates (under 50 percent), lower operating costs, improve security, and increase innovation. Google's top priority is designing and creating the employee experience. More and more other firms are starting to agree.

Another benefit of data mining is that the intelligence of an item will dramatically overshadow its material and functional value. For example, Four Seasons and Ritz–Carlton hotels charge a lot more for their luxury environments and the level of personal service. However, a hospitality consultant explained to me that the level of information gathered from clients is what makes the real difference. The premium comes from how they translate that information into a highly personalized experience.

Right now, the room rates of both range from $350 to $450 per night in the Dallas market. Marriott's room rates are approximately $150 per night. The cost of building or operating the Four Seasons was not double or triple Marriott's costs. The difference was the ability to gather and translate information into a unique experience.

Products and services are becoming more of a means to better understand clients than an end in themselves. The art and science for the new economy is creating the virtuous feedback loop that so gradually modifies and improves the user experience, it goes almost unnoticed. It is a new business model. This point really jumps out in the simple comparison between Ford and Google in Table 4.1.[3]

A few companies that we met with, like IBM and Google, have developed similar capacities for gathering employee experience

Table 4.1   The Value Shift of the Information Economy

	Ford	Google
Employees	171,000	44,777
Market Cap	$66.86B	$293.73B
Revenue	$134B	$49.96B
P/E Ratio	18.88	33.05

data and translating that into either work design or support services. Imagine the ability to gain a deep understanding of your workforce and what engages people, just as the Ritz-Carlton, Four Seasons, Amazon, or Netflix understands the unique habits and interests of each of its customers. The potential is not simply reaching full engagement but tapping into the invisible talents, knowledge, outlooks, and experience of people to find that exponential jump. Organizations will experience a Moore's Law[4] effect where the cost of innovation drops dramatically as learning capacity expands exponentially. As command and control recedes, replaced by internal and external network structures, we will certainly feel like Dorothy from *The Wizard of Oz*: "We're not in Kansas anymore."

Your Brain at Work

A Chicago company that designs and furnishes office interiors had recently moved into an open environment office. They used their new layout to let potential customers see an open workspace in action.

While working with them, I profiled the management team using Gallup's StrengthsFinder assessment, along with a tool that provides deeper detail called CoreClarity. I spotted something interesting in the results related to the new space. Two of the managers had profiles that suggested they were on the far end of the introvert scale. So I asked them, "How do you like the new office layout?"

Darren, the CFO—a deep-thinking, highly private, off-the-charts introvert—said, "I hate this layout! I feel like I am out in the open and can't get a thing done. I have to either get in early or take my work home."

The company president quickly pushed back, "Hey, you're in the back, away from the major traffic."

"Yes, I'm next to the printer. Every time someone uses it, I might as well go take a smoke break."

Darren represents up to 40 percent of the workplace—that many test as introverts.

When I share stories like Darren's at Case4Space gatherings, I'm surprised at how many people quickly express frustration at design concepts that are applied with little understanding or appreciation for the physiological or psychological dimensions they affect. Leaders must be aware that an engaging and effective workplace will consider the basic and general human comfort and needs. But they must also think through the individual personalities of all employees.

In 2013, workplace surveys began to show strong resistance against open plan solutions. The key complaints were noise, privacy, and the need for more areas for doing focused work. The successful implementations are better at thinking through individuality, providing sound conditioning for open areas, and producing a variety of work venues.

As work becomes more interactive, environments open up, and as health becomes an increasingly important issue, understanding the brain at work will become critical to successful design. It is already having a strong impact in health-care environments and hospitality. The Academy of Neuroscience of Architecture has become a central resource for bringing this knowledge and discipline into the workplace.

Gamification—The Mechanics of Engagement

Brain science is also entering the workplace through gamification. This process translates the mechanics of engagement into four elements: a goal, rules or constraints, real–time feedback, and voluntary participation.[5] It is not turning a program into a series of badges or turning work into a game. Work is work. But, you may have witnessed one of your kids or grandchildren engrossed in an educational game. A few companies are building that same bridge into the workplace.

If the ladder for innovation begins with engagement that leads to collaboration, then gamification offers a fascinating new tool for the workplace. One work application is that it unlocks and develops a particular kind of thinking that is key to innovation. Gabe Zichermann, founder and CEO of Dopamine and Gamification Co, identifies this as fluid logic.

The Aviators, a television show with a weekly audience of over nine million, asked, "Can a 12–year–old straight off the streets land a 737 in a major U.S. airport?" They invited Remie Aquino to try. With a little help at the start of his flight, Remie took over the controls and landed the simulator at LAX on his first try.

Several years ago I accepted the same invitation. The experience felt very real, stressful, and disorienting. It was so easy to overcorrect with a slight move of the control stick. Flying required a delicate touch while watching myriad digital readouts, meters, dials, and gauges and adjusting speed and pitch. Let's just say I was less successful than Remie. That seems to be the norm. Kids, raised with video games, do better than their parents.[6]

Remie demonstrated fluid intelligence, the capacity to solve unfamiliar or novel problems (vs. crystalized intelligence, which applies existing knowledge and experience to problems). Video gaming builds fluid intelligence, a vital component to thinking outside the box and leading to innovative solutions.

A second application of gamification is crowdsourcing to solve wicked problems (see Chapter 3). Many have heard the story of David Baker and his game, Foldit. A biochemist and professor at the University of Washington, David had been trying to map a key protein chain for an HIV–like virus. An international team of scientists had worked on the problem for over a decade.

In 2008, Baker approached David Sales, a computer game designer at the university, to create a game to tackle what analytical tools had been unable to solve. Foldit was designed to solve the complex folding patterns that define proteins. When Baker's team launched the game and the challenge, they allowed several weeks for people to sign up, form teams, and submit their ideas—but the protein puzzle was solved in less than 10 days. Even more astounding, it wasn't solved by scientists, but by gamers.

Gabe Zichermann concludes, "We must remember that the average player lives in a world devoid of daily positive reinforcement, surprise, delight, and meaningful sociability. By aligning our experience with their desires, and striving to make every encounter more meaningful, we can bring fun to every grey, dull corner of the world."[7]

From Wellness to Well-Being

When we held one of our summits at the Google campus, we immediately noticed the food and funky bicycles. Our conference room had a set of barn doors that opened into a micro-kitchen. A central table displayed a variety of fresh and local fruit. The glass-front refrigerator was stocked with bottled waters and naturally sweetened teas and juices. Off to the side, a cabinet prominently displayed healthy snacks.

After our snack time, Chris Coleman, our host, gave us a tour. He explained their wellness evolution and strategy. It all started when they realized that Googlers were getting a reputation for gaining weight in their first year of employment. So they redesigned the menu, offered smaller plates, made exercise rooms smaller and spread them out over the campus, and added more walking paths between buildings.

It was also clear that, as hard as people worked, Google accommodated their need to take care of personal business and break away for personal space. We saw quiet zones with sleep pods and Google electric cars that employees could use for personal errands. They could also drop their laundry off at numerous sites and pick it up at the end of the day. All of these services and conveniences added a dimension that went beyond wellness.

We were impressed with holistic approaches to work, health, and work–life balance. When we looked at Google, Cummins, W. L. Gore, Zappos, the Bill & Melinda Gates Foundation, and several other companies, we saw a real commitment to well-being. It is an old conversation, but it is now finding frameworks of reality.

The Intelligent Workplace

Mobility, transparency, intelligent environments, the low cost of information, big data, and human dynamics are converging in the incredible world of apps. As I recently drove home, I saw a traffic jam ahead with no view of where the bottleneck started. While stopped I turned to the crowdsourcing navigator app, Waze. It combines GIS (geographic information system), crowdsourcing, gamification, big data, and analytics to let me know what's up ahead and suggest alternate routes. Imagine pulling all of these elements together in the workplace. Waze showed the speed of the traffic and pinpointed the location of an accident that caused the backup. Since my car was not moving, I hit the icon that represented heavy traffic, and a little bubble opened and said I had earned 6 points and helped my fellow Wazers. I was in the game.

The Pandorification of the Workplace

Pandora is an app that allows you to create your own Internet radio station (or multiple ones). It builds your station around your own musical tastes. Right now, I'm listening to my "Kohala" radio station, made up of primarily guitar jazz. Pandora works by first selecting a song or an artist to represent the station's genre. The app will begin to play songs with similar attributes. If a song Pandora plays matches your taste for that station, you click thumbs up. If not, you click thumbs down. It's that simple for the user.

Behind the curtain, Pandora is the product of the Music Genome Project. In 1999, Will Glaser and Tim Westergren began to break music into what are now 450 fundamental attributes. The project developed algorithms defining relationships between these music genes. Some of the attributes fall into large categories such as Rock or Classical. Others are more esoteric and precise.

Each time a song is marked with thumbs up or down, the algorithm goes to work comparing its genomic attributes to previously chosen or rejected songs. In a very short time, the radio station finds that stream of music that fits your tastes based on the algorithm you participated in creating.

Lots of data, plus an algorithm with continuous feedback, creates what might be called a frictionless listening experience. I seldom have to hit thumbs up or down on my Kohala station. It knows me. Pandora is clearly better than listening to AM, FM, or even satellite radio. It is also easier than building your own playlist.

The Pandorification of work is here. *Now.* We have all the pieces and we have them in place. Companies are *now* breaking work into their "genomic" elements. We have assessments that allow us to profile how people are wired and how they best work. We have sensor technology to capture movement. Gamification allows us to engineer responses to and view engagement. SNA helps us see the vitality of team interactions. We can stream data and translate it into dashboards for quick and intuitive interpretations. Finally, we can begin to see patterns and design interventions and environments to influence behavior and performance. Let's take a quick scan at some of these pieces. Even though it's all in place, no one seems to realize that we can do it! Privacy and other concerns are keeping us from walking in to this new magic. But trust me; it is coming.

IBM's Susan Stucky described what sounds like a work genome effort at the 2012 International Facility Management Association (IFMA) Workplace Strategy Summit at Cornell University on the future of work. According to her bio, her work "comprises service system modeling and simulation . . . Her focus is on new ways to detect patterns of interaction that increase value and patterns of interaction that diminish value."[8] This sounds very much like Pandora's thumbs up and thumbs down. She told me that IBM has identified more than 4,000 attributes that make up the work they perform.

Can we begin to identify the genes for engagement? Matt Killingsworth is a researcher who designs studies to determine when we are most happy. He created the Track Your Happiness app to find some causal relationships. When you sign up for the app it will ping you several times a day and ask a series of quick and easy questions. Some of the questions:

- How happy are you right now?
- What are you doing? (It provides a scroll-down list of options.)
- Do you have to do what you are doing?

One of Matt's conclusions is that "a wandering mind (or distracted) is an unhappy mind." The ability to be fully present (engaged) in anything we do, even driving, is a key to happiness. What if companies could gather data on what, when, how, and with whom its employees are most engaged?

The *Internet of Things* plays a key role for understanding the relationship between the environment, performance, and behavior. "According to Cisco [in July 2013], there are an estimated 1.5 trillion things in the world . . . and approximately 8.7 billion, or 0.6%, were connected in 2012. The firm expects a 25% annualized decrease in price to connect between 2012 and 2020 and a matching 25% annualized increase in connectivity. That means we can expect 50 billion connected things by 2020 . . ."[9]

Both CoreNet and IFMA report that companies effectively use less than 50 percent of their space. That wasted space is a chronic symptom of an unengaged and underleveraged workforce. So, of course, many companies want to measure the effective use of space.

We will soon consider the office a work habitat and collect data on the roaming, working, grazing, and migration patterns of those who inhabit this environment. A simple smartphone app is the logical solution. An employee would turn it on, like punching a time clock, and then log off at the end of the day. Something like this will probably be an initial solution to relieve privacy fears. In time, however, the embedded technology in the building will document all the details of an employee's work presence and patterns.

The National Renewable Energy Laboratory is a living laboratory for the most advanced applications of energy technology in Golden, Colorado. Their live energy dashboard provides a real-time look at energy use in any area of their campus. It provides comparative data for time of the day, seasonal use, and other variations to continuously tune the building to optimal performance. They found the visibility of the data positively changed behavior to reduce energy consumption. Their Energy DataBus inspired our thinking around a similar Engagement DataBus.

The Pandorification of Work in Action

Darren, the introvert CFO we met earlier, settled into his new open cube near the printer. On the first day the company's new Engagement App pinged Darren with the question, "Rate your engagement level." In the last few minutes two people came by to use the printer, leaving Darren distracted and frustrated. Thumbs down. Over the next few days Darren's interaction with the app collected data on where he did his work and with whom. Darren, it seemed, never left his cube.

Within a few days the app gave Darren some feedback, recommending three work areas that Darren could move to. Darren reluctantly moved, another annoying change! After one day he noticed that the distractions had dramatically dropped. He completed two major projects that had piled up, and he actually felt . . . positive. His boss noticed that Darren seemed happy.

On the other side of the data, the Engagement Dashboard came to life. The maps clearly showed "live" areas of interaction, "dead" spots, bottlenecks, and vital hubs. After the first few weeks, the data painted a discouraging picture. Engagement levels were less than 30 percent, and portions of the company were near the toxic level. After week six, a shift began. The app was helping people find where they worked best and helping them link to people with talents and resources they normally did not interact with.

The Dispatch Team was struggling. The communication map spotted a key bottleneck making their coordination efforts more difficult. Dispatch relies heavily on Warehouse Receiving to let them know that work is ready for scheduling. However, that vital link showed up as a faint line of infrequent communication. With some minor adjustments, setting up coordination meetings and a shift in proximity, that bottleneck disappeared and the improvement showed up immediately on the Engagement Dashboard.

Within six months, the interaction among the data, the people, and the app was taking on a life of its own. The employees were breaking out of their departmental silos. The data showed them who needed to be involved in key meetings. Where the managers used to hear excuses for efforts getting held up or falling into black holes with people passing the buck, they began to hear things like, "We reserved the project room for two days so we could tackle the complaints we're getting on our invoicing."

The Engagement App facilitated the process by first reserving the room, and then pinging each of the department heads that had some role in the issue. This was just one of several just-in-time meetings now taking place that tackled a complex problem with all of the right stakeholders.

What if we could track people's movement and use of space, and mash that data up with a person's engagement level, the office's communication patterns, and an employee's optimized work conditions? Could you finally mash that up with an organization's ever-evolving culture? Could you create such an engagement app?

Imagine creating an Engagement DataBus. The dashboard might show the overall engagement level of the company and the ebbs and flows based on external events (i.e., stock price movement or news from the competition). It could track internal factors like a new product launch, a lost contract, or the hiring or firing of a top executive. That last feature could provide an interesting barometer. Companies can test new ideas, strategies, products, or programs before heavy investment is incurred.

Perhaps the DataBus could show the engagement level for different teams or departments and the factors that cause it to ebb and flow. What if it could show what areas in the office are hot spots for positive activity or dead spots? When analyzing contributing factors, you could zoom out to macro patterns or zoom in to view the social network patterns of particular teams.

Imagine building a social and gaming element into the app. An employee could quickly see how his or her personal or team engagement level compares. Maybe the app could take the aggregate data stream and, by matching algorithms, send recommendations, provide notice of a job opening more tailored to the employee's strengths, or connect with other employees that may have just-in-time knowledge for helping to complete a project.

Our idea of the Pandorification of work is simply stepping over and into the same information technology paradigm that companies like Amazon, Netflix, Google, and others use to understand the market. The first step is to create a data stream, then use algorithms to define relationships within that information that emerge into patterns and, ultimately, over time, a deep understanding of the causal relationships that drive performance and behavior.

On one level the process is quite simple. Start with some question about a behavior you would like to understand. Identify a handful of key variables you think influence one another. Then create an app that is engaging enough that people will play your game. Once the data stream begins, then the rest is easy.

The Power of Human Engagement

What company creates loyalty so strong that customers tattoo their bodies with its logo? Harley-Davidson.

That is because Harley-Davidson dares to remind us of the deeper craving we all have for freedom, affirmation, and affiliation. Ken Schmidt, former director of communications for Harley, is a living lesson and a bard for the power of engagement. Ken said that the single greatest discovery Harley made as they were pulling out of near bankruptcy was a choice. They could focus on building great products or they could understand the people who bought those hogs. In other words, they could be in love with their own product or they could fall in love with their customers. Love for your product can dull you to what your customers say. But if you listen to them, what you hear can help you make better products.

The Human Side to Technology

Every tool rests on implicit behaviors (social technologies) that are best suited for that tool. We pound with hammers; we turn screwdrivers. The tools of digital technology, however, are advancing faster than our social technologies. Therefore, many just cannot keep up. We all know those who prefer Windows XP. Books like *Death by PowerPoint* explain this gap. One of the big challenges facing us is the need to reduce the gap.

Fumbling around and wasting time just to get everyone online for a teleconference, crawling under tables to find a power socket, searching for someone with the right password for the Wi-Fi, or using a digital projector with an old bulb all reveal how social technology is lagging behind digital technologies.

"The pace of obsolescence is increasing faster than we can absorb. The ability to understand and deploy the space around us as a strategic element to connect and maximize people is critical to success."

—Erin Rae Hoffer, Industry Strategy and Thought Leader Marketing, Autodesk

Those at the forefront of or leading the digital revolution make the use and integration of technology a seamless and hassle-free experience. For example, CBRE made a big investment in teaching their digital immigrants how to access and use their cloud-based files. Today, many companies not only understand the mechanics, but are also spending the time and money necessary to bring the value of instant access, tagging documents and simple sharing, "frictionless design," and reliable equipment to the workplace.

Our companies are filed with digital immigrants, so our workplaces must ease that transition. *Everyone* will need a connected, networked, and mobile digital mind-set in the work of the future. Digital immigrants would benefit from it, but digital natives will demand it. The natives assume technology will work seamlessly. They are a vastly underutilized resource for moving companies forward from Gutenberg habits to a Google mind-set.

The next chapter will help you understand this historic cohort and the benefit they bring to business. Warning: Before you see their benefit, they may scare the hell out of you.

CHAPTER 5

What Every Executive Needs to Know about Millennials

Media is like an environment; it takes us over, and sort of consumes us in many ways . . . Media, in some ways, determines or dictates who can say what to whom, what they can say, how it will be said, etc. And so, when media change—our conversations change.
—Michael Wesch[1]

When I recently made a presentation to a company retreat of senior executives, I mentioned our research on Millennials (those born between 1980 and 2000). Immediately, the room temperature increased. Strong opinions bounced around the room like beach balls. Adjectives were barked and growled like profanity: "disrespectful," "entitled," "antisocial," "uncaring." Several snapped variations of, "They never answer their phones or e-mail" or "They're all like Justin Bieber, Miley Cyrus, or *Jersey Shore.*"

Wow. So that's your hot button.

I understand. Bob Johansen, author of *Leaders Make the Future,* writes, "The digital natives will be a disruptive force on a scale that we cannot yet imagine.[2]

Digital Natives and Digital Immigrants

"For my one-year-old daughter a magazine is an iPad that does not work. It will remain so for the rest of her life. Steve Jobs has coded a part of her OS."

—*YouTube Video*

Ten years ago I wrote, "When the primary means of storing and distributing information changes, our worldviews change."[3] When technology changes the way people see and experience the world, it remakes children into different human beings. They grow up to form different social structures and then new institutions to empower the changes and the new capabilities. This radical remake has happened twice before. The Gutenberg revolution and the expansion of print in the fifteenth century created a radical disruption for about 150 years. Television changed the media landscape in the 1950s, resulting in decades of disruption to industry and social institutions.

Today our kids have been wired by the most social, most expansive, most rapid, and most accessible media landscape in history. This is what defines this next generation more than any other factor. That is where we need to begin.

"Don't look at the new comers entering the workforce as 'know-it-alls,' but instead include us as a part of the team. We want to learn, to fail, and to experience the company. We want to make an impact, but from a way to help everyone—not just us. In the end, it's not who's been there the longest, but who has helped the organization succeed."

—Katherine Tracey, marketing coordinator, Cassidy Turley, and Millennial

If you are reading this book in paper form, you are probably a digital immigrant. You may use digital tools and use them extensively and well, but it's not your first media "language." For some, that first language may be found in books and other print media. For those born after 1950, television may be the way you best connect to information and events. In either case, digital technology is a second or third language. Even though we function in this digital world, we also miss most of the rhythm, pace, nuance, and value that only true digital natives understand.

We are the first generation to see that those entering the job market know more about how the world actually works than those in charge. Today's managers and leaders face a critical issue: How can we embrace a mind-set that is completely foreign to us? To make the challenge even more difficult, that mind-set is wrapped in the jarring and often offensive package of youth.

The generational model used by nearly every commentator, marketing firm, generational expert, and management consultant today was first introduced by William Strauss and Neil Howe in their seminal book, *Generations: The History of America's Future, 1584–2069* (William Morrow, 1992). Their premise: There is a cycle of four repeating generations, each lasting approximately 20 years and taking the shape of an archetype—pioneer, nomad, hero, and artist. Each generation goes through four distinct phases of life: childhood, young adult, midlife, and elderhood. Finally, society follows four stages of social development: prosperity, awakening, decline, and crisis.

As the theory goes, pioneers—baby boomers, born in prosperity—developed the strong hope and ideals that set the tone for a new era. Nomads (Generation X) grew in the shadow of the boomers' idealism and ambition. The contradictions they perceived between boomer ideals and practice, plus their dominance by numbers, led Generation X onto a path to pragmatism. Heroes—the Millennials—arrived at the decline of boomer culture. The Millennials also came of age in deep crisis—the 9/11 attacks, two wars, and an economic meltdown.

The Millennials' rallying cry and central narrative could best be characterized as correcting the "sins of the fathers." They struggle under the consequences of multiple wars, social injustice, national debt, poor job prospects, declining education, political dysfunction, economic inequity, a polluted and ravaged environment, pay inequality, and a general erosion in how society and institutions care for and regard one another.

If we follow the pattern, then the next generation, artists, will set the stage for a new cycle. They will bear the brunt of this hard economic reset and the arduous work to reshape social and economic institutions.

> "As a young professional, there appears to be an awakening in our industry. Specifically for the organizational architect—there is a social responsibility to acknowledge the passion that drive employees and respond with an engaging workplace that empowers change at all levels."
>
> —Julia De Rosi, GSA Space Planning, and Millennial

Strauss and Howe's generation model provides insight into some of the social values for Millennials, but it does not consider the defining nature of technology over the last 50 years, nor the more complex configuration of Millennials and future generations. Twenty-two of the 25 generations in Strauss and Howe's model predate the Information Age and its more rapid, changing, and complex nature.

Tech–Savvy versus Digital Native

> "We know that whatever media ecology is present at the time a child becomes an adult will influence that person for the rest of his or her life."
>
> —*Bob Johansen,* Leaders Make the Future[4]

Many label Millennials as digital natives. But that is not true. "Technologically savvy" may be a better label. Millennials provide a vital bridge, but are not the truly rewired brains that will begin entering the workforce around 2020.

Digital natives are those raised with digital technology as their primary media platform for understanding and interacting with the world. Though many Millennials had computer access through school and are quite comfortable with the technology, television still dominated their media experience. The digital native era began around 2000.

I believe that understanding shifting communication landscapes will provide better and more reliable guidance than the generation model. First, each media landscape behaves like a different kind of communication tool, reinforcing some forms of thinking and behavior, while making others more difficult. For example, print reinforces perspective, reflection, and linear rational thought, while television reinforces novelty, immediacy, and emotional connection. And we've clearly seen that television's forms of thinking and behavior have trumped print's over the past generation.

Second, the defining imprints of communication on cohorts have shrunk from 20 years to 6.[5] At that point, the generational model quickly breaks down. The Strauss and Howe model was built to describe a pre-Information Age time whose institutions and social norms remained relatively stable. Gen X and Millennials represent the first post–Industrial/Information Age cohorts, but digital natives had not yet been born when their work was first published.

By regrouping historical periods according to their dominant communication platforms, we find a clear acceleration of change that correlates closely with our earlier discussion of a world entering an era of complexity. The media landscape lens also provides a mechanism for anticipating the new rules that will govern institutional winners and losers, as seen in Table 5.1. (The start dates for each communication medium generally represent when they roughly reached a critical mass of adoption.)

Table 5.1   Communication Era Cohorts

Media Landscape	Dates	Years	Economic Era
Print	1650–1955	305	Industrial
Television	1956–2000	44	Information
Personal Computer	2001–2009	9	Digital
Internet/Broadband	2010–2013	4	Networked
Mobile, Smartphone, and the Cloud	2014–		Cloud
Wearable and Internet of Things			

Building on this framework, we can begin to project the rise and dominance of the next redefining media landscape—mobile. This will be the result of ubiquitous wearable technology converging with the Internet of Things.[6]

A generation immersed in a near-seamless experience of thought and environmental response, compressed intent to fulfillment, predictive of need and creating deep situational awareness, will produce a significantly different kind of person than even the digital native. Imagine walking through a facility and seeing the infrastructure behind the walls through your Google glasses, receiving notice that someone's laptop will need to be replaced in a week, or simulating a team's innovation cycle by modeling their communication patterns. These are current capabilities.

Amazon's "predictive demand" signals one of the features of a mobile, always connected era. That's right—our lives will be parsed into algorithms. Our smartphones provide enough information through normal use that each of us has a unique signature. Julia Angwin, author of *Dragnet Nation: A Quest for Privacy, Security, and Freedom in a World of Relentless Surveillance,* shared in an NPR interview, "There was a study that really surprised me that showed that if you had four separate locations of a person, where they had been over a period of a day, you could uniquely identify them. There would be only one person who had been to those four places."[7]

GIS data, 3D building, information modeling, and augmented reality will allow one to walk through the office and replay yesterday's activity. Google glasses will provide a visual simulation of which groups met where, which areas drew the most traffic, and which were left vacant. The media landscape is taking us further into an integrated Technoverse.

The Signature Academy

While doing research on Cummins Inc. in Columbus, Indiana, I met Jack Hess, executive director for the Community Coalition for Education and the former president of the local Chamber of Commerce. One of the keys to the success of both Cummins and Columbus was their partnership in building strong schools. Jack asked if I was familiar with The Signature Academy. This magnet school followed a curriculum called project-based learning.[8] The academy provides a window into the future of work; every manager needs to see it in order to fully understand.

Jack gave an example of an assignment. A class was assigned to research the history of the *Titanic*. But the assignment was more like a *Mission: Impossible* scenario.

The students logged on to their class computer to get the project details: Tell the story of the *Titanic*, covering the time line of events, the cause of the sinking, the social customs for the period (i.e., the class structure and how each class lived and was treated), the fashions, the engineering flaws of the ship, oceanography of the route, and the weather, and evaluate what went wrong and why. Furthermore, there was an equally important human element to the assignment; students had to form teams, organize, and complete the assignment together. Finally, the deliverable: a video that had to be scripted, directed, shot, and edited. In two weeks.

Several elements flipped traditional learning on its head, and would flip traditional notions of work. Jack explained, "In a traditional classroom, you learn something and then conduct a project to demonstrate what you have learned. In the project-based learning model, all teaching is done through projects where the students themselves take responsibility for their own learning, determining what roles they will play on the team, what information they have, and what information they need to collect."

As Jack was talking, I was compiling a list of subjects the kids covered: history, sociology, transoceanic travel, fashion, engineering, metallurgy, meteorology, leadership, team dynamics, scriptwriting, videography, and public speaking. Additionally, the role of the teacher was turned on its head. Teachers functioned as coaches and guides, sometimes as counselors, but not as subject matter experts.

I assumed the students were in high school. But Jack was quick to correct me; they were in second grade![9] At that point, I wanted to see the school. He gave me the address. I passed it a few times because I was looking for a school building, not a renovated auto painting and body shop (see Figure 5.1). Even though school was out for the day, I wandered around the outside of the building a few times hoping to meet someone. In a moment, Mike Reed, the principal, opened the door and asked if he could help. I told a short version of my long story and said, "Jack sent me." That was all he needed to know. Mike gave me an hour-long tour of the building, shared the school's curriculum and philosophy, and took me through what a day in the life of his students was like.

The building was designed for optimum flexibility. Rooms had more than one use, furniture was mobile and often reconfigured, collaborative technology supported every room, technology was central to the experience, and the space was designed to be social and engaging. The teacher's offices were a large, open room, and student work was posted on the wall, visible for everyone. Teacher meetings took place around a table in the center of the workspace. The building was designed to feel like a college student union building, and it does.

Figure 5.1   Signature Academy Entrance

The message from Mike was clear: This emerging, integrated form of learning required a different philosophy, a different social and organizational structure, and a radically different setting to support it. The need for flexibility also translated into a simpler design. That simple design carried a much lower initial cost and an easy adaptability to changing needs.

I traveled back to Indianapolis wondering if business leaders have any clue to just how different these kids are from the current workforce.

How Future Employees Will Get Things Done

The Signature Academy painted a picture of what work, and work environments, will look like in the future. The kids in that school are coming to the workplace—soon! That's why it is essential to reinvent our social structures. American business must leverage the technology that will fundamentally change how groups interact, learn, and get work done. Can you imagine the dissonance tech-savvy, team-based, and collaborative Millennials and digital natives will hit when they walk into the current workplaces? How do you think they might react to being assigned a single job, a cubicle, three-year-old technology, and firewalls? I'm pretty sure they will not accept technology or processes that make collaboration diffi-cult. I don't think they will tolerate IT departments that act like your local DMV. And they might have a serious problem with intranets that are more hassle than they are worth.

> "Bridging the digital knowledge and business intelligence gaps will help remove generational tension enabling engagement across departments and throughout the corporate ladder."
>
> —Tim Wakely, Balfour Beatty, and Millennial

The work structure at The Signature Academy will likely become second nature over the next five years. Companies such as Valve Software, W. L. Gore, Procter & Gamble's Connect + Develop, Zappos, Navy SEAL teams, and WordPress already have work models that will be attractive to Millennials and digital natives. Other more traditional organizations are migrating toward more team-based, tech-nology-enhanced work environments. CBRE and GSA, for example, are finding their younger employees fully engaged in their new surroundings and work structure. As CBRE's Lew Horne observed, "It was initially disrupting but turned out to be fully liberating."

Millennials and digital natives may provide organizations their best tangible barometer of what works and what doesn't. Techno-logical change has happened so quickly that we as digital immi-grants have yet to understand, let alone create, the social infrastructure to regain some sense of equilibrium. When we look back at the Gutenberg revolution, what followed was

150 years of wars and chaos until the Peace of Westphalia in 1648. In the interim, societies and institutions experimented and formed ways to harness this new game-changing printing press. Constitutional governments, a new model for science, public schools, commerce, and capitalism were born out of that era. They took full advantage of the new media landscape. We're currently in a similar convulsion of "out with the old and in with the new." Those who can figure out how to remake themselves faster will survive and have a great advantage in the future.

So, as a leader, if you are a digital immigrant fully wired and invested in a Gutenberg business model, you face three choices:

1. You can pioneer and lead your firm where few immigrants have dared to travel.
2. You can befriend and tap into the knowledge and instincts of Millennials.
3. You can do what you're currently doing a bit faster and cheaper.

We recommend a combination of pioneering and partnering with Millennials. The third option will become your tombstone.

The Internet Is a Collaborative Infrastructure

Companies cannot bolt Internet technologies onto a command and control structure and expect success. They also need a new philosophy, business models, work structure, and leadership roles that fit a new environment.

A collaborative and innovative culture goes against the nature of traditional organizations. That's why some exceptional and traditional companies that have a history of innovation set special groups apart from the rest of the organization. For example, Xerox's PARC or Lockheed Martin's famous Skunk Works both grew from a recognition that the natural DNA within a traditional organization kills new ideas.

Charles O'Reilly III and Michael Tushman's "The Ambidextrous Organization" in the April 2004 *Harvard Business Review* presented research on successful and failed innovation efforts. They described four logical approaches:

1. Innovation led internally with senior management support
2. Internally led skunk works with no management support
3. Initiatives outside the organization supported by senior management
4. External skunk works

The only approach that resulted in consistent success was the third, the management-supported external initiatives.[10]

From Disruption to Liberation

My tour of the CBRE office in Los Angeles gave me a good look at a Millennial-influenced workplace. When I exited the elevator on the twenty-fifth floor, I walked into a large, open space filled with daylight. "The Heart" looked like an upscale hotel lobby. The receptionist stood behind an elevated desk. She knew who I was and why I was there. When I asked her position she said, "I'm a concierge."

"And so, what does a concierge do?"

"My job is to make sure that all of our guests get any support they need. I stay connected with them through their stay and then follow up with any requests they may have." After a few minutes, I was introduced to Darcy, a Millennial, who gave me a tour beginning with The Heart. Behind the reception area was a long tabletop, or counter, where people could perch and talk. The table included drawers of food and beverages. At the end of the tabletop was a small group area that provided elevated tables with stools.

Darcy interpreted the area from her view: "The sunlight makes this one of my favorite areas to work. I get together with several of my colleagues, and we can get sooo much done. We like to push each other and pitch in together. This is the way I studied in college."

> "In a rapidly changing business world, it's important to step back and assess an individual's contribution to an organization. Understanding how all of the pieces come together to fit an organization's structure is essential in ensuring success in the next generation of the business model."
>
> —Janet R. Gonzalez, Millennial

Darcy took me through the office and explained the free-address workplace: No one has permanent personal space. They have a choice of over 16 work venues. She said, "You see a lot more interaction and work between my generation and the brokers. Our other office seemed to have clear territories. The brokers stayed in their world."

Lew Horne, President of CBRE, Southern California, described the same transformation, "We see the team effort evolving naturally. We had a lot of talent and knowledge, but no one really knew it was here or how to tap into it. Now, people run into each other daily and discover new ways to collaborate."

When I asked how the more tenured brokers and older staff handled the change, he said it was at first disruptive. "We gave everyone personal coaching to set up their computers, learn the software, and go through the hard work of migrating their files and data to our new systems."

I thought this was both obvious and brilliant. If you have experienced Apple's One to One training, you know how effective, reassuring, and encouraging the time can be. I recently needed help in migrating to my new MacBook Pro, so I naturally sought out the Genius Bar at my local Apple store. "Adam" took the time to help me simplify my life, improve my business, and just make my day. That is the kind of support that Lew provided his people.

The Mosaic Generation—It's Complicated

Millennials actually comprise several cultural cohorts. They are a mosaic of nontraditional families and gender identities, ethnic diversity, distinct cognitive categories, and third-culture kids (TCKs).

In 1950, 80 percent of families were headed by married couples. Today, that number is less than 50 percent. Our nation has migrated from the extended family of the early 1900s to the nuclear family of the 1950s to the fragmented family of the 1970s to the nontraditional family in the 1990s. Now, "family by design"[11] has found its way into the lexicon.

According to the Pew Research Center, 40 percent of Millennials are nonwhite. Nearly 19 percent are Hispanic, 14 percent black, 4 percent Asian, and 3 percent are mixed race.[12] On top of those identities, we have the TCKs, also known as cross-cultural kids or global nomads. Authors David Pollock and Ruth E. Van Reken tell us that TCKs emerge from a "culturally changing and highly mobile world during the formative years . . ."[13]

In December 2013, the *Huffington Post* reported that 61 percent of *Fortune* 500 companies have policies that prohibit discrimination against transgender workers or job applicants. Two-thirds offer health insurance and other benefits to same-sex domestic partners.[14]

Similarly, companies today have a greater awareness of those with Asperger syndrome (a high-functioning form of autism, accounting for about 1 percent of the workforce)[15] and adult attention-deficit/hyperactivity disorder (3–5 percent).[16] More recently the awareness that many in the workplace are introverts (up to 50 percent)[17] raises the question about how to effectively adopt more open workplace strategies. Companies are beginning to recognize that one size solution do not tap into the unique gifts people possess. Future workplace strategies will not simply accommodate but seek to embrace and enhance individual work styles.

This generation is more consciously aware of its uniqueness and, therefore, carries a deeper desire to belong. This circles back to

Simon Sinek's picture of the workplace as a safe harbor from the jungle that everyone faces outside the office. Wise companies will create safety for *everyone*. That will certainly require them to move away from a workplace of perks and entitlements into one where all employees are regarded as colleagues and peers. Designing space with these values in mind builds an organizational awareness and emotional intelligence that cannot be replicated by programs or promotions that try to marshal support for new causes. Inclusion and diversity must become integral attitudes and authentic components of the culture.

Invisible Diversity

I recently met with David Boatwright, Executive Director of Global Facilities and Real Estate for Cummins Inc. As we sat and talked in the new Commons building, an experiment in designing a space more appealing to younger, more technology-oriented workers, I asked how their new open environment accommodates introverts. David pointed to a red banner behind me that said, "Diversity Matters." He described it as a recognition that some people get overlooked for promotion because of our inherent biases. Invisible diversity is an intentional approach to embracing and making room for those differences within the company.

Tom Linebarger, Cummins's chairman and CEO, explained it further: "While race and gender are often easy to see, differences such as religious and political affiliation, work style, and cultural background that make people unique are not often noticeable."

It did not surprise me to learn that the source for this view traced back to Cummins founder J. Irwin Miller. He recognized that architecture and design were formational to the values and behaviors of any community, business, or civic arena. In fact, Linebarger attributes his journey to Cummins as starting with a Miller quote he saw in the Stanford Business School Career Center:

"In the search for character and commitment, we must rid ourselves of our inherited, even cherished biases and prejudices. Character, ability and intelligence are not concentrated in one sex over the other, nor in persons with certain accents or in certain races or in persons holding degrees from some universities over others. When we indulge ourselves in such irrational prejudices, we damage ourselves most of all and ultimately assure ourselves of failure in competition with those more open and less biased."

—*J. Irwin Miller*

Tim Solso, former chairman and CEO of Cummins, summarizes the opportunity and challenge for businesses bundled in this most diverse and complex generation: "The ability to manage diversity could well be the difference between success and failure for businesses, as well as the communities in which they operate."

The Millennial Opportunity

Eighty million Millennials cannot be easily analyzed, explained, or impeded by old attitudes, structures, and policies. Any group that large will have its way. By 2020, they will make up 50 percent of the workforce; Gen X will drop to 20 percent, and Boomers to 22 percent.

"Above all, this is an invitation to reflect on the essence of organization and the human experience in a deeply personal, holistic, and authentic way."

—Lindsey Etterbeek, Marketing Specialist, Architect + Design Programs at Haworth, Inc., and Millennial

As a generation, Millennials are not the lazy, entitled narcissists that we often imagine. Every generation has been accused of bringing more harm than good to the world as their influence emerged. Millennials are highly technologically savvy, culturally diverse, and open minded. Because the technology is assumed (and even boring for them), they expect it to work hassle free or in a "frictionless" way. In this way they can bring us to the business and social tipping point referred to by Clay Shirky: "It's when a technology becomes normal, then ubiquitous, and finally so pervasive as to be invisible, that the really profound changes happen, and for young people today, our new social tools have passed normal and are heading to ubiquitous, and invisible is coming."[18] They are also more selective about how and where they work. Businesses who want to attract this young talent will need to create work environments that support how they are wired to relate, work, and create.

CHAPTER 6

Changing Design from PUSH to PULL

People only see what they are prepared to see.
—Ralph Waldo Emerson

My 15-year-old son, Tyler, begins his school day by pulling up his class assignments on the Keystone curriculum website. Today he has to create a "virtual poster" on a biology topic. Tyler isn't quite sure what a virtual poster is, so he comes downstairs to ask me. Like most of Tyler's school questions, I have no clue what he's talking about. This quickly moves to, "Son, let's look it up."

We Google the words "virtual poster school." In 0.36 seconds the search delivers over 36 million hits. The first few say:

- Virtual Poster Session Archive | Earthzine
- Virtual Graduate Student Poster Session
- Virtual Posters with Glogster—YouTube
- Images of virtual poster school

We also found samples on a website called Slideshare.

Tyler and I learned that a virtual poster is basically a multimedia slide deck that fully explains a topic without presenting the information live. Tyler had what he needed to complete the assignment.

The authors of *The Power of Pull* (Basic Books, 2010), John Hagel, John Seely Brown, and Lang Davison, define PULL as "the ability to draw out people and resources as needed to address opportunities and challenges. Tyler had what he needed to complete the assignment. Pull gives us unprecedented access to what we need, when we need it, even when we're not sure what "it" is.[1] Many high schools still use a PUSH model. PUSH batches students into age groups traveling together along the same curriculum path. It only allows slight variations within the planned and batched approach. It's a planned one-size-fits-all model.

Tyler's school, Keystone, offers online courses that allow him to pursue his ambition to become a movie score composer. The music requires several hours of daily practice and composition work. He would not be able to fit the amount of music practice, composition work, and logistics into a PUSH environment. According to Hagel, Brown, and Davis, PULL represents a shift from the planned world of PUSH to an unpredictable world that favors those who can pull the teams and resources together in order to respond in real time. If you have ever used Wikipedia, Amazon, Google's search, Netflix, or Apple's One to One training, then you have experienced PULL.

Goodbye to Push

The TV show *Mad Men* captures the golden era of PUSH. Creative geniuses ask, probe, and research a client's problem and goals. They disappear for a period of time to apply their signature formula to the client's problem and then return and deliver the breakthrough idea—"Ta da!" This expert or professional model has been the bread-and-butter work for architecture, engineering, and design for more than 50 years.

PUSH assumes that:

• Leaders or experts have the answers
• They can accurately plan results

- Achieving results is based on a "proven" and often proprietary path
- This proprietary formula (body of knowledge) contains the company's secret sauce to protect, hone, and monetize

For two decades, the Internet's supply of cheap, abundant, and accessible information has torn down one PUSH domain after another. Media and entertainment were the first to fall. Health care and education are in the middle of watching their fortresses crack and crumble. A less visible but equally disruptive revolution is taking place within the professional service industries, including architecture, design, and engineering.

The wicked nature of our complex world erodes and wrecks PUSH assumptions:

- Leaders and experts do not have *the* answers. Problems are now buried within a network of relationships. Solutions have as much to do with the interaction of stakeholders as they do with the process. Learning our own way to the solution is the PULL alternative.
- Planning and forecasting no longer work. Clay Shirky, Columbia University professor and digital media expert, says that uncertainty has shifted our predisposition from planning to coordination. Any leader who thinks that he or she can set a target and then drive an organization to hit it is living in the past. Wall Street's model of reporting quarterly results and pressuring firms to use a PUSH style of management is meeting more resistance and coming under more pressure to change.[2] Leaders are increasingly refusing to play command and control and instead are moving to build long-term health. Project planning is also moving away from ideas like bid pricing and waterfall planning. More owners are selecting teams that can work well together instead of letting each supplier act out of its own self-interest.
- Creating and protecting a proprietary body of knowledge is obsolete. That is primarily because the shelf life of information

and expertise is short. In a volatile environment, rapid learning is more important than mastering dated knowledge. Those who can learn faster will win. And faster learning requires interacting with more people, with more variety of backgrounds, more often. Organizations gain more by opening their vault of information to others (inside and out) who can add, iterate, test, and spread.[3]

Stuck in PUSH

To illustrate the futility of PUSH, consider this imagined narrative. During the planning of StandFirm's eastern-region relocation, Jamil, director of real estate, goes over the numbers with his broker. The selection is narrowed to three locations in the downtown area. Jamil's primary directive is to reduce real estate costs by 15 percent.

The developer's architect creates some test fit drawings—simple plans with boxes to represent offices. The real point is to see which option allows for the most offices. After Jamil compares the plans and the features of each building, he announces, "The Uptown building will fit 15 more offices per floor with a slightly smaller floor plate. Based on the broker's comparison of features, this looks like the building to choose."

Jamil meets with Susan, the company's facilities manager, who has 15 years of experience in interior design. She begins the actual design. The routine is clear. Each position in the company has a standard cubicle or office size and configuration. The company outsources the actual layout work using a list of prequalified design firms.

Some of those firms provide additional services like workflow analysis, alternate workplace strategies, social network analysis, and even team and organization culture analysis. Susan has an interest in these areas but isn't high enough in the food chain to pick a firm with this kind of support unless they come in with the best price. Susan now hands off the scope of the job to Jeremy in Procurement.

"No program, school, or magazine has prepared business leaders to handle the decisions that need to be made regarding employee work environments. And certainly, there is little discussion on how to manage employee feedback about the decisions that are made. In that void, financial measures have become the only tool to make decisions regarding space. Using just a financial lens to make decisions regarding where your valuable personnel spend so much of their time is a narrow, underdeveloped thought process."

—Mabel Casey, vice president, global marketing and innovation at Haworth

Jeremy buys everything from copiers and office supplies to vending services and equipment replacement. He has a process for everything. Jeremy plugs in Susan's requirements and hosts a pre-bid Q&A session with the four competing firms. He tells them, as he always does, "We will look at best value; we're not obligated to go with the lowest price."

One of the newer firms, FutrWerks, actually takes his comments at face value. They include services in their proposals that could improve employee engagement and performance. These services cost more.

The FutrWerks team discussed whether to respond strictly to the letter of the bid or take the risk and add what they knew would improve performance. Design firms continually scan for the rare opportunity both to apply their deeper expertise and to get compensated for delivering added value. Was StandFirm cracking the door open to them? Their sessions with Susan and Jeremy made them think that StandFirm was looking for the best long-term value. They decided to step outside the box.

Jeremy likes the idea of adding SNA or other culture profiling tools that FutrWerks has proposed. But he's not sure what they really are and has no idea how to justify the cost. Bottom line:

When the award results were announced, FutrWerks did not receive its loss well. This seemed like another confirmation that owners only look for the lowest cost.

Of course, this loss is more complicated than the simple narrative that owners want cheap and suppliers are terrible at conveying the business value in their services. The system that separates the roles from the whole is a key culprit. The opportunity to bring change was lost somewhere in the handoff from the Business Unit leader's need for expansion to Corporate Real Estate's quest for the best deal to Facilities' application of corporate standards to Procurement's focus on creating an apples-to-apples approach to due diligence.

StandFirm was stuck in the same PUSH paradigm that my wife and I were when we tried to help Tyler's music aptitude and passion. PUSH only works when one size fits all, when the whole is the sum of the parts, or when driving efficiencies into each part has no unintended consequences on other parts of the system. More simply, the PUSH system caused StandFirm to lose site of the relationship of the less than $1 cost of design to the $82 the company spends on employees who are disengaged in their work and hindering the performance of others.

Changing space is rarely just rearranging bodies and cubicles.

We Are Stuck in PUSH

During our third Case4Space summit, we wanted to expose the planning and analysis mind-set behind PUSH thinking. In order to do so, we borrowed from a simple game: the Marshmallow Challenge (www.marshmallowchallenge.com). The challenge revealed the distinct difference between the planning and analysis of PUSH thinking and the PULL attitude: playing and experimenting in order to let solutions emerge

Our participants divided into several teams. Most of our Millennials were assigned to the same group. We wanted to see if they would approach the challenge differently. The exercise was simple. We gave each team a dozen pieces of dry spaghetti, some small marshmallows, masking tape, string, and a paper lunch bag. The goal was to build the tallest structure possible in 18 minutes that remained standing. They could use only the supplies provided. I held the tape measure and a stopwatch.

One team, made up primarily of younger members, was called the "experimenter team." They spent little time designing or debating; different team members just started playing with the pieces. The planning was going on simultaneously with construction. This team was far less time conscious. Their lack of structure between planning and building made their Case4Space facilitator anxious; she wondered if they would actually get around to building the tower. But she did notice more team conversation and cooperation. The experimenter team's presentation was not as eloquent as others'; they just said, "Here's the tower" (see Figure 6.1). Their tower won, standing 18 inches high. It did not fall down.

The Marshmallow Challenge has collected a large amount of data by tracking the height of towers from different demographic groups. The average height is 20 inches. Our best was 18. The

Figure 6.1   Millennial Led Team

towers for business school students average 10 inches. Kindergarten students, on the other hand, average *30 inches*! Researchers conclude that kids do better because they don't have existing frameworks for solving problems or expectations for how the spaghetti, marshmallows, string, and tape should work. They also like to play.

The point of the Marshmallow Challenge is that, on the surface, many problems look like straightforward technical troubles that can be tackled by the right expertise and execution. The game raises an important leadership question: How do we approach problems for which we have no prior reference point for solving? John Seely Brown suggests that we need to tinker, play, and experiment so that we can productively *fail* our way to understanding.

How to Move Away from PUSH

PUSH is still effective in predictable environments where efficiency is the driver. However, more problems today require real-time tailored solutions and a discovery attitude for solutions. The Marshmallow Challenge reveals that many of us understand the PUSH-to-PULL shift but our habits still reflect PUSH.

TAG Consulting has developed a tool called *The Leadership Triangle* to help assess when leaders are facing a pure PUSH challenge, a combination of PUSH and PULL, or one that requires a strong PULL approach. The first side of the triangle deals with tactical or technical challenges. These fit within an identifiable range of options. Leaders simply select the best option and execute well. Examples might include facing the need to add two new people to a team and adjusting the offices to make room.

The second side of the triangle tackles strategic challenges. These are driven by changes in the external environment and the need to set a new direction, realign priorities, and adjust the thinking to take the new path. The leadership role focuses on making the case for the new direction and making the hard decisions over what activities will stop and what new activities need to be added. This is a combination of PUSH and PULL and falls into the domain of classic change management.

PUSH—the world has changed and we are standing on a burning platform.
PULL—here is what the future can look like if we can make the change.
PUSH—those who try to stand in the way will be terminated.
PULL—we will empower early adopters as champions to help people navigate their challenges in adapting to the new normal.

The GSA 1800F Street project and CBRE's Los Angeles projects reflect this kind of strategic realignment. Both recognized that their key constituents were asking for new levels of service that their current structures were not set up to support. They needed a change in direction and environments that reflected and reinforced the new strategies.

The third side of the triangle deals with transformational or adaptive challenges. These are sometimes called the existential challenges because new conditions now question the fundamental purpose or viability of a product or organization. The distinct role of leaders dealing with transformational issues is facilitating the hard discussions, challenging the organization's assumptions, and developing a discovery mind-set (the kindergarten approach) to explore unfamiliar topics and opportunities.

Transformational challenges have no easy answers because they have no precedent. They are complex and have interconnected and embedded relationships. They are like living systems; when you introduce change, the system reacts like an organism, fighting invasion, rather than like a machine that is simply compliant with the engineer's tinkering.

Both the GSA's Martha Johnson and CBRE's Lew Horne faced transformational challenges as a result of their strategic redirections. They each saw their organization's relevance at stake; without fundamental changes in values and behavior, they would have no vibrant future.

As soon as the implications of change translate to the personal level, people consciously or unconsciously react to the different levels of loss they will experience. For some it is a loss of control, privilege, or influence. For others, change threatens to break up long-established relationships. Others fear going from a high level of competency to needing to learn the new order of things. People flinch at numerous projections of loss.

The collective loss often surfaces in the form of both overt and covert resistance. When management invests time and effort in achieving clarity and confidence about a new direction, they often think that should settle and clarify everything. But those affected by the new direction may feel a deep sense of loss, disorientation, anxiety, and fear. It is normal for employees to struggle through some of the following questions:

- Why are we no longer successful?
- Whose fault is it?
- If our team's work is good, why are we at risk?
- Who are we now that our core market has become obsolete?
- The market has so dramatically changed and our structure is no longer suited to compete—now what?
- How long will my job be around?

The transformational role of a leader helps the organization or a team process through letting go of its former identity and learning to embrace a new and unfamiliar way. This is not traditional change management. The organization will have a hard time hearing the benefits of change when focused on the message behind the message, the sudden awareness of a large threat and unfamiliar ground of uncertainty.

That is why both Martha and Lew reinforced what remained true about their core mission and values. They kept the conversation transparent and they were first to give up their status and go through the same experience they asked of others. They also paced the new with a series of small-scale experiments that gave access to everyone.

The best way to address the underlying social structure of legacy habits and PUSH is to use space as a tool for change. What better means do leaders have for moving into a PULL universe of tailored interventions? What better approach is there to understanding the distinct operating system that drives many new-generation companies than using space as a tool for learning? Changing how people live and work in the space is the best way to reveal the hidden dimensions of an organization and its shadow cultures.

> "Space is a powerful tool—it brings together people, technology, and ideas. It has the ability to communicate bold new concepts and define the culture of an organization."
>
> —Bob Fox, principal, FOX Architects

In the next chapter we will look at how to move from the PUSH approach to using PULL to successfully engage wicked problems. We will travel from the old expert-driven design process to a cocreative design mentality.

PART III

A New View of Space and Culture

CHAPTER 7

Using Space to Shape Culture

Consciously or not, we feel and internalize what space tells us about how to work.

—David Kelley, IDEO

On a trip to Columbus, Indiana, I met with a group of Millennial employees of Cummins Inc. As we talked, I said something like, "So you're in this small town and you make diesel engines. How exciting is that?"

Kimberly, a bright-faced 24-year-old, with just two years at Cummins, responded as if she had studied the question.

"A few weeks ago, as I got ready for work, I suddenly wondered, 'What if every Cummin's diesel engine in the world stopped at the same time?' "

She went on to actually name villages in Africa that would no longer have power, hospitals that would no longer run, mines that would have to close, produce that would not make it to the markets, and a few other consequences that blew me away. She ending by saying, "We literally make the world run."

My first thought was, *Okay, clever. Marketing came up with this little slogan and she memorized it.* So I did some homework; I Googled it. Her "slogan" was original. This was Kimberly's imprint of

Cummins's mission and value and her heartfelt attachment to both. How does a company reach a freshly minted college graduate and create the kind of connection that causes her to find such identity within the company's mission?

The answer to that question has more to do with culture than it does with strategy or training. Edward Hall describes this elusive key; "Culture hides much more than it reveals and, strangely enough, what it hides, it hides most effectively from its own participants."[1] We all talk about culture, but how would you describe it?

People in all times and all places have lived inside a set of "shared basic assumptions." Every company, school, town, neighborhood, church, sports team, and so forth is characterized by a distinct culture. But because it is often buried inside assumptions, attitudes, and rituals, we often become aware of it only when it changes. Culture can be more clearly seen in the spaces that facilitate life and work, like homes, places of worship, stadiums, offices, parks, restaurants, and stores.

Peter Drucker's recognition that culture reigns suggests that strategy may announce the path for the voyage, but culture is the gyroscope that holds the ship steady in all kinds of seas. It prevents "roll" and gives position, orientation, and momentum. Without that gyro of clear and healthy culture, leadership must continually monitor and apply external pressure to counterbalance the internal habits and inclinations.

Many consultants believe that strategy can produce a Kimberly. After they finish their complicated opus and turn it into a finely crafted 100-piece slide deck, they pass it along to senior leadership, who recontextualize the recommendations and then pass it on down to marketing, communications, or HR. It will then go through several iterations over several months to formulate the "right" message for management to convey to the organization.

All of this activity and rehearsal is typically behind the curtain and out of sight from the employees. However, we all know that these manufactured mission-and-values slide decks don't get the job done. Kimberly is not the product of a communications strategy, but rather a clear, consistent culture and value system that envelops her daily.

Every day she experiences congruence between the message and the culture. She has met senior leaders, been to their homes, and has seen them as real people. She sees them treat people with respect. That's why she embraces them, their values, and their vision.

Of course, few of Cummins's more than 46,000 employees have had Kimberly's access. At the same time, there was nothing extraordinary about her experience. That's the culture effect. Kimberly is a cultural "fractal" of what most perceive to be true.

What are the common expectations in your company? Fairness or entitlement? Transparency or secrecy? Accessibility or hierarchy? Trust or wariness? Learning or blame? Whatever you think those expectations might be or hope they become, you can find the real ones enshrined within the edifice of the office and the process that allocates and configures space. Leaders who wish to disrupt a legacy culture that no longer aligns with a new mission should begin by disrupting the norms of their office.

Leadership by Interruption and Disruption

"Leaders need to work along a continuum of interruption and disruption in order to continually adapt their organizations."
—*Martha Johnson, former administrator for the GSA*

A GSA director in the Midwest, hidden in his private corner office, felt isolated from the activity of his team. So he decided to sit in a vacant cubicle. That simple act disrupted the entire floor, spawned rumors, and prompted anxious questions and statements.

One peer asked, "Are we giving up our private offices?"

"No, I am simply more productive when I'm in the middle of my team."

A director stopped by and inserted, "You know, you'll lose your influence and authority if you sit out with the rest of the employees."

An intern was looking for a place where she could spread a project out over several days, not pack it up each night and then have to find a new conference room the next day. This GSA executive suggested she use his office. After a few days, another manager came by and asked, "Are you aware that some intern has taken over your office? Would you like me to deal with her?"

What this GSA executive began to notice was a strong but hidden cultural value around the status of the office his people occupied. He also found a way to reveal the hidden values by simply changing his own behavior. And it was also the way to shift the values of the office. He changed the space to reflect new values.

Changing Space Changes Culture

When Michael Bloomberg became mayor of New York City, he wanted to convey a value of transparent government and form people's behavior into coherence with that value. The first thing he did was to get rid of private offices, including his own, and sit in the middle of the mayhem.

A *Forbes* magazine interview with Bloomberg observed that "City Hall will never look like this again: The hive that is the 'bullpen,' with its desks strewn about the open space, and the staff—junior and senior—all buzzing around the King Bee himself, who sits in the middle of it all, just as he likes it. It's an open–plan workspace style that Michael Bloomberg brought with him from his days as the head of his eponymous data company, designed to be fluid, interactive, decentralized, and cooperative."[2]

The GSA's Martha Johnson and Bob Peck also started with their own offices when they led the large 1800F project that demonstrated how one could change the responsiveness of federal government.

Johnson said, "The building accommodated 2,200 people when we moved out 15 months ago. When we move back in 12 months from now, we'll be able to put 4,500 people in. How are we doing that? It's neither hard nor complicated; it has good precedent in the private sector, but it requires a rethink of how government approaches workspace. To start, we won't have any personal space. Private rooms, pull–aside areas, conference nooks, and quiet places? Yes. Personal, solely dedicated offices? No.

"And I'm walking the talk. My office in that building is the third largest in D.C. It's larger than a basketball court. It's got a fireplace and wrought iron casements. It's historic, it's steeped in history, and I won't be moving back in. Just like today, I'll be working out of a cubicle."[3]

When visiting the Zappos headquarters in Las Vegas, you will likely walk by the somewhat cramped executive "suite" called Monkey Row (see Figure 7.1). In this narrow sliver of space along the interior window of the building, you will find seven table desks lined up next to each other. Tony Hsieh, the president, sits in the middle, right next to Chris Nielsen, the CFO. The door is open, and when you walk in you will see whoever is on site that day. The gatekeeper behaves more like a gate greeter. Her title, "Time Ninja."

Interviewed for the *New York Times,* Ron Bundy, chief executive for the Russell Index Group, "believes the environment has

Figure 7.1 Monkey Row At Zappos

engineered a subtle but significant shift in the firm's culture, by eliminating the office as a status symbol. 'The big benefit is that there's a whole host of really talented informal leaders in the building, and they have an opportunity to shine and have more of an impact,' he says. 'This has really opened up opportunities for people without formal titles.' "[4]

You hear similar stories of how changing space changed culture from W. L. Gore, Google, Alcoa, Intel, Travelocity, eBay, Morningstar, Yahoo, Facebook, Chiat\Day, Menlo Innovations, Valve, Basecamp, Carfax, and an emerging number of both "old school" and high-technology companies. It is clear that leaders are creating interactive environments to spawn innovation.

Chiat\Day broke the cubicle habit early, in 1993, and learned some hard lessons with their Virtual Office experiment. Jay Chiat saw that the days of creative "geniuses" presiding over small internal empires (as in *Mad Men*) were running out of steam. Competitive pressures required better and faster ideas. In Chiat's mind, that meant teams would be connected by technology, fluid and self-organizing, rather than tied to office turf.

His method to drive that new vision was to dismantle their traditional 1970s-era advertising office, with no advance warning, and replace it with one that had no personal space—an open campus. It turned out to be chaos. If we look at it through today's lens of mobile technology, that kind of shift might have felt more like a speed bump to the work routine. But back in 1993, laptops were rationed and cellphones were anything but smart. It created a riot that some say led to Chiat's sale of the firm.

"Lost in the gee-whiz coverage [of the opening of the Virtual Office], however, was a tiny detail: Almost from the get-go, Chiat's virtual office was a joke in the advertising world, 'the laughing stock of the industry,' recalls Steve Rabosky, a former agency creative director . . . the ad agency became engulfed in petty turf wars, kindergarten-variety subterfuge, incessant griping, management bullying, employee insurrections, internal chaos, and plummeting productivity."[5]

Fast-forward to 1999, and you will see that TBWA\Chiat\Day continued to evolve their concepts, rooted in creating a sustainable creative culture. If you visit their West Coast headquarters, Advertising City, you will have a one-of-a-kind experience. "For clients, prospective hires, and other visitors, the design serves as an elegant summation of everything that Chiat/Day stands for. In fact, one unintended benefit of the new facility is that it has become a magnet for new talent."[6]

All these stories feature leaders who see a direct connection between the environment of the office and the cultures they hope to influence. Leadership, now more than ever, is really in the culture business. Sadly, the whole culture conversation is foreign to most leaders over 45.

The television show *Undercover Boss* captures the epic (and now ancient) era of leaders trying to make decisions that their followers can barely relate to. Each episode features a leader trying to walk in the shoes of his or her employees. The bosses display awkwardness, difficulty mastering the job, and sometimes sheer humiliation. The experience brings about a Scrooge-like epiphany and transformation.

A day in the life experience is one of the most tangible means for leaders to understand both their own culture and the whole "culture thing" as Michael Bloomberg, Bob Peck, Martha Johnson, Ross Bundy, and Lew Horne have done. A leader who takes this journey will never be the same.

Mollie: The Story of an Accidental Change Agent

"Culture is not about behavior. It is about someone's sense of identity. People choose to be in environments they can identify with . . . . Every organization has its own ethos, services, and products. Apple people believe that their sense of identity is tied to the Apple identity. The future of work is giving people a workplace that is tied to their sense of identity."

—*Uday Dandavate, President of SonicRim*

Most companies are caught off guard by the overt and covert resistance to new initiatives. After months of planning and thought, a company rolls out a project or program intended to improve work and performance. Right there, employee resistance snags it. Turf battles, political maneuvering, workarounds, bargaining for exceptions, and outright hostility reflect the true culture. Of course, individuals and groups react when they see life threatened. Shades of Kübler-Ross's five stages of grief.

Mollie is a tall, good-natured, high-energy, quick-thinking rebel with a cause. She has a productive, mischievous edge and takes advantage of it when she's given an impossible task. She is aware of her Gen X position within a Boomer leadership culture. They like her because Mollie understands both the mission and her boundaries. She is politically savvy but doesn't play politics; she just works to get the job done. She's low on formalities and "optics."

Mollie has a big job. She is the director for corporate real estate and construction for Center Health's 1,200 corporate employees and more than 55,000 other employees spread over 150 different companies. Center's leadership often asks how she gets so much done, given the large scope of her job. The fact that she doesn't play politics creates some headwind for her boss, the company COO. But she consistently gets results, so he protects her. He doesn't know much about design and construction. That works to Mollie's favor; she *does* understand design and construction, which gives her the freedom to try new things. She also knows she has a target on her back. Several people would like nothing better than to see Mollie crash and burn.

Center Health rapidly expanded over the last five years through mergers and acquisitions. This kind of growth means that it is now a collection of diverse corporate cultures, processes, and loyalties. The senior leadership team looks like a collection of tribal leaders who came together out of necessity, not from a shared history, mission, or culture.

Everyone came out of the last officers' meeting shell-shocked. The CEO made it clear that if Center was going to meet its objectives, it must reduce costs by almost $500 million over the next two years. That translates into every department doing more with less.

One strategy to reduce cost was to consolidate half of the corporate employees into a new building. They are currently divided among three 40-year-old leased buildings. Walking into those buildings felt like stepping back into the 1970s. Each department was walled off from the others. Within the "big walls" each employee had a private office. When Mollie described the feeling of the space, she compared it to walking through a submarine. Only top management had windows to the outside world. If the perimeter office doors were shut, the office had no natural light.

Mollie told me, "There are people who have lived their whole career in those caves! These offices describe our company, silo'd and segregated." There was little cooperation, great distrust, and continual conflict and politics. She said you can send a fresh-out-of-college, enthusiastic kid into those offices, and within six months they've been reprogrammed into a disengaged, bored, and unproductive employee.

Mollie knew she was going to hit her target simply by consolidating the three offices and shifting to a 70-percent cubicle ratio. The consolidation itself would reduce the square-foot cost by 15 percent. And Center was shrinking its footprint by almost 40 percent by using cubicles. Accomplishing this was not going to make Mollie a hero. The whiplash from this radical change would make her the target of vicious criticism. Even though the other offices were cavelike, many had lived in them for 20 years and longer. The culture said, "Leave me the hell alone; I love *my* private office and being out of sight and out of mind." The move had little to do with logistics and everything to do with culture.

Mollie knew that the company could not just simply transport people into smaller, improved, and lower-cost space; they would also carry the old attitudes and culture into new space. But, she wondered aloud, "What if we changed the relationships and interaction of the space? Could we shift the recursive behaviors or 'me-ism' and 'not-invented-here' to a climate of collaboration?"

When we talked, Mollie made a profound observation about the dramatically different experience of building medical facilities.

"When it came to building a hospital, there was a clear mission that unified everyone's agendas—the patient experience. It didn't remove all of the politics, but it provided a plumb line when competing interests arose. When a conflict emerged, we simply asked, 'Does this decision provide a better patient experience?' But when we planned internal projects, we heard a completely different narrative. You would think the user groups came from warring nations."

Then she made a second profound statement: "Changing space shines a spotlight on culture. All of the drama of a company comes to life when you meddle with the way people live. All of the subterranean politics and conflicts surface; they come to life. When you change space, you intersect with HR, IT, senior leadership, business unit budgets, turf issues, facilities, accounting—there is not one element of the company that doesn't have a stake and doesn't show up."

Mollie knew there was no upside for her if she only accomplished the logistical and cost goals for the project. These were already baked into the projections. But, because of the culture issues, she faced considerable risk and resistance. Her strategy was simple, bold, and a proverbial career choice. She would use the move as a vehicle to shift the culture of segregated and competing tribes to a single company culture.

In her conversations with the COO, they recognized their business had shifted to a strong focus on the patient experience. They seemed to execute this side of the strategy outside the home office very well. But that focus did not cross the bridge to corporate.

Those who worked in the medical facilities could see two distinct cultures: their patient-care culture and then the black hole at corporate.

She pitched the strategy to the COO: no private offices. He was all in. When this was broached with senior leadership, that idea was a bridge too far too soon. Political realities required a slight pivot. Only 10 percent of the offices would be enclosed.

The time line was short: less than six months to move 600 people from zero to completed move. Mollie also knew that if she floated the concept to all of the departments, they would resist and sabotage the effort. So, she activated her rebel-with-a-cause strategy, took counsel from a few of the business unit leaders she trusted, did her homework, and then implemented the plan.

Her personal theme was to break barriers. Many of the employees worked in the same buildings, on the same floor, but had never met one another. In addition to using a low-height cubicle layout, she also removed all of the private printers and consolidated the printing in one location per floor. Now people would have to walk to the printer and run into people they would otherwise seldom see.

Mollie was rolling. She got approval to cut out a section in the middle of the floor plate to build a staircase between the floors. That would allow people to easily walk up and down to meet one another. She designed a very comfortable micro-kitchen that was well stocked with great coffee. Then she put that kitchen next to the staircase and removed the coffee stations each group had in the previous space. She created restaurant-style booths with monitors and easy technology hookups. Why? So people would have to get up, walk to the micro-kitchen, and run into people they would otherwise seldom see. She brought the same creative magic to bathroom placement.

Mollie also convinced HR to create new, large print name tags for everyone. New conversations emerged: "Wow, so you're Jim? I've spoken to you over the phone several times; it's great to put a face and a name together. How long have you worked for Center?"

Next, she helped create a connection between the home office and the many sites in the field. Throughout the space, Mollie installed wall monitors that streamed live video of the field facilities, activities, or construction. If their mission was to provide healing environments, then the corporate employees needed to see what those environments were like.

Not everyone appreciated the change. Many of the managers assumed they would get private offices. The "no" brought one to tears. That kind of resistance and collateral damage was inevitable, considering the short time frame given to accomplish the work and the decision to withhold information in order to avoid the real threat of sabotage. Mollie learned lessons that would inform and assist future changes.

When I last checked in with Mollie, the space had been occupied for about nine months. Naturally she had learned a lot. For instance, the common banks of refrigerators needed a policy to prevent "ownership issues." The new conference room scheduling technology got caught in an old, territorial "I own it" attitude. Some conference rooms were immediately booked 24/7 for the full year—including holidays! That had to change. And Mollie had to ban fans, heaters, and even waffle irons. Obviously, human behavior left on its own reverts back to turf and tribal warfare.

Ironically, the head of HR was one of the key opponents, and he would not participate in the strategy to shift behavior. He advocated keeping the original ratio of private offices and tried to get management back along the window walls. He lost that battle but succeeded in securing private offices for C-suite executives.

This left Mollie with an interesting question for her COO: "Who owns culture? Who gets to define and steward it?"

HR saw their role as handling policy, benefits, hiring, and firing. Organizational Development (OD) defined their mission as creating training and implementing organizational assessments. On paper, it seems like shaping and stewarding culture would fall into either HR or OD's territory. But neither area really understands the true behavior, habits, and rituals of the company. That really falls to those—like Mollie—who touch the way people live in their space.

Mollie saw and knew how much the design strategy had become a catalyst and shaper of the new culture. The issue gets down to one of the most fundamental understandings of implementing change. *If you change the interaction of relationships, you change behavior, and that leads to a change in culture.*

Six hundred people moved in on time. The new space was beautifully designed, had the latest technology, and contained plenty of conference rooms (a longstanding complaint). The senior leadership team breathed a deep sigh of relief. They were also quite proud. The COO saw the power of the design for changing the culture. He wondered what could be done with a strategic approach to integrating cultural alignment into the design.

The strong, positive results for Center have given Mollie a platform to take things further in future planning. It has also shifted her interest from simply dealing with space, cost, and schedules to the importance of design and culture.

CHAPTER 8

Social and Engaging Design

Design thinking has come to be defined as combining empathy for the context of a problem, creativity in the generation of insights and solutions, and rationality in analyzing and fitting various solutions to the problem context.

—Wikipedia, "Design Thinking"[1]

On May 25, 1961, President Kennedy presented an audacious goal to a joint session of Congress. The United States would put men on the moon and bring them safely home before the end of the decade. After delivering his clear and compelling vision, Kennedy handed the ball to the engineers of NASA.

On July 20, 1969, Neil Armstrong stood on the moon. That's why Kennedy's speech has become the gold standard for presenting a grand vision and marshaling the people, energy, and resources to accomplish it.

That was then.

In 2011, Lew Horne of CBRE, had a vision for the future of his office. But he knew that achieving the goal would come through collaboration rather than the "Kennedy model" of leadership. He could not just make a speech and hand the ball to others. Lew had to remain engaged with those who would work the plan. He did not need to know much about design, technology, or the work-place of the future, but he had to be willing to work, experiment, and learn.

The problems faced today do not respond to the old-style "expert solutions." No one benefits from the designs that parachute in from high altitude. Today, the human factor is more important than ever. We live in an era of design thinking and, more impor-tantly, empathy for those caught in the problem. We must join with those who live with the problem every day to discover insights and solutions, and then adapt the solutions to the context.

What Is Design Thinking?

Speaking of the human factor, let's consider a residential real estate story in order to envision design thinking. You and your husband, in your early sixties, decide to downsize from the 4,000-square-foot home where you raised your family. So you find Brenda, a good buyer's agent (a realtor who works for buyers, not sellers). You tell her what you want. She asks questions about you, your life, your dreams, your concerns, your financial parameters, and other life details. She very carefully begins the search. You don't hear from her for several days.

One day, you drive along a mountain road 25 miles from your home. As you round a corner, you see it: the red-steel-roofed two-story cottage nestled in the pines, beside a beautiful duck-filled pond. And it is for sale! You instantly fall in love; Norman Rockwell must have painted this place.

You quickly dial Brenda and tell her you found "the house." She finds it on her computer and sets up a showing. Your husband, Rick, agrees to meet you there at 10:00 AM. the next day.

You know it's not perfect, but oh, the pond, the drive-up appeal. You can just imagine how your friends and family will squeal with delight as they round the corner and catch first sight of the place. The next morning, as you walk slowly around the property and through the cottage, Rick and Brenda make positive comments. You so want them to be in love with the house. But they are not. Finally, you all walk outside and stand beside the pond talking. Rick looks at his watch and says, "Honey, I have to get back to the office for the staff meeting. We can talk about this over dinner tonight."

As Rick's car disappears around the bend, Brenda starts slowly. She talks about the oh-so-cute ducks on the pond, the movie-set charm of the place, and the excellent square-foot price. Then, she slowly says, "Look, I need to be your agent here. So let me just point out some realities. I know you are looking at this as a retirement home. I would be concerned about the distance from here to the hospital. It's 26 miles on a gravel country road. And do you really want two flights of stairs with your knee problems? I mean, think about it: The master bedroom is on the second level and the laundry room is in the basement. You will spend a lot of time on the stairs. And Rick travels out of town two or three times a month. Do you want to be alone out here in the mountains for six to ten days a month?"

Design, for many, follows the old realtor model. A realtor shows you five houses the first day. One of them could work if you cut down that majestic oak tree and added a room. He is really good; he sells you the house. And you regret it for as long as you live in it.

Brenda represents a new kind of design thinking. She steps into the details of your life. She has been paying attention to all you told her and all she has observed. You slowly realize that Brenda heard what you said and what you didn't say. Her textured understanding of your life's context gives a tailored and nuanced approach to finding the right home. She actually understands value through your lens. True empathy is part of the challenge. After listening to her, you realize the cottage in the mountains will simply not do.

Many space decisions can be well served by the 1960s realtor approach—just find it and close it. More and more leaders, however, are taking the Brenda approach of addressing complex questions and discovering how to tailor their environments to the purpose, culture, and goals of the client. They will help the company spur innovation, improve culture, or recapture engagement. The questions they address require that deeper connection to context. These leaders also shift a fundamental mind-set. Their solution is no longer a prescription that will serve clients for several years before they return for a quick adjustment. The engagement is now a journey that will require continual monitoring, cultural conditioning, and adaptation.

Design Is Now Complex

Once upon a time, when your company required new space, you quickly agreed to the pretty building sitting near the easy-off, easy-on freeway exit. The complexity of our times has changed all that. Today, leaders must consider the changing nature of work, a very diverse population, the need for an safe and enjoyable workplace, disruptive technologies, pressing concerns about health and wellness, sustainability, the emergence of soft-skill demands, the squeeze for talent, and disruptive business models. They all create a radically new role for the workplace and require new skills of those who plan, deliver, and support them.

One consistent theme throughout our research is that a traditional design approach producing that "Ta da!" solution is unable to penetrate complex challenges. It provides ample expertise and insight but fails to grasp the context of culture, which turns a great solution for one project into an exercise in missing the point for another.

"I believe the architects' role needs to transform from one of 'expert' to 'facilitator' in order to support an organization's people and culture by building upon their expertise and experiences. Working with an organization's people and culture will positively impact both stakeholders and shareholders."

—Sabret Flocos, Principal, FOX Architects

We are seeing more workplaces adding cafés, concierge services, open collaborative spaces, more natural light, and fitness centers, and expressing more concern about wellness and emotional intelligence. These efforts are headed in the right direction, provided they too don't become the next silver bullet or one-size-fits-all.

For example, Jerry, the head of corporate real estate for a big financial firm, met with a large project team from a national contractor to see what they had to offer for a new regional headquarters.

He was frustrated before he walked into the presentation room. After introductions, Jerry said, with some emotion, "I just want someone to listen to us." They had just completed another large corporate building project using the latest ideas the design world had to offer. Yes, the space was far better than what they had before, but, he explained, "it is just not who we are. We hired one of the best architectural firms, and they sold us on their concept, but they did not listen!"

In that sobering start to a conversation, Jerry was asking for someone to walk in his shoes, not interview the team and then come back with, "This is what we did here." His request was, "Are you willing to come alongside, tap into a day in our life, see the company through the lens of our people, and help us materialize what we're probably not capable of articulating?"

Very few design firms and consultants have a heart and mind to respond to such a cry for help. Even if they did, the obstacles and constraints in traditional procurement practices strip the ability to provide this level of partnership. Jerry's challenge gets to the heart of a growing practice: design thinking.

Design Thinking for Leaders

Roger Martin is the former dean of the Rotman School of Management and the author of *The Design of Business* (Harvard Business School Press, 2009). He has spent as much time in design thinking as anyone in the world today. He describes design thinking as merging two competing domains, reliability and viability.[2] Think about it:

Business ultimately aims for reliability, which depends on analytics to turn solutions into algorithms. Reliability allows solutions to scale by repeating the past in a better, faster, and cheaper progression. Martin's concern is that the reliability side of the equation has become the overriding bias within business for the last 50 years. And that kills the risk essential for innovation.

"Often times the discussions around customers' space needs tend to focus on the costs side. However, participating in Case4Space reinforced the importance of identifying each customer's interest in improving their culture through engaged leadership and employee collaboration."

—Bill Hollett, SVP leasing, Cousins Properties

Viability anticipates the future that markets and customers may need, desire, and use. These are the seeds of innovation. Anticipating the future always begins as an educated hunch. Innovation falls in the realm of transformational change. Reliability, on the other hand, fits well into the realms of tactical and strategic challenges described earlier. Martin offers design thinking as the bridge that links the two mind-sets. Business has built a bias through its MBA programs, engineers, and financial managers that instinctively distrusts discovery as a wandering pursuit, hoping to uncover something useful. Martin concludes that Management Science allows no room for the intuition necessary for innovation or the creative approach to problem solving that design provides.

In today's world the hunch with no data or proof has no value. The kid with the spreadsheet has been winning over the kid with gut instinct. But *right there* is where today's business narrative is incomplete and where Martin would like to insert design thinking. What if the kid with a hunch had a process to test that hunch in a way that arrives at a hypothesis? Design thinking provides a framework for going from hunch to hypothesis to heuristic (rules of thumb).

And that creates a bridge for the kid with a hunch to cross, contribute, and cooperate with the kid wielding a spreadsheet.

Culture and engagement belong in the fuzzy unknown; they don't fit on a spreadsheet. They can't really be gauged by assessments, either.[3] However, we know they respond to their environments. We've established that space can be a proxy for understanding and influencing culture. We'll also make the case that design thinking can become a proxy for engagement.

To address culture and engagement, design thinking begins with the environment or habitat of work. Traditional design begins by defining a problem or goal and attempts to isolate the issue from its context to break it into separate competing categories.

For example: Cost, schedule, form, and function are four common design categories that architects and designers will balance against a client's stated goals.[4] In design thinking, the solution reconciles these competing subgoals. It does so by adding empathy to the situation. For instance, a hospital trying to reduce inpatient stays would begin with, "How do we improve the patient experience?" A company trying to improve collaboration would begin with, "How do we improve the team experience?" It's a subtle, but crucial, distinction. It gets to the real human issues instead of addressing cold systemic issues and symptoms.

The Rush to Form

If you've sat through a design presentation, you'll readily recognize the routine. A design team learns a little about what a client wants to accomplish. "We need a call center that doesn't feel like a call center!" Armed with that information, a head count, interviews (programming) with managers, and a few more details, the firm goes back to their office and returns to present the latest research on call centers, images of past call centers they have designed, and, finally, sketches and drawings to capture what this firm's next call center could look like. *Voila!* The client reacts positively or negatively to the images, completely unconscious of the thinking behind these designs. It's truly a lottery for the designer, hoping that the prospect lands on an image and falls in love with it. This is the rush to form.

The now ubiquitous Herman Miller Aeron mesh-back ergonomic chair almost never existed. It was prejudged by its unusual form. Here's my recollection of the story. Andy McGregor's design team discovered that the heat from foam cushions in office chairs made people adjust their posture, on average, every six minutes or stand up. Neither was good for productivity or health. But they also discovered that a mesh-back relieved the heat buildup and also reduced pressure on the ischial tuberosity (butt bones) to allow comfortable and healthy seating for longer periods. However, the chair looked weird when compared to what everyone understood as an office chair. Andy kept the prototypes hidden from most of management. He knew that the form was so radical that unless people had a context for the new design, they might reject it.

When it was time to present the chair to the board, it was put in the back of the conference room under a bed sheet. As board members mingled before the meeting, a few went back and peeked under the sheet. Their noticeable shock and negative reaction set the tone for a long and hard boardroom debate on whether to go forward.

When Andy's team presented the research for how they arrived at the materials and design, they put the discussion in the context of individual health and the corporation's commitment to sustainability. Suddenly the chair made sense. Chastened by this near disaster, McGregor's team changed its marketing rollout to first tell the story. They didn't even show the chair until later. Today, of course, the Aeron has become an icon and a great success story, because the design team chose to focus on the actual experience of using the chair rather than the chair itself.

A Human-Centered Approach

A human-centered philosophy and methodology sits at the heart of design thinking. Stanford's engineering professor John Arnold is most often credited for this shift from focusing on the "thing" as the center of an engineering solution to the user's experience. It was a radical departure at the time (1958) and is still an outlier discipline. It collided with the engineering mind and culture. No wonder engineers, like lawyers and politicians, have become a genre of jokes.

You Might Be an Engineer If . . .
   . . . all your sentences begin with "what if."
   . . . Dilbert is your hero.
   . . . while everyone else on the Alaskan cruise is on deck looking at the scenery, you are still on a tour of the engine room.
   . . . you read a computer manual on vacation, turning the pages faster than others would read a John Grisham novel.
   . . . the salespeople at Best Buy can't answer any of your questions.
   . . . at an air show you know how fast the skydivers are falling.[5]

Design thinking has taken on an interesting migration by jumping from one "left-brained" discipline to another: science, industrial design, architecture, construction, and business management. Roger Martin describes this invasion of human-centered thinking as the vital counterbalance that will save business from its left-brain domination. It gives leaders two essential skills for leading in complex times: common sense and a common touch.

Design thinking is built around these common principles:

- *Empathy:* The ability to address complexity begins with understanding the live experience of the stakeholders within a system. This is now referred to as human-centered design or user-experience design. Empathy, the ability to put yourself in the shoes of others and care about them, lays the foundation. It is also the weakest skill.
- *Patterns:* Complexity defies analysis. But complexity visualized will often reveal patterns. Asking each stakeholder to provide a narrative of their experience allows the group to identify themes. If the themes are then captured on a wall surface through sticky notes or graphic scribing, the group will be able to see more of a whole view of the system they need to influence or change.

- *Values:* How do we define the value proposition for a project or a solution? Too often it is narrowly defined as meeting a cost, schedule, or quality outcome. Dick Bayer, principal at The ReAlignment Group, argues, "A value is something that we get up out of bed for. Cost, schedule, and quality are simply constraints, not values."[6] Creating a "values matrix," a lean tool, offers one the means to construct a deeper discussion and alignment around the value of a project.
- *Positive Outliers:* These are people or organizations that defy conventional wisdom but get better results. It's what Steven Spielberg brought to movies in the 1970s. The movie *Jaws* represented a breakthrough in promotion from public relations to mass marketing and cemented the idea of the summer block-buster. Spielberg changed the business model where film making was only one of several new revenue streams. Spielberg was a positive outlier who became a tipping point. The search for positive outliers works especially well when you have no precedent and experts have no more clue than you do about the path forward.
- *Ideas to Prototyping:* This is learning by doing. Modeling complexity reveals the key, but hidden, relationships and attributes. Prototypes are not solutions; they are tools for visualizing questions and ideas.

The Sleepover Project

In 2008, David Dillard, then president of a large firm in Baltimore that specialized in senior housing, created the Sleepover Project®. The new demands in senior care created the need for more patient-centered solutions. Dillard felt that the traditional delivery process insulated designers from clients, caretakers, and, most importantly, the residents themselves. So he had another idea. And his idea transformed his design practice.

Dillard himself, in his fifties at the time, was wheeled into a skilled nursing community in Los Altos, California. He played the role of a stroke victim, someone who had lost the use of his right arm and leg.

"Until you try to lean over and get something out of your suitcase, and it takes you not 20 seconds but seven minutes, you don't appreciate the game of inches that seniors play. Good architects have good hearts and minds, but they haven't been able to empathize enough with physical constraints."[7]

Dillard's experience became company policy. Several times a year, his staff members and selected partners go to the senior community both to experience and document their insights. The difference between traditional design and design thinking stands out as Dillard reflects on a moment in his day in the life simulation: "During lunch, a group of visiting musical bands came in and asked if anybody wanted to play along. I've been playing guitar since I was 14, but I realized I was a stroke victim and couldn't use my right arm. That hit me like a hammer to the heart, realizing I would never be able to do that anymore."[8]

Dillard's idea also gives leaders an opportunity to step into the user experience of their workforce and feel firsthand what a day in the life at his or her organization is really like. This will not only better inform the design choices but will also reconnect a leader to the pulse of the firm. The engagement of stepping into the shoes of the organization creates a connection and a common touch that requires no special expertise or innate talents.

Undercover Boss

Sheldon Yellen, the CEO of disaster recovery firm Belfor Holdings, told *Inc.* magazine that he agreed to appear on the TV show *Undercover Boss* because he had a hunch he was out of touch with his 6,400 employees. So, disguised as a rookie water tech, he traveled through the crawlspace of a house to find the extent of damage to a customer's home from a water leak. When he complained about the cramped and dangerous conditions under the house, his supervisor announced, "Welcome to a day in the life of a water tech at Belfor."

Sheldon was taken aback by the conditions that their water techs often encounter, and was even more deeply pierced by the uneven impact his pay freeze had had on his entry-level employees.

His previous decisions and expectations took on a new context. Employees became personal, not numbers on a spreadsheet. *Undercover Boss* reveals the role that empathy, or the lack of it, plays in the decisions leaders make. It uncovers how easily managers become removed from the context of the work and the lives of their employees. Does your company have its own way of signaling a similar disconnect? Do you have a way of actually listening to an honest complaint? Can you hear them say:

"I know and do my job. Why didn't they ask me about changing that procedure?"

"Do they know or care what this insurance change will mean for my daughter's cancer treatments?"

"The twelfth floor doesn't even know we exist."

That disconnect is a leading cause of disengagement, and a disengaged workforce cannot drive innovation. Empathy connects ideas and solutions with context.

Emotional Intelligence

How do you take a powerful idea or cultural value and not dilute it with growth and complexity? Magic conjures images of surprise, mystery, fascination, wonder, and delight. It is an experience that feels immediate, not formulaic. At the same time, we know that great magic is completely disciplined and rehearsed. It's an interesting metaphor, but I had no clue what it might look like for an organization or with space.

A few days after initially pondering the "magic" concept, I sat next to Starlette B. Johnson on a flight to Washington. She was the former EVP and chief strategic officer for Brinker International and the former President of Dave and Buster's. Quite a résumé.

So I had to ask, "How do you scale the magic? I mean, you create a restaurant concept in Dallas, and it has to work in Peoria *and* Poughkeepsie. How do you do that?"

She was clear: "To start, it's clarity about the culture and hiring people who fit that culture." That sounded similar to what Case4-Space had heard from Google, Cummins, and W. L. Gore. She continued, "Hospitality is the last industry where you can be highly successful without an advanced degree because it is based on *emotional intelligence.* Success is judged by the customer's experience and your ability to read in real time how to create a memorable experience. The experience begins when you see the restaurant, walk in and are greeted, feel the atmosphere, and look through the menu. This is all part of a designed and well-executed experience."

She had introduced a theme we had not yet explored: emotional intelligence.

Dr. Daniel Goleman, author of *Emotional Intelligence* (Bantam Books, 1995), pioneered the application of emotional intelligence in leadership and worked closely with Stanford University to refine this first pillar of design thinking. Emotional intelligence includes self-awareness, self-regulation, motivation, empathy, and social skills.

At Case4Space, we commonly use Gallup's StrengthsFinder assessment to identify the talent themes for management teams. One talent, empathy, provides a natural capacity to put oneself in the shoes of others. Empathy seldom shows as a top-five talent among senior level leaders. That's why leaders must also overcome neurology when it comes to empathy. This ability to feel what others experience is a function of the mirror neurons. They allow you to mimic or simulate the swing of a golf club or the wipeout of

> "It is easy to look at the current state of corporate America and say that business leaders don't care about their people or the spaces that they spend one-third of their life in. I disagree, they do care . . . they just do not have the language nor frame of reference to understand what to do."
>
> —Mabel Casey, vice president, global marketing and innovation at Haworth

a skier. Research now shows that, as leaders rise in their organizations, that ability begins to shut down.[9] Competition, hard decisions, cutting losses, isolation, filters, and layers all contribute to losing touch—and the drama of regaining that common touch, as on *Undercover Boss,* makes captivating television.

Empathy provides the beginning pillar for design thinking. It can become one of the avenues for leaders who need to build or reestablish that personal and visceral connection with employees and to the nature of the work they do. When we spoke to leaders who successfully led transformational efforts by using a new approach to their space, it was clear how transforming it was for them. Participating in the discovery process of design gave all of them a deeper understanding of the link between the environment and the work. Walking the talk did more than provide credibility to ask others to change. It added context to concept, what the military calls "situational awareness."

PART IV

Change Your Space— Transform Your Culture

CHAPTER 9

The Untapped Potential of the Workplace

Space is one of the most basic, underlying organizational systems for all living systems—particularly for people.

—Edward T. Hall

While talking to Steve and Jim, two directors of facilities for a large medical device company, I could see that both men wanted to make the case that space might improve productivity. So I shared some of the Case4Space research and offered a few stories. Steve said, "If I put a proposal on the table, it's going to be evaluated strictly on hard costs and savings. None of this soft cost; they must have proof!"

Both Jim and Steve believe there *is* a clear connection between space and productivity. They told me the story of a new building project that consolidated three locations. The new building provided a nice open cafeteria where people liked to meet, versus the old break rooms. The space had more sunlight and an upscale workout facility.

Jim said, "After we moved the first group in, the others couldn't wait. People really like coming in to the office. And here's my measure: People brought their families to see where Mom or Dad worked. That tells you something!"

The clear success with employees suggests something, but it's not enough to make a case on its own. After all, the C-suite speaks a different language and uses a financial lens to evaluate the value of spending one dollar on improving the workplace versus the return on that dollar if spent on new equipment.

I asked Steve, "What work behavior would you like to improve?"

"Breaking silos and getting more cross-pollination going on."

That flipped our conversation over to the concept of value. Here's the deal: Over the life cycle of a building, 82 percent of the company's cost will go to employee wages and benefits. Five percent will go to design, construction of the building. Michael Brill, founder of BOSTI,[1] conducted client-based research with over 100 organizations and 10,000 employees to explore what effect the workplace has on productivity and job satisfaction. When facilities departments work to reduce costs, BOSTI raises a simple question: "How will it impact employee performance?"

That is the untapped potential of the workplace. And that is where managers need to see the big picture. They must discover the link between the quality of design and the quality of the experience for those who work in the building. The question is how to tie the following cost percentages together into understanding each system's relationship to the whole (see also Figure 9.1):

- Employee cost—82 percent
- Technology—10 percent
- Facilities—5 percent
- Operations and Maintenance—3 percent
- Design— less than ½ of 1 percent (part of the facilities 5 percent)[2]

Brill makes a clear argument that space should be seen as a tool that will enhance performance. If companies invest in high-quality space, they increase the overall corporate performance. Vivian Loftness, former Head of the School of Architecture at Carnegie Mellon University, also says it is easier for managers to see the

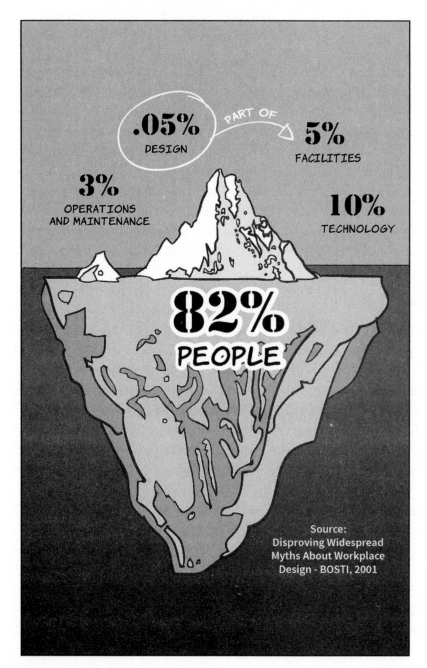

Figure 9.1   The Tip of the Iceberg

connection between technology and performance than the connection between space and performance. The same managers that have little problem justifying a $3,000 computer over a $1,000 computer will choke on a construction cost of $300 per square foot. They always want to get to $100—even though the design and construction costs are a small percentage of the employee costs.

Thankfully, many architects and designers are waking to the need to make a clearer and stronger business case for an investment in well-designed space. Companies that are moving toward more multidisciplinary teams; experimenting with pods, clusters, or cells; developing ways to collaborate; and looking at alternate work strategies already see the vital role the space plays.

Great Stories

Many novelists, screenwriters, and mythologists understand that most stories in literature and film follow a mythic structure. Although that structure is presented in slightly different ways, they all tell of the universal and sometimes heroic reach for goals like redemption, success, reunion, and completion.

In that very same sense, work is part of the great story of humanity. People work in order to leverage their muscle and brains into a means of realizing a better life story. That's why people in the workplaces of the earth deserve respect; they are doing their best to conquer poverty, insignificance, futility, and failure. And that's why the terrain of commercial real estate is never a cold science to me and I cannot be cynical about it. That terrain is the landscape of human dreams.

Almost everyone understands the effect of home space on a family. That's why we consider the investment in a home, yard, furniture, appliances, interior décor, and safety systems to be essential to the health and well-being of the family. But we have trouble seeing the same kind of impact of a workplace on the "family" of employees. We would have little respect for parents who spared no cost in designing their master suite and furnished their children's bedrooms with garage sale furniture and décor. Yet that has been a common practice in traditional workplace design. Spend it all on the executive suites, boardroom, and the lobby. But that misses the whole idea of the untapped potential of the workplace.

Likewise, in our search for workplaces that bring out the best in everyone, certain myths and mistakes are posted as guards; they fight those who try to get close to the solution. Let's look at some of the gatekeepers that keep excellence away from the system. First, there are four myths that we all must try to conquer:

1. *Bidding secures the best players at the best price.* The hard facts are that bidding adds unnecessary cost (up to 10 percent), and the selection process creates a complicated structure that is inefficient to coordinate, dysfunctional, and unreliable.

   Obviously, everyone must conduct their due diligence when hiring the contractors needed to do their work. As we documented in *The Commercial Real Estate Revolution*, early adopters of alternative procurement methods have found great results by using collaboration models—that is, bringing the entire construction ecosystem together at the very start of a project and giving them all a chance to collaborate on issues of design, constructability, and costs from the outset.

2. *Great design is an expensive luxury.* This grows from the stereotypical view of design as style and aesthetics. But design can be a great tool for accomplishing the objectives of an organization. Creating a process around the whole instead of dividing it into parts bakes health and wholeness into the project at the very beginning.

   Cummins patriarch J. Irwin Miller believed that design had the ability to improve how we work *and* to elevate our aspirations. He saw design as integral to the human story. Design for him was more than aesthetically pleasing buildings; it was a way of solving business and community problems. Design was key to Cummins Inc.'s process of innovation and becoming a global market leader. Miller said, "It's not good design that is expensive, mediocrity is what is expensive."

3. *Contractors make their money on change orders.* Bidding and delivering a project are two separate processes. In some cases, contractors do see the contract as an opportunity to increase the price for the project without competition. But most contractors work on very low margins (between 1 and 3 percent). They make commitments on price and schedule based on partial information about the full requirements of the building. They must also work with unpredictable weather and site conditions. That is part of "the system that causes good people to do bad things."

4. *Owners hire third-party representatives as cost-squeezing, performance-policing, schedule-streamlining quarterbacks* rather than as advocates for their clients' higher-value goals. When hired as the former, they, like any of the members of this supply chain, are more than willing to comply. However, the role to streamline and cut costs turns the process into a transactional, low-trust, marginal-impact project.

These myths are the legacy of a dysfunctional system. Lew Horne reflected, "What we [at CBRE] did was disruptive. It changed the way everyone had to play the game. But it was liberating for our people!" Overcoming these constraints and dispelling the myths is like breaking the sound barrier: Peace and clear flying wait on the other side.

Mistakes

Mistakes are not as ferocious or as damaging as myths. But they too are gatekeepers; they will prevent us from finding success. So the wise builders are vigilant and relentless in trying to conquer them.

Groupthink

Groupthink tends to capture everyone at some point. Developers, for example, base project choices on what they see others doing successfully. Replicating what seems to work sounds like a good formula. But it means that little thought is invested in understanding the needs of tenants. Templates and rules of thumb are handy tools, but they can also lead good people into the path of least resistance. For example, low design fees drive architectural firms to cut and paste designs that worked in other times and other places. There is no reason to reinvent the wheel, but every client's unique mix of business, culture, business model, and external forces requires and deserves original thinking to understand how design can generate value for them. Our muscles for holistic thinking and problem solving are grossly underutilized in the current system. So, when a new idea emerges and receives positive press, we see a great rush to imitate it and capitalize on the buzz.

An Undefined or Ill-Defined Problem

Symptoms in a world of wicked problems are seldom what they appear. When an architect, designer, or consultant interviews a client to understand "the problem," the first principle is, "The stated problem is not the real problem." It is a symptom, and that symptom has to be viewed as part of a larger system or put within its context. For example, the contractor's view of the problem is often, "If only the architect could provide properly detailed drawings. . . . "

The architect retorts, "If only contractors understood 'design intent' and could read drawings. . . . "

Underneath these symptoms is a deeper problem: a system that drives distrust. Part of that distrust is a lack of understanding about what each participant on a project team actually does.

Getting no deeper than an interview level of understanding is a recipe for a fuzzy understanding of the real problems, the ones at the root of the symptoms. Dermot Egan, cofounder of Studio Tilt and coauthor of *Codesigning Space: TILT,* describes their process of finding first principles. First principles are one of the frameworks for identifying root causes and core objectives instead of a "rush to form." If you're not sure that you've reached the core drivers for a space solution, use Toyota's "Five Why" model. For example:

"We need a more open work environment!"

Why?

"So we can improve communication."

Why?

"It takes us 45 days to process invoices and we get constant complaints."

Why?

"If a question comes up with an invoice, it can sit in someone's inbox for a week or longer before it gets resolved."

Why?

"Because they have to chase down the person who can answer the question."

Why?

"Because we have four or five people who all need to sign off on the invoice before it goes out. Any one of them can hold up the process."

"Why do four or five people need to sign off?"

What began as an identified space requirement worked its way deeper into a process problem. Further digging might actually find that the number of sign-offs is tied to a lack of trust in the process itself.

Ray Lucchesi, principal at Renovus Collaborative and member of Case4Space, shifted his architectural practice to one focused on helping clients understand these deeper questions. He found that taking this deeper dive often resulted in simpler solutions that actually addressed root-cause issues.

An ill-defined problem is often the result of waiting too long in the process to bring in expertise. Traditional design-bid-build projects engage the trades—which make up 80 percent of the cost, risk, and knowledge—after all of the major decisions, and big mistakes, are made.[3] If you participate in construction meetings, as the trades walk out you will likely hear a comment like, "If they had only included us when they locked in on the air handling system, we could have saved them a bundle because this building doesn't really need one with that capacity." The process, the solution, and the key stakeholders can no longer be separated.

Owners make the common mistake of selecting players rather than a team. It is just part of the procurement model of bidding out architects, contractors, and then specialty expertise. Why do successful projects usually happen by luck, not by design? Because of the distrust embedded in the bidding process, the adversarial structure of projects, and the lack of familiarity or understanding of how each firm actually does business. This mistake was described earlier as a sports franchise assembled with low-cost players, with no incentive to work together, that only play together for one game. Some companies are getting great results by spending more time getting the team right, even with procurement practices that require competitive bidding.

The last big common mistake designers make is thinking only about the form of the space. They need to help owners make better holistic decisions by addressing the business case for the decision, providing the return on investment, and looking at the larger culture implications.

An airport facilities director had just finished a terminal modernization project. It looked very impressive. When I asked how he liked the new design, he said, "The building is beautiful but it is a nightmare to maintain!" This mistake ties directly to a narrow design scope and the owner's terminal modernization project. Once a project is defined as a space issue, people tend to think of form and aesthetic and do not consider the other interconnected and human elements in their thinking. They do not see the untapped potential for the space.

We've learned that the least defensible mistakes generate one of two responses:

1. "This is how WE do things!" (The not-invented-here syndrome.)
2. "Our business is unique and that's why you'll have to do it our way."

Any manager who has been with their firm for more than five years is likely infected with this malady. This bubble of isolation is common for managers within their company; in reality, this kind of feeling or pushback is based out of fear and distrust. Dick Bayer, a colleague of mine and Case4Space member, and I were with a global firm who openly admitted their process was so onerous it was likely costing them a premium in the marketplace. In addition, none of their projects were meeting schedule and most were significantly over budget. Despite these open admissions and the recognition that my colleague and I had a solid track record helping firms develop a more trust-based, holistic project approach, they still said, "Our business is unique and this is why we do it this way!"

Dick simply said, "What are you afraid of? Let's deal with that first so we can address it and not hide behind a convoluted façade that isn't working!" As a result, the company began exploring their self-imposed constraints and myths and began moving toward a more trust-based dialogue with their suppliers.

We need a cohesive and coherent story of the workplace. It is a story of building workspace with the same intentions and sensitivities brought to the process of building homes. Perhaps if we learn and tell that story, we will stop sabotaging innovation, creativity, and engagement. That would be the real power of using space as a means to reveal, refine, and transform culture. The next chapter further builds our understanding of the intimate relationship between space and culture and why it matters.

CHAPTER 10

They Did It, You Can Too

In the 1990s, Jerry Sternin with Save the Children accepted an impossible mission: Stop the childhood malnutrition affecting more than 65 percent of Vietnam's children under five years of age. He was given six months to show progress or shut the program down. Remaining tensions and distrust toward the United States set very difficult conditions for his mission. These constraints, along with the tragic conditions of the situation, led Sternin to an epiphany that would change future aid work.

Sternin had to discard traditional aid work, which relied on supplies, expertise, knowledge, care, and food from outside. It would take too long. He knew the answer had to be hidden in plain sight. He also knew he needed new eyes.

Sternin started by asking the mothers to identify children based on their poverty levels: poor; very poor; and very, very poor. Then he asked the question that changed everything: "Are there any healthy babies in the very, very poor families?"

The answer was, "Yes!"

Some very, very poor mothers fed their babies smaller portions more frequently and went out into the rice paddies and gathered small shrimp and snails for them (viewed as unhealthy and even dangerous for children), which added vital protein. Their babies were healthy!

That horizontal, peer-based learning, instead of relying on experts teaching about nutrition, allowed Sternin to make progress that outside agents could never have achieved.

Sternin learned that, very often, innovation bubbles up from the ground. It frequently originates in those who live in the middle of the gritty, even deplorable, details of life. At Case4Space, we have seen the same kind of grassroots brilliance. The solutions and breakthroughs that the universities, think tanks, and *Fortune* 500 companies miss will often percolate within those who daily face the crises.

Future Travelers

Case4Space heard a lot of "Yeah, but . . ."'s when we shared our mission and belief that space mattered: "Yeah, but . . ."

- You can't measure white-collar productivity.
- Google can do it, but they are special.
- It's too expensive; owners will never pay the premium.
- The industry is too entrenched and will never change.
- No one has been able to answer your questions.
- There is no direct relationship between the office space and engagement.

So we wanted to find those who hadn't heard that what they were doing wouldn't work. They represented the only doors that could lead out of our boxes.

Patrick Donnelly, principal at BHDP Architecture, led a team named Future Travelers. He identified Future Travelers as companies that had built great cultures, broken with conventional norms, and done things that surprised us. Patrick's team included Sabret Flocos with FOX Architects, Markku Allison with Scan, Paula Bedford and Josh Schierbeek with Haworth, VIMTREK's Arol Wolford, Daniel Homrich with WH[Y] MANTRA, Balfour Beatty's Haley Smith, and Richard Kadzis with Kadzis Consulting. Patrick described their job as "finding the healthy babies . . . focusing on the successful exceptions, not the failing norms."[1]

Naturally, we had some hurdles to overcome. We had our own theories of what worked, because we were experts. But we had little experience looking for solutions hiding in plain sight. We were used to *bringing* the solutions.

We heard these Future Travelers talk about their suppliers as facilitators, partners, stakeholders, and guides. Most were selected more for their cultural fit and willingness to learn than their portfolios and résumés. In many cases, owners had to retrain the habits and instincts of their outside team to appreciate what made the company and its environment distinct. It was the difference between creating a great-looking house and building a place that felt like home.

We met with several companies. Because we could only include a few, we chose some of the "successful exceptions" that precipitated some of the most interesting questions and conversations: Cummins Inc., Google, W. L. Gore, CBRE's L.A. offices, GSA's 1800 F Street project, Red Hat, Zappos, Cousins Properties, Haworth, and Balfour Beatty D.C.

Cummins Inc. and Columbus, Indiana— Engagement with Stakeholders

While in Indianapolis for business in 2012, I heard a story on NPR—"Columbus, Indiana: A Midwest Mecca for Architecture." I had never heard of Columbus, but the reporter said it was just 45 miles south of me down Interstate 65. How could such an obscure town contain more than 80 buildings and sculptures designed by some of the most famous modern architects of the 20th century? I called David Dillard, a Case4Space colleague and architect: "Hey, David, you'll never guess what I ran across. There is this town called Columbus, Indiana—"

He cut me off and said that most architectural students make the pilgrimage to Columbus. My curiosity increased.

Something in this little town sounded a bit magical. I thought it might provide clues to some of the work we were doing in Case4Space. To get the story, I drove down to Columbus with Tom Miller, partner of Darwin Branded Environments, specializing in integrating a company's brand to its workplace, for the first of many trips. I met Jack Hess, Executive Director of the Institute for Coalition Building, downtown at Gramz Bakery and Café. He had moved to Columbus in 1993, expecting to stay only a year or two. That's what happens to people who come to Columbus expecting it to be a career stop. It turns out to be an incredible place to live.

Jack told me the story. It began with a vision that J. Irwin Miller—head of Cummins Inc. and a lifelong resident of Columbus—had in the 1950s. The town had a problem. How could a small town attract the best engineers in the world with underperforming and poorly built schools? A failed school project in the mid-1950s became the spark for transformation.

Cummins funded the next school's architect, Harry Weese, who built the Lillian C. Schmitt Elementary School in 1957. The school was transformed. In fact, it was so successful that it led to an ongoing partnership between Cummins and the city. Jack's story led me further into the cave.

Tom Miller and I interviewed John Burnett, President and CEO, Community Education Coalition; Mark Gerstle, Retired as Vice President of Community Affairs, Cummins Inc.; Tracy Souza, President and CEO, Heritage Fund; Sherry Stark, Retired President and CEO, Heritage Fund; and David Boatwright, Executive Director of Global Facilities and Real Estate at Cummins. I also met with a group of young employees at Cummins. Finally, I met Will Miller, president of the Wallace Foundation and son of J. Irwin Miller, surely an under-recognized luminary for his time and a relevant thinker for today.

The magic was not the architecture, although it is a treat to any tourist who appreciates mid-century modern design. The magic was how Miller saw architecture as a way to create social capital, a framework for the art of civic discourse and democracy.

Miller recognized that managers who advanced tended to be more naturally outgoing. He saw an unintended filter that left many highly talented but more introverted employees (typically engineers) behind. So Cummins initiated a program called "Invisible Diversity" to better identify, embrace, and support those who were often overlooked.

Cummins was at the forefront of the civil rights movement and remains a beacon for creating a culture of respect. Columbus was a pioneer in project-based learning. The Signature Academy was one of the most innovative and impressive elementary schools I have seen. The schools in Columbus are years ahead in thinking, design, and results. The company's partnership with higher education is a great demonstration of the power of engaged stakeholder action.

Between 1989 and the early 1990s, Cummins survived near-bankruptcy and a hostile takeover attempt in a dramatic story of a community coming together. The Columbus/Cummins partnership was a commercial version of barn-raising. As such, the collective participation formed strong and intimate social connective tissue.

Will Miller presented a 50-year study of community growth, economic health, and school achievement comparing Columbus with similar communities in Indiana and across the nation to a chapter of the American Institute of Architecture. Columbus excelled in every category. In fact, the town had no peers. Miller reminded this audience that there was architecture, and then there was a social and engaging form of architecture that had the power to transform and create a virtuous cycle of compounded value. Cummins had invested a little more than $19 million over 50 years. By any measure, Cummins and Columbus realized an incredible return on their investment.

J. Irwin Miller believed that the kind of architecture that elevated the human spirit required great thinking, and great thinking required structured and open process with engaged stakeholders. "Every one of us lives and moves all his life within the limitations, sight, and influence of architecture—at home, at school, at church, and at work. The influence of architecture with which we are surrounded in our youth affects our lives, our standards, our tastes when we are grown, just as the influence of the parents and teachers with which we are surrounded in our youth affects us as adults."

Google—Engagement by Design

Dave Radcliffe is vice president of Real Estate and Workplace Services for Google. When I first shared the Case4Space story with him in 2011, he responded, "If we gain one key insight and can apply it through the organization, it is worth our investment." That was my first lesson in Google and Dave.

Learning and the speed of knowledge transfer are Google's lifeblood. Simplicity and proximity are key factors to achieving this. Radcliffe's mission is to leverage space to increase learning and to rush and scale that knowledge. The office must become smarter and smarter to quickly adapt to the unique needs of each team, improve the user experience, and anticipate change.

Imagine the challenge of reducing the gap between a continuously changing online world and a constrained offline world. That is exactly what energizes the work of Radcliffe's team.

There is no place on the planet that studies their employees and understands what engages them more than Google. Senior vice president of People Operations Laszlo Bock said, "When an employee starts on their first day, we know that if the manager says, 'Hi, nice to meet you, you're on my team, we're gonna be working together,' those people end up 15 percent more productive in nine months."[2] Radcliffe's team even has research on what colors, materials, lighting, and configurations attract or repel people. The continuous experiments, data collection, and analytics provide Google with insights that filter back into the workplace. The goal is to improve innovation and creativity.

At Google, workplace engagement begins with engaging work. Google believes that people want to do interesting things. That is supported by a culture that grants voice and choice to its employees. The office shells are kept unrefined to encourage experimentation. Teams are provided with broad square-foot parameters and then are aided by Dave's team to cocreate a workspace for that team. If a new team leader takes over, Dave's team revisits the design of the space.

Transparency and openness support learning and the rapid transfer of information. When you walk through a Google space, you will find walls covered with notes and visual forms of thinking. Google believes that a "home" destination creates a predictable connecting point, improving the opportunities to connect with others. There are also the famous micro-kitchens, dining booths, and gourmet cafeterias to improve the number of human encounters each day.

Google is also contrarian in some areas. For example, they do not have open and free-address spaces, and they do not promote distributed work (work from home or other remote sites). Google has extensive research and data that support the value of working together. For them, commuting is simply a constraint; it does not shift the nature of their business. They use a variety of solutions to deal with the challenge: Google buses, more than a thousand bicycles on campus, electric cars that employees can use to run errands, and concierge-type services.

Few realize the massive and ever-changing enterprise Google has become. In addition to search, YouTube, and Android, they also have divisions in life sciences, robotics, unmanned cars, wearable technology, fiber optics, and manufacturing, and its Singularity University. Dave said that they continually ask questions like:

- What is the culture of search?
- What is the culture of content (i.e., YouTube)?
- What is the culture of social (i.e., Google+)?
- What is the culture of manufacturing (i.e., Motorola and Nexus)?
- What is the culture of distribution, as they look at companies like Zappos and Amazon?

In addition, Radcliffe's group has to ask how the legacy culture of one group influences and inhibits another.

The buildings that Radcliffe's team designs both optimize the work experience and perform as laboratories to test new ideas, technologies, materials, and environments. Dave told me, "Diner booths often work better than traditional conference rooms . . . Casual collisions are what we try to create in the work environment. You can't schedule innovation, and you can't schedule idea generation. So we really look for little opportunities for our people to come together."

If companies like Google are early trend finders, then we should expect to see a focus on healthier workplaces, more flexible space, design focused on the user experience, integrating sustainable thinking into all aspects of the business as good business, and collecting data as a means for creating a more emotionally intelligent organization.

W. L. Gore & Associates—The Human Scale of Engagement

At the outset of Case4Space we identified companies with reputations for unique and engaging cultures. W.L. Gore was certainly one of them, but getting inside the company was like trying to get inside Augusta National when the Masters is not being played.

"Firms of endearment" updates Freeman's Stakeholder Theory following a good-to-great approach, but it also compares business results between firms that are loved and those in Jim Collins's research. In almost every category, these stakeholder-focused firms outperformed the good-to-great companies. Another way to distinguish these companies is to call them "emotionally intelligent" in addition to "business smart." We also found it affirming to see that Cummins Inc., Zappos, Google, and Harley-Davidson were also considered firms of endearment.

In September of 2012, I attended the IFMA Workplace Strategy Summit held at Cornell University. It was a very productive conference. But the best part was that I met Jay Steimer, head of facilities and real estate for W. L. Gore.

Over the two-day event, I learned about Gore's unique culture. Hearing Jay speak about their culture felt like we were listening to a '70s counterculture refugee—except it was not utopian. It was clear, worked out, bottom-line focused, pragmatic, and proven. Jay disrupted my image of a large chemical company spawned from the command and control culture of DuPont and still living in its Delaware shadow. I have visited some hip high-tech firms lauded for their bossless or self-organizing cultures. They are cool and energetic, but their cultures feel more like wet paint. With Gore's 50-plus-year track record, their paint in corporate democracy had long since dried and held up.

Jay invited Sabret Flocos, a principal at FOX Architects, and me to visit their campus in Newark, Delaware. Two months later, we did. I knew very little about W. L. Gore outside of Gore-Tex, a material that protects my hiking boots and my feet from moisture. The first object we saw there was a rock of flourite and, next to it, some white flourspar powder. When the powder is heated, it turns into a very unique and adaptable polymer. The magical polymer was discovered at DuPont. They trademarked it as Teflon, and Gore uses it in Gore-Tex. Sabret and I learned about dozens of different applications for this highly stretchable, heat-resistant, lightweight, permeable, and inert substance. It is used in delicate applications like heart valves and insulating space suits. Everyone uses Gore products. Gore has one business, Teflon—or, more accurately, polytetrafluoroethylene (PTFE). Someone at DuPont figured that Teflon would be a better name.

Bill Gore left DuPont in 1958 because he wanted to pursue the application of PTFE for insulated cable ribbon for computers. He also left to create a culture of engagement. Bill Gore found that his work on task force teams was far more productive and energetic than the isolated work he did as a chemist in his department. He wanted to create a company that felt and was structured more like a work group than a series of departments. Gore's own website says they are "a team-based, flat lattice organization." They have "no traditional organizational charts, no chains of command, nor predetermined channels of communication."

Over time, the company arrived at about 150 people as the ideal size for a business unit within a facility. Bill Gore said in an interview, "We found again and again that things get clumsy at more than 150."[3] Research from evolutionary psychologist Robin Dunbar arrived at a similar threshold of people that one could know and care about in a social network. It is often referred to as Dunbar's Number. Jay Steimer told us, "It's important that people know and care about who they work with."

Each W. L. Gore business unit has autonomy. There are two job titles within a business unit: that of the business unit leader, and then associates. Each associate has both a voice and a vote on priorities, spending, and the execution of work. It is a meritocracy. Peers evaluate performance, compensation, and each idea. Each new hire receives an advocate to help them adjust to the culture and find a business unit where they best fit. They also understand that the cost they represent to a business unit will be judged against the value they can deliver. There is no hiding. It is highly tribal in structure, culture, and unit identity.

W. L. Gore's values must be understood to fully appreciate their mechanics of corporate egalitarianism. You can find Gore's values on their website, but in our conversations with Jay they came through clearly at a very personal level. For example, when we talked about Case4Space, Jay said, "I want to make a commitment to you . . .," but he would first need to make a case for his time and expense to his peers. Their democracy and "team-based, flat lattice organization" are very real—so real that the head of facilities and real estate for a multibillion dollar company must get the approval of his peers in order to commit to Case4Space.

When the word *commitment* was spoken from their unique tribal context, it became one of those "aha, now I get it" moments.

In the Gore world, no one assigns work to others. Teams determine how the work will get done through a practice of making commitments to one another. It seems less efficient but has the benefit of great clarity, alignment, and accountability. It is a counterintuitive "slow in order to go fast" mind-set that is deeply embedded in the culture. So Jay's personal commitment also committed his peers to some degree.

The magic of W. L. Gore is that it operates as a network of work commitments rather than assignments. In Glenn Ballard and Greg Howell's[4] three-year study of the reliability of planned work on construction sites, they found that only 54 percent of job site commitments were completed as promised. The bottom line of traditional construction processes and culture results indicates that up to 50 percent of project costs are a waste and 70 percent end up late and over budget.[5]

With 10,000 employees, few bosses, autonomous business units, divergent markets, a slower and messier way to reach decisions, and employees spread out across buildings of less than 200 people, W. L. Gore is like the proverbial bumblebee—it shouldn't be able to fly. Yet Bill Gore has been able to harness, scale, and sustain the small teams idea. His disdain for creativity-killing hierarchy has translated into a culture that provides freedom for people to pursue their passions based on merit. The human scale of work and space has become one of W. L. Gore's distinctive traits.

Keeping commitments is the glue that holds their democracy together. Trust is the medium for reducing friction. And they've maintained and grown that tribal democracy for over 50 years.

CBRE—Smaller and Smarter
Leads to Engagement

The CBRE headquarters story signals the mainstreaming of alternative work strategies. It shifts thinking away from squeezing costs and instead focuses on the efficiencies of space for the employee experience. They have moved the conversation from wellness to well-being as the first Delos-certified commercial space.[6] They created a luxury hotel experience for the workplace, with concierge-trained lobby attendants. Most significantly, they cracked the code of spending more and costing less.

CBRE spent $180 per square foot per person in the new space, approximately 50 percent more than a conventional Class A finish out.[7] At the same time CBRE will save hard costs of over $9 million over the life of the lease.

Lew Horne, president of CBRE, Southern California, left a clear trail for others to follow. He represents the leadership of engagement, a kind of leadership that doesn't depend on expertise, position, or force of will. His simple approach was, "We've got to change. Let's figure it out together." He did not use consultants in the traditional mode to analyze, assess, and announce solutions. They were invited to go on the discovery journey, too.

The new headquarters turned out to be a great success. In the first six months, more than 4,000 clients and prospects toured the space. Companies are now coming to CBRE to see and hear the story in hopes of walking away with some of the secret sauce. They made it look easy, but while Lew was confident and clear on the need for change and had some ideas of what a new future might look like, getting to the other side of the mountain was difficult and improbable.

CBRE is the largest commercial real estate broker in the world. Los Angeles is one of its largest markets and its headquarters. Successful brokers earn millions of dollars a year and function like moguls under the umbrella of the firm.[8] In many cases, brokers function as independent contractors. Naturally they are prized, pampered, and protected.

CBRE's former office looked like a traditional law or accounting firm. Large private offices lined the windows with administrative support cubicles in the center. Private offices symbolized success and respect. Inside these offices you might see family pictures; photos featuring poses with celebrities or while standing on top of Mount Kilimanjaro; signed baseballs, footballs, and sports jerseys; framed front-row Eric Clapton concert tickets; autographed guitars; etched silver-plated shovels from ground breakings; trophies; and the like. Each broker was well protected from interruption or intrusion. Each employee had a place to call his or her own. But this dedicated high-cost real estate was only occupied 51 percent of the time.

Paul Stockwell, one of the veteran CBRE brokers, told me that he used to arrive at the office and shut the door, never feeling the need to leave. His team was near and his administrative assistant offered all the support he needed. Paul had a comfortable, effective, and common island within the office. When the idea of a more open environment was first broached, Paul was one of many skeptics. He wondered where he would put his years of memories and trophies and how he would access his years of files.

Lew was about to embark on a mission that would require these brokers to exchange the symbols of success for a laptop and a chair, somewhere in the open office. He would have to be able to pull this off without losing a broker who could take his or her memorabilia and clients across the street to set up shop with a competitor. In fact, John Zanetos, one of the young rising stars, probably captured the aspirations of many when he told Lew that he joined CBRE to build his business and to one day have an office like Lew's. He may have said to eventually take Lew's office.

Lew was not technologically savvy and did not have a background in workplace strategy or design. He was not acquainted with mobile work and not tuned in with the younger culture. Lew's daily routine consisted of overseeing large transactions, meeting with investors, building relationships with community leaders, and working with corporate officers on the oversight of his 1,200-employee region. He readily acknowledged that he was best at making mistakes, in the open, and learning from them.

When I met Lew, it was clear he was a student of his business and industry, with a keen sense of the shifting market and a willingness to go out and learn from others. He also set an early tone by making it clear nothing would be developed behind closed doors and he would not expect anyone to do something he wasn't willing to do first.

The financial crash that hit hard in 2008 didn't just cause companies to retrench; it drove them to think differently about their real estate, to ask new questions and demand new solutions. Lew's clients wanted less space, more flexible lease agreements, more amenities to improve work–life balance, the ability to handle a more mobile and fluid workforce, and better use of technology.

Lew saw that CBRE had to lead by example. That meant it had to experience the new challenges of work and change just as their clients did. The nature of the business had to shift away from team islands to leveraging collective knowledge. Lew did have a strong workplace strategy team to guide him in his research. Beth Moore, Lenny Beaudoin, Georgia Collins, Chris Hood, and their team were familiar with alternative workplace strategies. They recommended that Lew first see their Amsterdam office and that of Eneco, an energy company. CBRE Amsterdam provided an image of a more open approach to work, but Eneco created the epiphany and the compass for Lew. There he experienced the energy, the people traffic, the casual encounters, the feeling of the open space, and what looked like higher engagement in the work.

The first step in the process was to engage his employees in a similar discovery and education process. So he sent key skeptics and influencers to visit Amsterdam and companies like Bloomberg, Russell Investments, Autodesk, Google, AT&T's Foundry in San Francisco, and others. Seeing began the believing. More than 25 percent of the office, over 60 people, worked on teams researching technology, furniture, culture, health, art, recognition, and moving to a paperless office.

One small area of the office was set aside to test and try ideas. This included testing different work configurations, furniture solutions, and technology. It was vital to pay attention to the details of how equipment worked. Those little details were key to the user experience. Things as simple as having enough outlets and easy plug-and-play electrical and digital connections were crucial to creating a frictionless work environment. This experimental zone also provided a platform where ideas could evolve. For example, they originally planned to maintain some permanently assigned private offices. But because of the open testing and dialogue, people saw the benefits of the more dramatic open approach.

The level of leadership engagement allowed CBRE to lead their consultants, not follow. That was a critical shift because consultants provided vital technical expertise but did not possess the contextual and tribal knowledge needed to cocreate solutions. CBRE's consultants did as trained; they aggregated the best of what they had already done and then worked on variations of that theme. CBRE sent them back to the drawing board several times. They charged them with the following:

- Don't bring us what you've already done; help us think in a fresh way.
- Don't impose your trained orthodoxy of what you think is "the right way."
- Understand what we are trying to accomplish and the experience we want to create.

Lew's extensive homework, the workplace strategy team, employee participation, the open place of testing, transparency, and allowing a vision to evolve created a pace of change that brought everyone along. The result was an office designed around several distinct activities that produced a wide variety of choices for how and where to perform work.

CBRE provided "digital coaches" to help employees move their files to the cloud. They also trained them in how to organize, find, and live as a digital native. CBRE invested heavily in technology. Each seated area provides dual monitors. Tables are designed for easy plug-and-play access. Offices are equipped with sit-to-stand desks. They partnered with Google Galaxy to provide life-size high-definition satellite images of any major market, so a client could tour any location virtually and get a realistic impression of the site. This replaces hours and days of walking through buildings. Even the traditional employee break area has both a high-end hotel feel and a high-tech touch.

CBRE went from private offices, cubicles, and conference rooms to over 16 different kinds of configured spaces. Every one of them is glass, an expression of transparency. Even the main conference room of this *Fortune* 500 Company is completely glass—no curtains.

Bob Fox noticed the unspoken communication that he thought made the experience special. "People walk by and smile, wave, or actually stick their heads in to say 'Hi.'"

Paul Stockwell talked of running into people he had never met. One day he decided to work in the accounting neighborhood and discovered a lot of valuable knowledge he could tap into with that group. At CBRE, employees can work in their own neighborhood or anywhere else they want.

CBRE's headquarters staff decided they wanted to be part of the space after the design had been completed. It turned out to be an easy adjustment. The headquarters team was given a neighborhood for identity but could (and does) work throughout the space like everyone else.

GSA—Moving a Battleship through Engagement

Martha Johnson, former administrator of the GSA, started her career at Cummins Inc. When I talked to her, I could see that the Columbus/Cummins ethos still gave a clear and resonant tone to her thinking, even after several decades.

Martha led the initial charge for the 1800F project. It integrated four functionally separate organizations, consolidated six locations, and restored a 100-year-old historical building. Like many break-throughs, the 1800F project came about out of necessity. At the time the GSA faced:

- Dramatic budget cuts
- President Obama's directive to achieve a Zero Energy Footprint in 10 years
- A historic 1917 building that still had air conditioners sticking out windows
- Space that was 40 percent occupied Tuesday through Thursday and almost half of that on Monday organizations, and a frag-mented organization operating in multiple locations—their archaic silos reinforced office turf divided by status
- Money made available through the American Recovery and Reinvestment Act

Martha had strong support. Bob Peck, who headed up the Public Buildings Services at GSA, was aligned and active. They both realized the rare opportunity. If they were going to go through the major disruption of displacing the workforce for two years while renovating the building, they should use that transition to rethink and reinvent GSA.

Many people may not realize what GSA does. Martha described GSA as the government's front door. It provides the physical presence for the government to the public. The GSA manages 360 million square feet of office space. It is the world's largest purchaser of nearly anything. It also creates the world's largest carbon footprint. Without dramatic change, that would increase 70 percent by 2050.

If GSA took the lead to change its command and control culture to a service and performance organization, the phenome-non had the potential to ripple through the entire government. If GSA could pilot a dramatic reduction in energy consumption, it could mark a turning point both for government and commercial office space.

They would start with 1800 F Street. Martha said, "GSA needed to take advantage of the disruption of a once-in-a-century building renovation in order to demonstrate to the entire government that interrupting long-standing workplace norms was possible and positive. We used the 1800F project as a catalyst to become a more open, collaborative, and customer-serving organization. The revamped space set the stage for inventive answers to old problems."

Martha's was a historic office, the third largest in DC. She described it as larger than a basketball court, actually 2,000 square feet, with a fireplace and wrought-iron casements. She exchanged it for a cubicle in an open space. Walking the talk was a first step in changing the GSA's culture of entitlement.

In standard government culture (as in much business culture), space equaled status and power. So everyone had permanent office space. That permanent space cost $14,000 a year to operate each desk. GSA was spending more than $20 million a year just to maintain empty offices.

In the new environment, stripping away entitlements, taking away turf, and creating transparency with an open environment was aimed at rewarding performance (not position), encouraging and increasing chance encounters, and creating a culture of transparency. Creating a free-address environment and using a reservation system would also change the attitude from owning space to thinking about workplace as a service.

Two years in temporary space provided two key opportunities. The disruption created a season of transition and an opportunity to build new attitudes and concepts. Of course, strong pockets of resistance emerged. But the GSA team knew that going in, so they made active change management part of their overall strategy. GSA had a culture that excelled in doing a great job if told what to do. They would now be asked to lower costs, reduce carbon emissions, and deliver high customer service.

The GSA team also saw and learned from leaders of alternative workplace strategies. They looked at Accenture, Deloitte, Google,

IDEO, and Microsoft. The end result of the 1800F transformation included:

- Increasing the capacity of the building from 2,200 employees to over 4,000
- Combining six locations and three organizations into one facility
- Reducing lease costs by $24 million annually and saving $7 million annually through integration of services
- Attracting weekly tours from other agencies and businesses to observe the positive climate and noticeable engagement in the work environment

The spark for the transformation was the crisis of cost reductions and grinding inefficiencies, forcing the need to rethink government. This was held together by a unifying vision of an innovative service culture that would ignite change throughout the government. GSA administrator Dan Tangherlini continues to promote and improve upon the lessons learned at GSA's headquarters throughout the federal government.

Red Hat—Open-Source Engagement

Red Hat, Inc. is a 20-year-old offspring of the open-source software movement. Open source (like Linux, MySQL, Firefox, and Wikipedia) allows free access to use, modify, and distribute software's source code or platform. Red Hat is the first and perhaps only open-source company that has exceeded a billion dollars in annual sales revenue.

Red Hat's culture demands and thrives on full disclosure, status through performance, candid debate, and the power of self-organization to get work done. This is a company where the power lies in the hands of the people, not management.

Red Hat's innovation has been the ability to successfully merge the structures of a large public business with the creative side of open-source culture. There seems to be magic in their formula to navigate the ostensible disparity between free software and profit, and freedom and accountability, while maintaining a core culture despite strong growth.

Jim Whitehurst, Red Hat's CEO, found his paradigm flipped when he came aboard from Delta Air Lines in 2007. He was used to people readily adopting his ideas—command and control. That didn't work at Red Hat. He would provide an idea and later find out, "We didn't do it. We thought it was a dumb idea."[9] That opened new thinking around the role of leadership in an open-source culture. "You can't lead a group of creative, passionate people [by saying] 'Go do this.' I've got to be more of a catalyst. In some ways I'm a head cheerleader."[10]

We had the opportunity to see how these dynamics played out when learning about their headquarters' move to Red Hat Tower in downtown Raleigh, North Carolina, in 2013. Louise Dixon Chapman, global senior manager of Workplace Planning, told us that the workplace is a key strategic tool to reinforce Red Hat culture, express the brand, and attract and retain employees. By 2011 rapid growth had spread employees over several leased buildings in Raleigh and Durham. Although downtown Raleigh had declined in recent years, Red Hat still wanted to establish their headquarters there and revitalize the area.

While Red Hat had originally wanted to build new head-quarters in downtown Raleigh, a perfect series of events allowed Red Hat to take space in an existing building. In 2011, Progress Energy had merged with Duke Energy. That merger would relocate most of the employees to Charlotte, vacating 300,000 square feet. That happened to be the same requirement that Red Hat needed, especially in light of their swift growth. Red Hat's move into the former Progress Energy space symbolized a changing of the guard from a legacy twentieth-century fossil fuel corporation to a twenty-first-century technology firm. That renovation reflected a new culture that would occupy the building and help energize downtown.

The old Red Hat environment was a holdover from the early high-tech days. They had taken over a building from a former telecom giant, and Red Hat had inherited that organization's Dilbert-like cubicle farm. Associates made their own modifications by removing panels and opening the space up for more interaction. It was clear they were eager for an environment that was better suited to their work dynamic and culture.

In preparation for the new building, Red Hat's project team created a very open approach for people to see and participate in the process. Louise described the level of transparency throughout the process, and how the team worked very hard to "communicate, communicate, communicate." As part of this effort, Red Hat project teams engaged with associates and partners early, practicing their value of defaulting to open discourse, which resulted in early collaboration with partners like Balfour Beatty. This initial interaction allowed these partners to align the appropriate services needed to work with Red Hat's very unique and participative culture.

Uprooting is always a challenge, even when moving to a new and better place, so Red Hat took steps to make the move as exciting as possible. Mock-ups, discussion groups, seeing what others had done, and communicating a compelling vision of the future created positive expectations.

Recreational and workspaces were designed to provide associates with a sense of community. The new spaces included a high-ceiling cafeteria on the ninth floor, breakout areas, and a gaming area, the last having become one of Red Hat's unexpected areas of high energy and pride. The eighth floor opens up to the outside with a large Wi-Fi-equipped patio. Associates love to bring family members to the facility; they want to show off their workplace.

Red Hat recognizes how unique their culture is and what the adjustment might mean to new hires. They created an area with interview rooms that allow potential hires to see and feel what it might be like to work at the company. The area provides large images of locations and associates from around the world, company activities, a subtle display of the many languages Red Hat does business in, and a sense for the kind of work and work atmosphere new hires can expect. Red Hat created two distinct interview rooms to allow candidates to select the environment they are most comfortable in. One provides a small but more formal presentation space well equipped for any kind of presentation or videoconference needs a candidate may have. The other is a more relaxed coffee shop atmosphere, also well equipped for presentations.

We recognized several common principles during our visit to Red Hat. The company maintains an associate-first philosophy where the work experience drives design. The organization is also evidently committed to extensively testing ideas before rolling them out. They invest a great deal of time in educating, taking feedback, and opening up the process for anyone.

Red Hat sees the workplace as a laboratory and a catalyst. The move gave the organization's employees a great opportunity to enhance their ability to better connect and collaborate, while reinforcing Red Hat's open culture. Louise sees all of this as a work in progress. Changing work styles, new technologies, and welcoming new colleagues means that the learning and improvement must keep pace and continue to evolve.

Zappos—Scaling Engagement through Culture

Zappos is an online retailer that started by selling shoes and became a multibillion-dollar company, bought by Amazon in 2009. I toured their new headquarters in downtown Las Vegas a few weeks after they moved in. I expected to see another cool high-tech space. It was all that. It struck me as a mix of Google's collegiate casual atmosphere, Southwest Airlines's visual celebration of their people, and an atmosphere of fun and weirdness.

The cab dropped me off at the Zappos entrance—the former, newly renovated city hall. The old city hall once held about

800 employees. Zappos was able to redesign it for 1,500. The Zappos culture celebrates individuality and fun, and the space reflects that. Most of the workstations have personal decorations, license plates with names, and many employee nicknames.

The new space is open, flexible, loud, and playful, sprinkled with individualized and unrefined surprises. Zappos offers a life coach, work–life balance assistance, a Genius Bar–kind of help with technology, a nap room, fitness center, adoption benefits, and pet insurance. A large patio attached to one of their cafés has garage doors that are opened when the weather is nice.

The executives sit side by side, open and accessible, along "Monkey Row." (The only "gatekeeper" is the friendly "Time Ninja.") The interior finish out is unrefined and flexible, with high ceilings and electrical cords dangling to plug into the work clusters.

The story line began to take shape in my head. A young, hip, high-tech culture, cheap real estate, a 24-hour business in a 24-hour town, employee-centric—but then I hit a disconnect. This was not a Google or an Apple. These were not high-paid engineers from top universities. This was essentially one big call center.

I have walked through dozens of call centers over my career. By and large, they live up to their dismal reputations as a sea of mind-numbing sameness. If there is a cognitive version of repetitive stress injury, call centers were designed to create it. Eighty percent of Zappos employees relocated from California to Vegas in their 2005 move for an average pay of $13 an hour. Their turnover was 25 percent of the industry average in 2008, and that included people receiving promotions.[11] While Teslas are common in the parking lots of Google and Apple, tattoos, piercings, and interesting hair are more common badges of status at Zappos.

Zappos visited Google, Nike, Apple, and other campuses before they created their new space. But they came away with a different strategy. Unlike those suburban campuses, they saw their setting more like the NYU campus, a community surrounded by a city. Their purpose was similar: Create chance encounters to spark innovation. However, they felt it would be more interesting to create these "serendipitous" interactions with the community surrounding the site.

An emerging neighborhood called Fremont East was just a few blocks away. It was attracting local business owners who were building restaurants, bars, and retail shops. Tony Hsieh, CEO of Zappos, saw the opportunity to help turn downtown Las Vegas into more of a community-focused neighborhood.

From this vision, Tony Hsieh launched a nonprofit called the Downtown Project. His organization is investing $50 million in small businesses, $50 million in tech startups, $50 million in arts and education, and $200 million in real estate development.

I listened to Tony's presentation. He stated two metrics for success: ROC, return on community, and ROL, return on learning. His goal is to accelerate serendipity, learning, productivity, and innovation. His case for space begins with Zappos's core values, which create a unique and engaging culture. This is a company, not unlike Cummins Inc., that sees beyond the strategy and efficiency of space; they see place as an integrated whole. Space is a reflection of and a catalyst for the kind of company and community Zappos sees itself to be and hopes to become.

Cousins—Engagement through Integration

Tom Cousins started his development company, Cousins Properties, in 1958. He is widely acknowledged (along with John Portman) as playing a major role in reshaping downtown Atlanta in the 1970s and 1980s. Tom bought the St. Louis Hawks basketball franchise and moved it to Atlanta in 1968. He may be best known today for his philanthropy and his tenacious pursuit and transformation of the most crime-ridden section of Atlanta, East Lake Village and restoring the once exclusive and famous East Lake Golf Club to become a community asset open to the public.

When I met John McColl, executive vice president of Cousins Properties, I could see that same steady and tenacious pursuit of a better and reimagined future. John's interest in Case4Space was to gain a better grasp of the changing demands of the workplace. The DNA of the firm is not simply to keep up with trends and meet demand but to look years ahead. Cousins' reimagination of what a developer might be began in 2009 and took shape in their early 2011 relocation. That thinking has become an ongoing part of everyday life, built into their culture and reinforced by their space.

Cousins moved to 191 Peachtree Tower in 2007. They were a traditional high-end developer taking 61,000 square feet, spread over two and a half floors, for 240 people. Most of the space was divided into private offices; about a quarter of the space was for administrative support cubicles, and about 15 percent was allotted for conference and project rooms. It was an environment of five separate fiefdoms with no common space to congregate. They didn't even have a mailroom (the mail was hand-delivered then). The CEO at that time felt that the executive area should be a quiet, invitation-only zone.

That all changed in 2009 with the financial crisis. The commercial real estate market dropped by half in many markets. Companies like Cousins had to fight for survival. It was not enough to simply cut costs, reduce head count, get lean, and ride out the storm. This signaled a sea change for leadership. John began a reeducation process to adapt to a new normal. In his mind, technology, a rapidly approaching digital-native workforce, and the repercussions of the financial meltdown would translate into companies looking for smaller, smarter, and mobile building solutions. Developers would also need to help companies improve the health and well-being of their employees.

That became the road map for Cousins's new space. The need for change was radical; John and the CEO maintained a tight, confidential lid on the project. In order to walk their talk and create a compelling proof of concept, John selected one of the worst spaces in the building, the fifth floor. It was adjacent to the parking garage, meaning there was no gorgeous view of the skyline. John hired Hendrick Design for their historical knowledge of Cousins and ability to help them envision a workplace of the future.

That space today is open, with small and larger teaming spaces spread throughout. My favorite area is called the Commons. It is a large, open area divided by three connected zones. One area is a large glass conference room that opens into a second area for casual meeting, relaxation, eating, or catching up with someone. The centerpiece of this room is a large wooden table with bench seating. This is adjacent to a well-stocked kitchen area. The Commons is a high-traffic, high-energy area that attracts people.

Cousins Properties is a company with a strong and resilient culture. They navigated dramatic change and used it to transform their business. Cousins dramatically restructured its practice. Instead of five divisions working as separate business units, they merged them into one focused practice. Leadership hoped and proved that they could be more agile and innovative by reframing their business as an integrated practice. Creating an open and collaborative space reinforced the strategy.

As a result, 70 people now produce higher revenue than 240 people did in the old environment. They cut their footprint in half. Their space is not only an office, but a living laboratory where clients can come to see a highly engaged work environment and hear the story of using space as a catalyst to change the culture.

Haworth HQ Renew—The Human Connection of Engagement

Haworth, Inc. is an office furniture manufacturer headquartered in Holland, Michigan. G. W. Haworth, a shop teacher with a gift for creating custom retail displays and simple room dividers, opened for business in his garage in 1948. When Dick Haworth, his son, took over in the mid-1970s, the company became an innovator in modular office furniture. It grew from sales of $10 million in 1974 to over $1 billion in global sales today.

Haworth's culture reflects the conservative and self-effacing Dutch Reformed heritage of the area. The 45-mile stretch west of

Grand Rapids is home to three of the largest office furniture manufacturers and is the hub for some of the most famous and influential modern industrial designers of the twentieth century. Haworth, Herman Miller, and Steelcase created the modern office and have continued to reimagine what the workplace might be.

Haworth's current building evolved from a distribution center in 1978, adding manufacturing in 1979 and then administrative offices in 1981. The building, reflecting a shop teacher's frugality, was created as the home for engineers designing cubicles and bending metal. Now, fast-forwarding to the mid-2000s, Haworth has adapted to keep pace with transforming ideas about work like those referenced in Bill Gates' 1999 book, *Business @ the Speed of Thought.* At the same time, Haworth moved out of product-focused R&D to a broader understanding of behaviors, culture, and new ways of working. That included a team of product designers, but also behavioral psychologists, industrial designers, ergonomists, workplace strategists, and sustainability experts.

It was now time to create an environment that reflected Haworth's current research and work philosophy, the global nature of its business, and provided a stage for testing new ideas and studying work behavior. Haworth also wanted to create a place where clients could come and see how Haworth handled the same challenges they faced.

The renovation of the old M-40 building became known as HQ Renew. The two-year transition required the administrative offices to move across the street to an industrial park called the ATS (Across the Street). It not only provided space to work, but also space for testing new ideas and products.

Haworth partnered with the University of Michigan's Ross School of Business to test and refine organizational culture analysis and translate culture types into a workplace strategy tool. The temporary space also allowed experimentation with mobile and distributed work concepts. During this period, Haworth evolved their products from several distinct offerings into an agile, integrated platform that includes modular interior construction solutions.

Haworth moved back into the completed renovation in 2008. When guests first arrive, they usually pause at the stairs next to the greeting station that lead to the ground floor of the atrium. The view from the top of the stairs provides an unhindered view of an open and expansive ground floor tailored for casual gatherings or private reflection as well as an unhindered look into each floor cantilevered over the atrium space. As such, it gives an astounding sense of scale and intimacy (see Figure 10.1).

Because Haworth hosted Case4Space twice, we became familiar with many of the collaborative spaces. Each is well equipped with technology and easily adapted for the several different configurations we used. In addition to the different kinds of spaces, we were also able to conveniently gather in the atrium, order coffee, and sit in one of many booths or at stand at a table and continue our conversations and work.

Michelle Kleyla, workplace knowledge/marketing manager at Haworth, told us that Haworth values basic research into human behavior and design principles. But they also believe there is a deeply human side to work that you learn one way—by observing. Culture and context mean that a solution that worked great for one group may not work well for another, even one doing similar work. When Haworth designed a Refresh area (a casual space with coffee and drinks) using an expensive stone surface at bar height along with contemporary seating, they saw that it did not attract much traffic. That was an opportunity to test some of their recent research into the importance of grounding elements in a space. A grounding element taps deeply into our early encounters with space; they are places that we are naturally drawn to.

The facilities team changed the space; they replaced the stone table with reclaimed timber hewn by a local craftsperson. They added overhead pendant lighting and exchanged the contemporary seating for a sectional sofa. It quickly became one of the

Figure 10.1   Haworth HQ Atrium View

most popular spaces in the building. The natural quality of wood, the hand-crafted human connection, the story behind the reclaimed table top, the new intimacy from the lighting, and the casual seating all played a role in changing the story of the space. It became a magical space, and Michelle said, "Our journey is to learn how to create this magic on purpose. We know that it begins by putting ourselves in the shoes of those we design for."

Balfour Beatty, Washington, DC—Engaging the Process

At the outset of many construction projects, the principal stake-holders will sit around a table with the owner and their attorney to address the terms and conditions of the contract. There is not much of a dialogue. It's a time to clarify and complain in an attempt to make changes to reduce liability. It is a game with the umpire on the home team's payroll.

Bob Fox, principal at FOX Architects, came to the kickoff meeting prepared to play the game. Balfour Beatty was moving to a new regional headquarters, and they would be both the owner and the contractor. As Bob shared his reaction, "The attorney asked me what I wanted out of this project, and it blew me away! Nobody had ever asked me that in a kickoff meeting before; in all of the other projects we have worked on, my goal is to focus on achieving client needs while limiting our exposure." This was certainly a new playbook that Bob had not seen before, a new way of thinking that would transform their business.

Will Lichtig, the attorney for Balfour Beatty, is a pioneer of relational contracting for construction, one of the tools used to configure collaborative project teams. After Will went around the table with the same question, Bob thought, "Maybe we can do something positive, create something great." It changed his outlook of what might be possible and tapped into a new level of engagement. Bob Fox expressed, "In a traditional project you go in with good intentions and trust. But as soon as the first hiccup happens, the gloves come off and everyone retreats to their corners for the next round. Now we had a big incentive to help each other to find a better way to execute our work—it's all in the *project's* best interest."

Balfour Beatty recognized the industry was changing fast. Traditional partitioned projects were getting harder to deliver without strong muscle and tight reins. What was really needed was deeper cooperation and earlier integration, which meant a new mind-set and new practices. The relocation would give the company an opportunity to test the emerging trend toward trust-based projects.

To join this fresh conversation and have an opportunity to lead it, Balfour had to find a way to walk the talk. Mark Konchar, Balfour's Chief of Enterprise Development, said, "Our approach to selecting suppliers was to have a simple conversation. We weren't focused on skill or capabilities. We picked firms we knew could do the job. Our questions were around trust, cultural alignment, and the willingness to work together on a process that was new to all of us. Our office was making a huge leap from a very traditional space to one that was designed to promote collaboration and flexible work teams."

With a year's lead time, they studied how work was actually getting done. The office created an early-adopter team to test ideas and solicit feedback from the other employees. They learned that most people are only in their office 30 to 40 percent of the time. And when they were in their offices, they were using only a small area.

Mark and his team visited several furniture showrooms to learn about work trends and see new office applications. Balfour found that the manufactured furniture solutions did not provide the customizing features they wanted. For example, one important consideration was working with large sets of drawings; they are a construction company. The employees wanted to showcase their craftsmanship and let people see the quality of their work. The design must allow for some personal customization of their space. That led to the use of millwork and the design of a flexible "kit of parts." Balfour and FOX put a lot of attention into the details—that included lighting, materials, the technology, and the fit.

The hard conversation had to do with reducing 70 private offices down to three. If they wanted more collaborative spaces, then the room would have to come from private offices and storage. They were able to purge a large number of files, and made it fun by throwing Purge Parties. A large number of files were also digitized and sent to the cloud.

In the end, the space was significantly reduced from the previous office, even as the office increased from 80 employees to over 100. The amount of space designed for collaboration increased by a factor of 10. Balfour made a heavy investment in upgrading technology and making sure that the collaboration spaces had current tools that were easy to use.

The use of the space was transformed. More used the space. It became a favorite venue for civic, trade, and larger team sessions, often by outside organizations. It also became a living story for clients and trade partners to see and hear work trends and more collaborative approaches to running projects. Mark offered a few lessons: "The first is to get the cultural conversation going earlier and look for any behavior or value shifts that could improve the work and the business. Second, drive the guiding principles for the project before beginning design. Finally, the more testing and iterating you can do, the better the final outcome."

Their human resources manager commented, "When people come in here, they are happy. This is our home." Bob Fox said he felt vested. "We now work out issues instead of protecting our rear." When engagement starts at the beginning and is modeled by management, the result is an engaging outcome. Balfour followed IBM's innovation ladder. They started with the culture and created a context for engagement, which led to collaboration and resulted in innovation-inspired transformation.

"Doing good work lifts and validates the human spirit. Why would we not celebrate that in workplaces that honor and encourage great work?"

—Dick Bayer, principal, ReAlignment Group

In his book, *Outliers: The Story of Success,* Malcolm Gladwell wrote, "Three things—autonomy, complexity, and a connection between effort and reward—are, most people agree, the three qualities that work has to have if it is to be satisfying."[12]

Based on our experience with these companies, we would add the following dimensions to Gladwell's observation:

- Deep respect for the individual and desire to help employees find and experience their unique ability to contribute
- An organic complexity where culture rules over policy and procedure
- Clear identity expressed as genuine connectedness among coworkers
- The places of work capture the soul of the company, so that those who work there feel at home and those who visit feel that hospitality

Finally, we saw authenticity in these companies. None of them took the easy path of imitating what they saw others do. For example, Google did not go the way of distributed work or free-address workstations. They had to research their own culture, external forces, and business goals in order to create a campus that reflected their unique identity. That was true of every company included in our research.

CHAPTER 11

Break Out of Insanity

It is expensive to be mediocre in this world. Quality has always been cost effective. The tragic mistake in history that's always been made by the well-to-do is that they have feathered their own nests. Today we know that society does not survive unless it works for everybody.
—J. Irwin Miller

As a historian, Stephen Ambrose saw the critical role that environment plays in life. He opened his epic saga of Lewis and Clark's Western expedition with this line: "From the west-facing window of the room in which Meriwether Lewis was born on August 18, 1774, one could look out at Rockfish Gap, in the Blue Ridge Mountains, an opening to the West that invited exploration."[1]

Clearly, our surroundings influence what we envision and produce.

The organizations highlighted in this book have discovered—and many of us are still learning—that we have a deep connection to space. We impart meaning into space by the very approach we take to defining it. Space becomes the context for culture, and culture has the power to release (or constrain) engagement, creativity, and productivity. We all seem to understand that when we speak of homes, museums, art galleries, places of worship, or airports. But we often undervalue space when we think about our places of work.

One of the managers at Google described their workplace evolution this way: "During our 1.0 phase, we were interested in fast and cheap. During our 2.0 phase, we ventured into iconic design; we looked for space that was cool. Today, in phase 3.0, our energy is invested in user experience, wellness, and sustainability." Google is very progressive and recently was ranked one of the best places to work. From their point of view, this next evolution seems like common sense. It is certainly supported by their track record of growth, innovation, and ability to attract top talent.

But why would this kind of common sense seem so progressive?

Google, born out of the digital revolution, operates from a different set of values than traditional corporations. Their universe places a premium on intelligence, problem solving, creativity, and decision making. These only surface when employees feel engaged. The evolution taking place in their universe represents a revolution for many.

The digital revolution has sparked new possibilities, novel social frameworks, business model disruptions, and organizational remapping, and it is now reaching the workplace. In one sense, the workplace is catching up to what has already taken place—a networked world collaborating to get things done.

Our research documents that this sea change is now coming to the workplace. As in every sea change, certain riddles once appeared unsolvable. Then suddenly someone resolved the challenge, and the answer became obvious to everyone. It was then taken for granted as part of the new common sense. The riddle of choosing between cost, schedule, and project quality has hounded owners for decades. This riddle has now been solved.

Design was once considered a commodity, a transaction to bid to the marketplace. But early adopters have discovered good design as transformational, a game changer with the right partner in a cocreative process. Companies are defying conventional wisdom by spending more on space—up to 50 percent more—but lowering overall cost and experiencing a measurable increase in engagement.

Does space influence productivity or engagement? It's no longer a question. Of course it does. It's been done. Those who say there is no link or way of reconciling the competing interests are simply stuck looking at the isolated pieces of an old puzzle. We've provided examples of companies who have been living this reality for decades; new-generation firms that instinctively default to culture and engagement, and legacy organizations that have found transformation. They all discovered new vitality and market relevance using space as a catalyst for a renewed vision.

Proof of Concept for Case4Space

Patrick Donnelly of BHDP Architecture and I recently met with executives from 12 large national firms. We quickly saw that they were struggling with the riddles of change in our industry. They asked for our perspective, so we gave them sticky notes and asked two questions: "What's working, and what's not?" What came back looked like the table of contents to this book. "Collaboration" and "adapting to change" were each written 11 times. "Millennials" and the problem of workplace engagement were listed nine times.

We shared some of the Case4Space discoveries with them. It was clear that we stirred their imaginations and raised some anxiety. We heard story after story of internal battles to overcome the riddles and misconceptions addressed in this book. In our debrief with the group, their number-one request was, "We want more time on these topics!" One CEO said that had he known the topic, he would have set aside the day.

But Patrick and I had no topic. We just happened to be in town together and coordinated our schedules to meet with a service provider, who literally pulled this event together on the spur of the moment. So, from an impromptu presentation, we tapped a deep response to the challenges of the sea change.

The war that price once waged against design and culture is coming to an end. Design and culture are both now part of a powerful new algorithm for effectiveness.

Everyone Wants the Same Thing

Someone famously said, "Insanity is doing the same thing over and over and expecting a different result." Regardless of who said it, that statement certainly describes the traditional (and current) matrix of the commercial real estate system. And it has produced a pervasive "code red" of stress, waste, poor health, and detachment. As we documented in Chapter 2, that matrix costs the U.S. economy about a trillion dollars every year!

> "Organizational health spurs the release of genius [in our people]. It can magnify its effect channeled toward purpose-driven outcomes. We see this link in our own business in the form of innovative problem solving and a culture willing to learn and share."
>
> —Mark Konchar, Chief of Enterprise Development at Balfour Beatty Construction

All of us at Case4Space want to help good people break out of the insanity. We have noticed something: One of the ironies of the current broken system is that all of the stakeholders want the same thing. Owners, developers, architects, contractors, manufacturers, vendors, and employees want workplaces that release everyone to do his or her best. We all want innovation, collaboration, engagement, efficiency, and safety. No one yearns for inefficiency, stagnation, conflict, stress, unsafe workplaces, failure, bankruptcy, or similar disasters. All of that is insane! We all want to tear down the walls that prevent a great place to work. So how do we do that?

First, we have to break out of the insanity of the current system to see this new common sense.

I think it's happening. The degree of disengagement, wasted office space, and the dis-ease and discomfort of the common work experience is bringing everyone to a collective "OMG" response. When we wake up from "no way" to clearly see "no wonder," we will have broken out of the insanity. If we simply list and then eradicate everything that makes work a hassle, disempowering, and draining, we will find the path to rethinking the workplace.

A new common sense requires that we invest in the whole life of our employees. We can't create an isolated column called WORK and just focus on that. We must view the workplace through the eyes of those who spend time there. In a very real sense, they are family. Their health, wellness, openness, engagement, and productivity are of equal value. That's because life is not fractured; it is integrated. We cannot afford for the workplace to dis-integrate our people when they walk through the front door.

When we think of workplace design as an area for the "experts," we trade meaning for efficiency. Furthermore, our space can take on the expert's identity, not ours. But when we open up the process and allow all the stakeholders (including employees) to participate, space can take on a company's collective identity. We know we've succeeded when that space feels like "home" to those who work there.

The typical path of selecting and building commercial real estate has become a matrix of experts, procurement practices, template buildings, tight schedules, risk, and (too often) litigation. That matrix is what one leader Case4Space interviewed called "the system that makes good people do bad things." Even worse, the "undertow" of that system makes it almost impossible to back out once the suction starts to pull everyone under.

That is why this book features leaders and companies that have crossed over from insanity to a new common sense. We did that because once people decide to break out of insanity, they run into resistance and rejection. It just takes time and relentless grit to break through the engrained habits and vicious cycles. And it takes more time to find that it's okay to have an original (and sane) thought. Once people press through that wall, they and many others will wonder why they had not done it before.

So you need the stories of those who have already traveled beyond insanity.

Change Your Culture

Leadership, now more than ever, is really in the culture business. And that means changing the conversation away from the *things* of innovation, collaboration, and engagement and creating a *culture* of those values. Programs and initiatives ultimately default to the prevailing culture. Creating a healthy culture builds a collective identity in a common journey. That is the only way to keep the corporate ship on course when it's hit by the forces of a changing wind.

> "People can't live or work without places—they define who we are. Places are becoming more connected and complex as we learn more about people and what drives our organizations."
>
> —Bob Fox, Principal, FOX Architects

A question most companies will have to answer is, "Who owns culture?" That is not a trivial question. We're not suggesting creating a chief culture officer or a chief workplace officer. But culture permeates everyone's turf, and yet few companies have a process that connects culture to HR, corporate real estate decisions, space design, technology, finance, and business strategy.

The unpredictable nature of innovation requires that all channels inside and outside a company become open sources of renewed questions, thoughts, and energy. To simply create an innovation capsule within a company is to live in a segmented world where untapped potential will never be realized. Without a culture of innovation, any attempt to move beyond the familiarity of the past will encounter a thousand pushbacks. Marshall McLuhan captured it well: "The idea department of a big firm is a sort of lab for isolating dangerous viruses."

Every company faces the law of the S-curve. Innovation travels like a wave from inception. It grows, peaks, and then disappears back into the sea. In today's S-curve, the lengths are shorter, the crests and troughs are deeper, and the external conditions of changing winds will generate larger, more formidable, and eventually destabilizing forces. But innovation creates a wave that others have to navigate. Resiliency is the capacity to handle external waves and to come through on top.

We began by listing the conditions for success in the turbulent seas of corporate life. They include high engagement, simplifying complexity, bounce-back resilience, constant refreshing and reinvention, and the ability to gracefully adapt the culture to the unpredictable and disruptive turbulence of external realities.

To attain those conditions means creating a culture of innovation—as the default mode. We must have a default that will automatically lean into:

- Direct experience over analysis
- Understanding context more than relying on data
- Inquiry over advocacy
- Meaningful connections instead of efficient transactions
- Conversation instead of messaging
- Pacing instead of pushing
- Embracing the journey equally important as the destination
- Building strengths as the focus rather than fixing flaws

Act Your Way into a New Mind-Set

In Chapter 10, we told the story of Jerry Sternin who worked in Vietnam in the 1990s. His job was mountainous. His mandate to address childhood malnutrition in Vietnam was constrained by lingering distrust toward the United States and an impossible six-month time frame. Jerry was forced to find an out-of-the-box approach or fail.

He felt that the answer probably lay hidden in plain sight. And he was right. He saw something: Although most babies were malnourished, some were very healthy. He watched the daily routine of their mothers. He focused on the healthy anomalies, those that deviated from the cultural norms but produced positive outcomes.

Out of that experience, Sternin made three key observations that Case4Space adopted:

1. *"Focus on the successful exceptions, not the failing norms."* [2] We were constantly reminded that our effort to change the broken system was a search for the Holy Grail. We simply looked for companies and leaders who had not heard it was impossible to link space and culture together and achieve high engagement.

2. *Finding someone, a positive outlier, with the answer doesn't mean we truly grasp the elements that create their magic.* Sternin said, "All [failures] had occurred exactly at the moment in which . . . the solution (aka the 'truth') was discovered. The next, almost reflexive, step was to go out and spread the word: Teach people, tell them, educate them . . . we realized that [failures] occurred because we were acting as though once people 'know' something, it results in the 'doing' something." [3] We did not stop with the case study but dug deeper into "the rest of the story" because the context for success revealed the true magic.

3. *Changing behavior changes behavior.* For Sternin, training, messaging, and indoctrination did not work. He brought mothers of malnourished babies together to work side by side with the mothers of healthy babies. That led to new norms. That's how you act your way into a new attitude or mind-set. It is so simple that it sounds stupid to say it. But, "Changing space changes behavior." Changing workflow changes behavior. Changing whom people sit next to changes behavior. Changing technology changes behavior. When applied with intent and good design, all of those simple acts become powerful change agents. People can act their way into the new.

Listening for What Matters

I recently heard Ken Schmidt, Harley-Davidson's director of communications for nearly 10 years, [4] speak at a conference. He knew his job for that audience was to get them outside their own heads, full of conference data and case studies, and stretch their imagination muscles. So he told a story of taking Wall Street investors to Sturgis, South Dakota. He wanted to get those "spreadsheet wonks" out of their comfort zone and onto Harley's turf. "Let them see 400,000 Harley fanatics and experience the mass confusion and a twinge of fear."

One of his guests commented, "Wow, this is incredible marketing!" That statement made Ken angry. He told the man, "These aren't customers. They aren't transactions! These are disciples who attract more disciples!" He repeated their famous caption: "What we sell is the ability for a 43-year-old accountant to dress in black leather, ride through small towns, and know that people are afraid of him."

Then he asked all of us, "What's the point in meeting Wall Street expectations? That barely moves the needle!" Ken reminded us that we only tell stories about experiences that exceed our expectations. What stories are people sharing about your company? How about your employees? *Are* there any stories?

Ken gave a 45-minute sermon on what it is to take people to the mountaintop, to pierce the veil for creating a culture of engagement. Think that is overstated? How many employees or customers have *your* logo tattooed on their bodies? Later, in a private conversation, Ken told me a story of when Harley was in serious trouble; they faced extinction. With their back against the wall, Harley needed to become a different kind of company. But they did not know what that was.

So they talked to hundreds of customers and bikers. In short, they listened, and then they listened some more. When they felt they saw the world through the eyes of their most ardent supporters, they moved forward. The new mission was to become important to and admired by the people who could make a difference for them. Ken said, "At first that was our customer base, but then we realized that we can't keep the promises we're making unless the company became something special to our employees."

He told me, "Our facilities and showrooms used to be filthy." So space became a key catalyst for transforming the culture. Today, if you go to the headquarters or any Harley showroom, you will enter Harley's alternate reality. I recently did that; I spent a few hours at a Harley-Davidson dealership. The 45,000-square-foot showroom offered themed vignettes that reminded me of a modern museum. One area showcased vintage bikes; others had futuristic concept bikes, apparel, training, and accessories; and then a view inside the large garage showed bikes being transformed and tailored for their new owners.

What I especially liked about Ken and the Harley story is the deeply human connection they have tapped into. They talk and they listen to the people who matter: those who make as well as those who buy the Harleys. In an hour of crisis, of possible extinction, Harley got out of their cloistered mind-set of thinking they were a manufacturer making stuff to sell. They had to begin to understand what the stuff really meant—and they did. That migrated to reengaging with their workforce, and that led to transforming the workplace, accelerating the cultural transformation. Harley became a place that made a difference to those who could make a difference for them; the rest was simple assembly.

Michael Vance, the former dean of Disney University, has said, "The more you are like yourself, the less you are like anyone else, which makes you unique. It's the unique factor that people are attracted to." He went on to say, "No one wants to go to kind-of-like Disney."

Finding that unique factor takes work, hard work. This is what people pay a premium to experience. Ken Schmidt says, "We are emotional, and therefore our emotions transcend rational thought. Is it rational to part with perhaps $24,000 for a new Harley Davidson when you can buy a perfectly good Honda for $8,000? The brain says buy the Honda; the heart says buy the Harley."

That is the cost difference between a Harley Sportster and a comparable Honda Shadow. Not only does the Harley command three times the price for essentially the same bike, it outsells the Honda 13 to 1.

Every workplace should create a unique experience that reflects the work, the people, and the culture. To what level? When a new manager takes over a team at Google, the facilities team provides support to reconfigure or adapt that space to the way the team decides it now wants to work. It should feel like a home away from home. Otherwise, it is simply an industrial knock-off that may look like the real thing but lacks the soul and distinction that creates its value.

Make the Investment

It has been said that leaders are measured by the timelines of their investments. Some invest in the next year. Fewer can see and invest in the next decade. Very few can invest in a long-term future of several decades. But some, like Cummins Inc.'s J. Irwin Miller, Google's Larry Page, and Zappos's Tony Hsieh see generations from now, and their investments reflect their vision. That's why we call them "visionaries."

Miller had the foresight to know that his Cummins could not build their diesel engines unless world-class designers, engineers, and the other professions essential to their business would actually relocate their families to a small town in Indiana. And they would not do that for any amount of money if local school systems, roads, businesses, public spaces, churches, and infrastructure were not first class. He once said, "Architecture is the visible expression of something much larger and important going on within a community." So he knew he would have to invest in architecture that would outlive him.

> "For too long I focused on business plans—before learning that our success was driven by focusing on engaging the creativity and passions of our team."
>
> —Craig Janssen, Managing Director, Idibri

The biggest failure of the broken system addressed in this book is that it has stopped investing in the future. When all the roles and metrics build a system in which the expense of building is known as "sunk costs," we will always see designed space as a cost always to be minimized, regardless of other factors.

But if we could see space as the way to shape culture, we might begin to understand that it is an investment in and beyond our own timeline. J. Irwin Miller could see that the investments in designing space would grant a great return on investment. And, as we wrote in Chapter 2, that investment compounds the return!

That's why Miller had the confidence to say, "It is expensive to be mediocre. . . . Quality has always been cost effective."

Another way to say that very thing is this: "Break out of the insanity." Break out of the insanity that insists on the exorbitant expense of mediocrity. Make the investment. Who knows? Perhaps the Meriwether Lewises of tomorrow will be influenced by what we envision and design today.

An engaging workplace is the expression of an engaging process and intent.

The difference between a cool space and something you really talk about is how the people in the space impact you.

The New Common Sense

Everyone understands that we live in a time of global conflict, disruption, fragmentation, and isolation. Playwright Arthur Miller famously said, "An era can be said to end when its basic illusions are exhausted." What we often consider to be unsolvable is just a crisis waiting for a new generation of leaders. That's why the metaphor of the churning sea provides an opportunity for new thinking about how we live and work.

In much the same way, a new generation of leaders—Millennials—is bringing new ways of thinking to the workplace. They seem to be arriving just as some exhausted illusions are collapsing. New generations always provoke and frighten. This reaction is typical. But not only do the Millennials understand the digital revolution; they are also more collaborative by nature than those who went before them. They bring a new kind of intelligence, creativity, decision making, and problem solving to our workplaces.

They are simply an example of new generations being better equipped to deal with a new era of crises. Every generation sees what was once called normal to be insane. And they also see what was once considered impossible to be the new common sense.

The good news for the rest of us is that crossing over the digital divide is easier than it looks. There is a barrier, but it is primarily a mental barrier. Leaders like Lew Horne, Martha Johnson, and John McColl discovered that to be true. As Lew Horne said, "At first it felt disruptive, but then it was truly liberating."

We began our journey in Case4Space as a search for the secret to creating engaging workplaces. We were trying to solve a 40-year unsolved riddle. What started as questions among colleagues turned into 15 months of discovery, challenged assumptions, and a new mind-set about the new nature of work. Joseph Campbell described the kind of absorbing adventure we experienced: "We're not on our journey to save the world but to save ourselves. But in doing that you save the world. The influence of a vital person vitalizes."

At Case4Space, we were not out to change the world. But we do think we have found some answers for those who face the questions. We certainly discovered a renewed vitality—and, in essence, the secret to engagement: Work at its best is social and engaging. We came away with a conviction that we will soon see a cultural revolution that views all work as connected, integrated, purposeful, and grand. The spark for this revolution is survival through innovation. When we do, it will be, at least in part, because we reshaped our environments to value these human qualities.

The Case4Space Approach

One resists the invasion of armies; one does not resist an idea whose time has come.

—Victor Hugo

I f you want to get a look beneath the promises and formulas from the latest business book and hear what really works, come join us at the Pancake House Roundtable the first Wednesday of each month. More than 10 years of these Wednesday morning meetings have given us countless lessons in common sense and a ringside seat for the changing trends of business.

The same eight colleagues that were introduced in *The Commercial Real Estate Revolution* still attend. All are owners of companies that play a role in commercial construction. The companies range from millions to several hundred million dollars in size. We are at that point in our careers where handing off the baton to the next generation of leadership has become one of our common subjects of discussion. We still talk about the market, competition, change, and, yes, our families.

We are all survivors. We made it through the incredible downturn that caused our industry to collapse in 2008. All of our businesses retrenched and restructured. Today we are all healthy and growing.

Our companies are not as quick to add people to the payroll, we are more selective of the culture fit, and we are all focused on making sure our work is close to our core strengths. We all feel fortunate for weathering the storm and grateful for the deposit of resolve and respect it salted into our interaction with each other.

The changes we have experienced over the last five years have taught us the new reality for business and life: Adapt or die. Each month, eight "object lessons" share their latest chapter in the art of change. Some are deeply transforming.

Over the years our menu orders have shifted from eggs, bacon, and pancakes to oatmeal and egg white omelets. The loss of a child, the addition of a grandchild, the struggle of a mutual friend, and several health battles all seem to strip theory away and make us more aware that life's complexities don't follow a time line. We all have fewer easy answers. There is something stabilizing about a monthly ritual of a meal with friends and colleagues. It seems to filter the noise of busyness; we all find a clearer signal for hearing what's coming down the road.

Technology has transformed each of our businesses. The topic of work–life balance has changed from something we might have joked about five years ago to a serious challenge, for ourselves and for our organizations. Our markets are increasingly complex, more demanding, and are forcing us all to rethink our strategies and business models. Our times together, however, have allowed us to continue to adapt. We have no formula, but we've found a rhythm. Our time is unplanned but our conversations have a purpose. We have often laughed at stories about our clueless encounters with digital natives. When asked how we've been able to maintain our group for over 10 years, one of the owners said, "We're a bunch of old dogs who happen to be looking for a few new tricks."

The Evolution of MindShift

The Pancake House Roundtable reflects the soul and values of a MindShift: deep respect, open trust, strong debate, and a drive to learn. Rather than promoting our own agendas, we have learned to focus on helping one another.

The MindShift model was the platform for Case4Space. Think of MindShift as a high-tech barn raising. The process and the journey have been and continue to be transforming for us. So, who are we? Patrick Donnelly, one of the Case4space leaders, answered that by saying, "We are an odd mix of talented people who have a common cause and use engagement to move the group from one state of mind to another."

I agree. We are a fellowship of thought leaders intent on changing the conversation about engagement and the workplace. Our goal is to see anyone interested in a proven approach to innovation or tackling a wicked problem launch a MindShift of his or her own.

The Roots of MindShift

The roots of MindShift go back to 1986, during a deep economic downturn in Texas. Businesses were reeling, especially commercial real estate, architecture, and construction. At the time I met regularly with five colleagues—an architect, a local bank president, a commercial carpet representative, a furniture manufacturer's representative, and an interior contractor—to share leads. We sort of made a pact to help one another through those dark days. We agreed to share our full client and prospect lists and to open the door for one another to our best client relationships. This level of cooperation would never have happened under normal business conditions. What was born out of necessity became a standard part of my approach to business for the next 25 years.

That fall, two friends, Pat Sullivan and Mike Muhney, created the first contact management software called ACT!. I had recently bought a 17-pound, luggable Compaq computer with a memory capacity of two floppy disks. I volunteered to organize all of the client and prospect names with ACT!.

The combination of our mutual cooperation and a tool like ACT! helped us to survive the downturn and to actually do pretty well. And it accelerated my career. That's how I learned what a virtual organization could do. All I needed was a little structure, a tool to multiply efforts, someone willing to organize, and a pay-it-forward attitude.

Over the next 20 years, I refined the model, and it eventually became known as SWARM (Smart Work and Referral Marketing). SWARM captured our philosophy of helping one another. In 2007 I used this same structure, called MindShift, to recruit and launch *The Commercial Real Estate Revolution.* I used it again in 2012 for Case4Space.

The most important criterion that transferred to MindShift was that we only recruited people with a common philosophy and commitment. I learned the hard way that talent and strong connections were less important than attitude and chemistry. For that reason, we found an early shakeout period with each MindShift where we politely and discreetly dropped the skeptics and free riders.

Case4Space started with a core of five people from our construction MindShift—Mabel Casey, Mark Konchar, Craig Janssen, Markku Allison, and Ray Lucchesi. Eleven more who were familiar with that initial effort joined, and the rest grew out of relationships. Careful selection and a clear purpose to change the conversation around engagement allowed the team to align early and commit.

A second key has been the diversity of participants. The range of expertise for our core group included architecture, design, construction, commercial real estate development, furniture and equipment, journalism, corporate real estate management, facilities management, decision economics, neuroscience, biomimicry, strategic foresight (a discipline that builds future scenarios for business application), equity capital, acoustics, data analytics, ethnography, Millennial culture, organizational health, workplace engagement, culture change management, branded environments, Video Information Modeling, tenant representation, project management, Building Information Modeling, workplace strategy, master planning, academia, procurement, graphic design, infographics, and lean practices.

Creating the Platform

In early 2006 I told Dick Haworth, then CEO of Haworth Inc., that I thought the industry was ready for a changed conversation around working cooperatively and collectively in the client's best interest. Dick liked the idea and asked for a proposal. The next month I presented the proposal to a leadership team.

The team liked it, but an initiative like that simply did not fit into marketing, sales, architecture and design support, product development or even the research department. After numerous meetings and phone conversations, we could not find a way to move it forward. Seven months later, Franco Bianchi, Haworth's CEO and president, asked me to make one more trip to meet a new executive. When I arrived at Haworth's transition head-quarters, I met Mabel Casey. After 30 minutes she said, "We need to do this!" Mabel actually saw more than I did about the potential for changing the conversation. The next step was to schedule a pilot session and see what might emerge from the conversation. That was a first lesson. Mabel understood how to pace and measure as we moved into the unknown.

In March 2007, architecture and design firm Gensler (the world's largest architectural firm) hosted 18 leaders at their Houston office. It was clear we had distilled the initial thought into a conversation whose time had come. That session launched the first MindShift.

Mabel Casey, Lew Horne, Martha Johnson, John McColl, Mark Konchar, and Dave Radcliffe each have abilities to see what others don't and then create a platform for engagement that allows discovery, testing, and then proof of concept.

That first MindShift reflected Mabel's unique ability to see the big picture, connect the dots, and bring diverse talents together. At one point in our discovery we identified other groups tackling the same frustrations. We wondered if our efforts would be better channeled supporting an existing group. But Mabel saw the opportunity to make a unique contribution by providing an overarching narrative. That insight provided focus and an identity that carried over into Case4Space.

Mabel, Lew, Martha, John, Mark, and Dave are highly engaged in building teams and setting the tone. They also know when to step back to let the team find its own sense of identity and traction; they all have a unique combination of high expectations with low control. Mabel set a tone for MindShift to push boundaries, appreciate how space matters, focus on changing the conversation, and select and create a team of respected colleagues—not easy tasks. Her ability to remove clutter, prevent rabbit trails, and find meaning in the work gave us a compass that allowed navigation into the unknown.

Content without Context

When consultants are hired to help companies tackle complex problems, their reports typically follow similar formats. They define the problem, provide statistics and pie charts about its size and significance, warn of implications if circumstances do not change, offer stories that promote different strategies that achieve positive results, and suggest that if you follow the recommendations, you will succeed. But that is usually content without context. Therefore, they create a false sense of understanding.

There are enough case studies, reports, and business books, each with a new study, theory, and polished packaging, that anyone can find a conclusion that fits the purpose. Over the last few years, some reports pushed business to get rid of cubicles to improve collaboration and spark innovation. Then new reports claimed that openness creates distractions and interferes with focus—and that impedes innovation. Another report questioned our ability to increase interaction if only 16 percent of work time is spent in face-to-face collaboration. The implication was that we shouldn't be too quick to tear down walls. We chose not to follow the traditional compilation of case studies but instead to set each company's approach within their unique cultural context. One size does not fit all. When success is as much about the dynamic of the stakeholders as it is about strategy and execution, we need to get behind the veil of case studies and hear the dynamic of the stakeholders. Lew Horne described his problem in confronting this blind spot with many experts and their reports: "They give answers to other people's questions, not mine." Lew repeatedly sent them back to the drawing board to return with original thoughts! He does not like the experts and reports that simply point to past projects and ask, "Which one of these would you like?"

The Chicago Kickoff for Case4Space

We proposed a one-day meeting near O'Hare Airport. The threshold for the meeting was low: *Come and see if there is good reason to pursue this conversation further.* I expected that half of the companies who expressed interest in coming might continue. But many came for the six-hour dialogue and debate (see Figure 12.1).

Figure 12.1 Chicago Kickoff

I think most of us assumed we were doing good work and making a positive difference. That's the problem with any closed system. We were measuring ourselves against our industry's metrics. By that account we all looked pretty good. Sure, we each had frustrations and complaints. But there was nothing on the surface that implied a need to fundamentally challenge our profession. We certainly faced nothing that might call for a revolution, unless it was framed with a different question.

Some came to Chicago because they hoped to shift the conversation away from what we do to why it should matter. It wasn't really clear, however, what we were searching for or whether it mattered to anyone. Like the first MindShift, I was in search for that deeper irritant that might bind us together in a common cause.

Changing the Conversation

It's hard to nudge strong professionals into a different kind of conversation. So I used a few props to set the context. Well before the meeting, I sent them a copy of Gallup's most recent annual employee engagement survey, a DVD of the movie *Moneyball,* Jonah Lehrer's book *Imagine,* the book, *Harold and the Purple Crayon,* and a purple crayon.

Gallup's report created the deeper irritant I was looking for. "If our industry is so good, then how can we live with more than 70 percent of employees who would rather be anywhere but the workplace?" Prior to this report, most had never considered a link between the workplace and engagement. The conversation around Gallup's work galvanized the group in such a way that the statistic was labeled the "OMG Factor." Too big to believe and too unsettling to ignore. How could anyone know those numbers and just go back to business as usual?

As discussed in Chapter 3, *Moneyball* tells the story of the general manager of the Oakland A's, Billy Beane, and his unorthodox approach to dealing with an unfair system—rich teams in major media markets could and did far outspend teams like the Oakland

A's. Beane was forced to challenge the operating assumptions of every team if he stood any chance of competing. We used the OMG Factor and *Moneyball* as vehicles to force us to challenge our assumptions and to think about the possibilities that we might change the game.

Harold (in the *Purple Crayon* book) is a kid with a huge imagination. Whatever he draws with his crayon becomes reality. So what could our work look like if we started with a blank sheet of paper and a purple crayon?

My instructions were simple: "When you come next week I urge you to sit on your analytical urges, your expertise, and your checklists. Bring your curiosity, openness, and experience. The temptation is to think we're coming to solve a problem. My hope is that we'll come to have a deeper conversation about what we really care about and what we would love to see if we had a blank sheet of paper."

What Do You Care About?

At the end of the six-hour dialogue, we were convinced that an engaging workplace does make a difference. We were equally convinced that a detached leadership and an isolated and fragmented process for creating space results in workplace disengagement. To find and demonstrate a better way, we made the following declarations.

Purpose

We believe design matters. It has the transforming power to address many of the chronic challenges leaders currently face.

Values

We value challenging the status quo, embracing positive outliers, and coming together as a diverse coalition willing to tackle tough questions. Design at its best is social and engaging.

Mission

Our mission is to tackle the chronic challenge of high employee disengagement and the incredible waste of space. The two are linked.

When Transaction and Coordination Costs = $0

Case4Space and the book *Change Your Space, Change Your Culture* could not have happened five years ago. We had a single sponsor for the first MindShift, and we had 20 participants. By contrast, launching Case4Space turned out to be much easier in recruiting core members, securing funding, and tapping into a much larger and more complex network.

So what changed? Social media.

In the past, trade associations, universities, or consulting firms would have handled this. Each would look at the topic through a narrow range of constituent interests. Getting support or sponsorship for an idea through institutions is difficult. But even if you achieve that, you would have a band of volunteers with no power to command. Coordination, cooperation, and accountability within such a venture is like herding cats.

The Case4Space initiative broke these constraints by leveraging social media to connect and coordinate across many institutions and with freelance experts. This permitted us to operate with a core of 38 leaders from 24 companies and more than 85 contributors.

An effort like Case4Space is constrained by cost and management bandwidth. But collaborative technologies like social media tools dramatically change all of that.

Case4Space had a traditional team structure made up of about 38 leaders. We increased participation through virtual involvement. We received some of our best, though unplanned and unexpected, contributions from those outside our core of leaders.

Most of the peripheral members simply watched our online conversations and postings. For example, Chris Hood, a CBRE

managing director for workplace strategy, was a peripheral participant. As Chris watched our work take shape, he reached out and
suggested I tour their new Los Angeles office. Chris paved the way
for an extensive behind-the-scenes look at the entire process. And
theirs was one of the most exciting stories we had seen.

W. L. Gore's Jay Steimer was another peripheral contributor.
He offered a behind-the-scenes look at a thriving company with
a very clear philosophy of culture and space. Furthermore, their
50-plus years of experience validated their approach.

Jack Hess in Columbus, Indiana, provided an inside look at
the history, philosophy, and people (past and present) that built
Columbus, Indiana, and its relationship with Cummins Inc.

None of these serendipitous encounters would have been
possible without the tools that allowed them to watch and engage
in our work.

The MindShift Format

Case4space's work was carried out through summits, team research,
site visits, interviews, and expertise.

Summits represented our primary work. We added Michael
Lagocki as an event designer and graphic scribe. He added a high
level of engagement. We did not meet in retreat facilities, but
instead chose to meet in highly engaged companies with unique
work settings. Michael and I approached each summit as a three-act
play that unfolded over a day and a half. The first act began at noon,
diving deep into a problem or question.

It opened with a dramatic frame for the big idea, sometimes
using TED videos, movie clips, or stories. This was followed by an
exercise designed to push the boundaries of our assumptions,
expectations, and comfort zones.

For example, in our first summit we identified a deep communication gap between the advocates of design and financial decision
makers. Instead of discussing or debating the reasons, we created an
exercise, "Pitch to the C-Suite" (see Figure 12.2). We divided into

Figure 12.2 Pitch to the C-Suite

four teams with each preparing their best case to a CEO, CFO, COO, or CMO for making workplace design a priority to improve engagement.

The teams went to work, selected their presenter, and made their pitch to the group. No group gave a compelling case. But the exercise revealed and clarified the gap we all complained about in Chicago: "Clients just don't get it." Suddenly, we could see why. The problem is us.

Each summit launched with a similar "experience the challenge" exercise.

The evening was an intermission, designed for social interaction and an opportunity to get to know each other in a personal way. Many of our good ideas began in the social interaction. The next morning, Act Two, was designed to generate ideas and prototypes for answering the previous day's challenge. Each team was given tools for creating compelling stories.

Act Three, on the second afternoon, tried to integrate each team's efforts. We identified key themes, metaphors, and questions that guided future summits and became central ideas in this book.

Fresh Perspectives

Selecting the locations for each summit had equal significance in shaping the events. We looked for locations that would broaden our view of what an engaging work environment might look and feel like. We looked for companies that had a story to tell about their workplace journey and its impact on the company's culture and its bottom line. Finally, we sought locations that offered different ways to arrange our group interactions; we wanted to examine how space influences our conversations, collaboration, and presentations.

Some of our great and even inspiring locations included:

- The National Renewable Energy Laboratory in Golden, Colorado
- The Google campus, Mountain View, California
- The Haworth headquarters in Holland, Michigan
- The Haworth showroom, Chicago
- Cousins Properties in Atlanta
- Balfour Beatty's new Washington, DC division office

Small Teams to Divide, Conquer, and Run Fast

Any team tackling a complex issue runs into the challenge of going deep or wide on the topic. Engagement is a good example. Coming out of the Colorado summit, we seemed to settle on four aspects of engagement: individual engagement, team flow, organizational health, and what we called "Future Travelers." As noted in Chapter 10, Future Travelers represented companies that seemed to defy conventional wisdom on culture and its relationship to the workplace. At the same time, they outperformed their competition. These companies have provided many stories throughout this book.

Each team found they were able to go deep, run fast, and make progress on the issue. Then a curious thing happened when we came together to share the work. Each team's presentation seemed to create confusion. The debate shifted to one team's aspect falling into another team's domain. They questioned the assignment. Were they doing it right? Is this what I really wanted?

The truth is, I wasn't sure what I "wanted." That was the point of the process. The topic of engagement is highly complex and interconnected. When we saw how quickly we fell into our habits of divide, analyze, and solve, we started to make real progress. Instead of analyzing the four groups as separate, we began to map the conversations as connected.

The teams seemed to take four paths with engagement:

1. The individual engagement team latched onto the massive power shift away from organizational control and the need to accommodate individualized work demands. Their creative approach to making this point took the form of a *Workplace Manifesto,* a declaration of many of the new qualities of engaged work.
2. The group researching team flow decided its mission was to help leaders understand the value of engaged collective work and what that looks like. Their research found high-performing teams shifting more attention to getting the right team composition, providing a context (setting) that felt collaborative, and creating alignment.
3. The team working around organizational health looked at the role of design at three elevations of value. First, they considered design as a tool for creating a better space (utilization, workflow, etc.). Second, they weighed design as a tool for creating a better process (communication, coordination, and collaboration). Third, they reflected on design as a tool for improving relational connection, cohesion, and community.
4. The group searching for Future Travelers called their effort the anthropology of the workplace. They identified almost 20 companies taking very different paths toward engagement. Two interesting examples were at polar ends of the spectrum. IBM has developed an algorithmic approach to designing work to facilitate their virtual employee network. Each work element that IBM might perform traces back to its most basic

component, like a work gene. When someone submits a work request, IBM's "work configurator" assembles the genes for the project and then searches for the individuals who best match the profile. W. L. Gore, on the other hand, takes an approach that is highly tribal and organic. Business units are designed to be between 150 and 200 people. That allows each business unit the intimacy to design and assign their own work.

"Go and see" became such a vital part of our work. It was the bridge we used to travel from one mind-set into another. We instinctively knew that our challenge was changing our mind, not our knowledge. We had abundant knowledge and evidence but needed to experience engagement and cultures with a deep appreciation for the value of workplace.

Connecting the Dots

"Never doubt that a small group of thoughtful committed citizens can change the world. Indeed it is the only thing that ever has."
—*Margaret Mead*

The days are gone when smart people can come together for a day and expect to solve complex problems. It doesn't matter whether it's a production issue, a market strategy, a geopolitical crisis, safety, engagement, or launching a change initiative. MindShift created a safe haven to journey into what was unknown territory for each of us. It revealed how insulated we are from the people who live with our decisions—and how to reconnect with them. We saw how our knowledge and expertise get in our way when we try to solve novel problems. It also created a setting to play and experiment and achieve breakthroughs. For example, we were able to work next to Millennials for several months; that removed some of the mystery and helped us see their unique outlook in action (see Figure 12.3).

Figure 12.3 Millennials Join Case4Space

MindShift allowed each leader to explore deeper questions, sit with seasoned leaders who were asking similar questions, take part in activities that revealed blind spots, see examples of what's to come, and feel what it's like for complexity to unhinge our analytics. We preferred to learn through activities in small groups. We found that unique environments can change perspective.

Our journey allowed time for solutions to take shape. Guidance brought continuity. We each felt ownership over the direction of our processes. Clear patterns emerged out of the complexity, and that provided key principles and tools. More importantly, Mind-Shift provided confidence for a kind of leadership in an era of no easy answers.

It has been a high-tech form of barn raising—easy to start, adaptable in structure with minimal cost and risk, but with the potential of achieving significant breakthroughs in problem solving or innovation.

Case4Space Core Team

Markku Allison—Principal
Scan Consulting—(616) 460–2211
markkuallison@gmail.com
Workplace Consultant

Dick Bayer—Principal
ReAlignment Group—(858) 613–6305
dick@projectrealign.com
Lean Consulting

Paula Bedford—Marketing Manager
Haworth, Inc.—(616) 886–1045
Paula.Bedford@Haworth.com
Furniture Manufacturer

Phil Bernstein—Vice President Industry Strategy & Relations AEC
Solutions
Autodesk, Inc.—(781) 839–5380
phil.bernstein@autodesk.com
AEC Software

Kevin Burke—Principal
PARABOLA—(434) 981–4790
kevin@parabola-architecture.com
Architect

Carrie Meinberg Burke—Principal
PARABOLA—(434) 960–3135
carrie@parabola-architecture.com
Architect

Mabel Casey—Vice President of Global Marketing and Innovation
Haworth, Inc.—(616) 393–3343
mabel.casey@haworth.com
Furniture Manufacturer

John Coates—Director of Sales & Marketing
Build I—(206) 384–4456
john.coates@buildingi.com
Technical Services Consulting Company

Julia De Rosi—Space Planning/Project Management
GSA—(312) 886–3983
julia.derosi@gsa.gov
Federal Government

Patrick Donnelly—Principal
BHDP—(513) 271–1634
tdonnelly@bhdp.com
Architect and Workplace Strategy

Steven Elliott—Principal
Investor/Entrepreneur—(480) 388–1500
steven.f.elliott@gmail.com
Equity Capital and Real Estate Development

Lindsey Etterbeek—Marketing Specialist, Architect + Design Programs
Haworth, Inc.—(616) 393–3000
Lindsey.Etterbeek@Haworth.com
Furniture Manufacturer

Sabret Flocos—Principal
FOX Architects—(703) 821–7990
sflocos@fox-architects.com
Architect

Bob Fox—Principal
FOX Architects—(202) 659–0929
bfox@fox-architects.com
Architect

Janet Gonzalez—Consultant, ENV SP, LEED AP BD+C
HDR—(312) 470–9501
Janet.Gonzalez@hdrinc.com
Engineering and Architecture

Chuck Hardy—Chief Workplace Officer at GSA Public Buildings
Service
GSA—(312) 886–0205
charles.hardy@gsa.gov
Federal Government

Bill Hollett—Senior Vice President, Leasing
Cousins Properties—(404) 407–1664
BillHollett@cousinsproperties.com
Real Estate Developer

Daniel Homrich—Strategist for Good
WH[Y] MANTRA—(404) 454–6820
danielhomrich@gmail.com
Generation Y (Millennial) Branding Expert

Cathy Hutchison—Random Thought Connector
Idibri—(972) 239–1505
chutchison@acousticdimensions.com
Acoustic Engineering and Experience Design

Barbara Jackson—Director, Franklin L. Burns School of Real
Estate and Construction Management
University of Denver—(805) 610–6130
barbara.jackson@du.edu
Construction Management Education

Craig Janssen—Principal
Idibri—(972) 239–1505
cjanssen@acousticdimensions.com
Acoustic Engineering and Experience Design

Richard Kadzis—Principal
Kadzis Consulting—(678) 687–9724
rkadzis@comcast.net
Market Research, Editing, and Writing

Michelle Kleyla—Workplace Knowledge/Marketing Manager
Haworth, Inc.—(616) 393–3000
Michelle.Kleyla@Haworth.com
Furniture Manufacturer

Mark Konchar—Chief of Enterprise Development
Balfour Beatty Construction—(703) 297–9225
mkonchar@Balfourbeattyus.com
General Contractor

Michael Lagocki—Scribe/Live Artist
Art Love Magic—(214) 687–8561
mike@artlovemagic.com
Event Facilitation and Design

Ray Lucchesi—Principal
Renovus Collaborative—(702) 263–7111
RaymondLucchesi@gmail.com
Regenerative Architecture and Planning

John McColl—Executive Vice President
Cousins Properties—(404) 407–1000
johnmccoll@cousinsproperties.com
Real Estate Developer

Tom Miller—Principal
Darwin Branded Environments—(317) 714–4824
tom@darwinbe.com
Branded Workplaces

Katherine Molyson—Development Manager
Cousins Properties—(404) 407–1000
KatherineMolyson@cousinsproperties.com
Real Estate Developer

Mark Pleskow—Principal
Jacobs Engineering—(703) 599–6834
mark.pleskow@jacobs.com
Engineering and Program Management

Dave Radcliffe—Vice President, Real Estate
Google, Inc.—(650) 253–3218
dradcliffe@google.com
Internet and Technology Firm

Erin Hoffer Rae—Thought Leader
Autodesk, Inc.—(781) 839–5380
erinrae.hoffer@autodesk.com
AEC Software

Josh Schierbeek—Web Marketing
Haworth, Inc.—(616) 393–3000
Josh.Schierbeek@Haworth.com
Furniture Manufacturer

Haley Smith—Communications Project Lead
Balfour Beatty Construction—(615) 889–4400
hsmith@Balfourbeattyus.com
General Contractor

Celeste Tell—Workplace Strategy Manager
The Bill & Melinda Gates Foundation—(206) 406–0146
celeste.tell@gatesfoundation.org
Charitable Foundation

Katherine Tracey—Marketing Coordinator
Cassidy Turley—(443) 465–7004
katherinec.tracey@gmail.com
Commercial Real Estate and Property Management

Tim Wakley—Research and Development
Balfour Beatty Construction—(678) 921–6800
twakely@Balfourbeattyus.com
General Contractor

Arol Wolford—Principal
SmartBIM and VIMtrek—(770) 628–0272
arolw@bellsouth.net
AEC Software

APPENDIX B

Image Recap of Key Events and Summit Sketch Notes

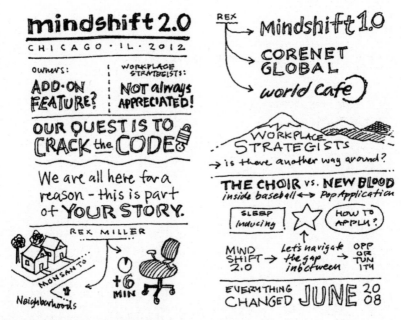

Figure B.1   Chicago Kickoff: Introduction

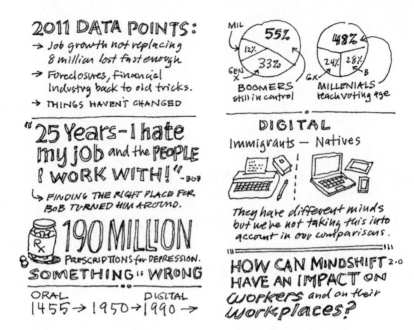

Figure B.2   Chicago Kickoff: The Scope of the Problem

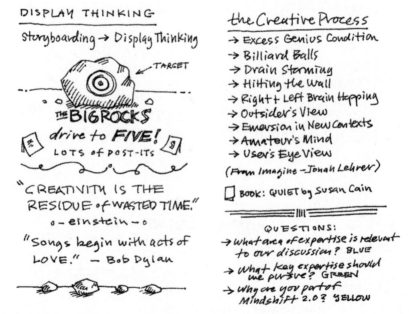

Figure B.3   Chicago Kickoff: The Mindshift Process

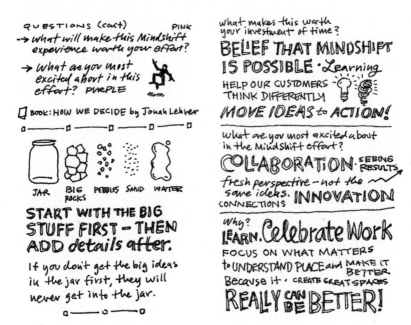

Figure B.4 Chicago Kickoff: Process and Goals

Figure B.5 Chicago Kickoff: Next Steps

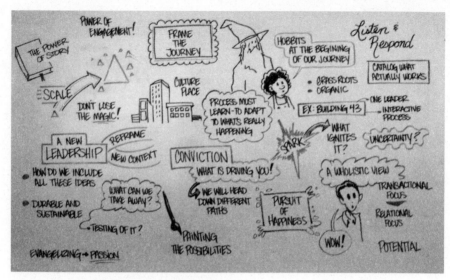

Figure B.6   Denver Summit: Recap

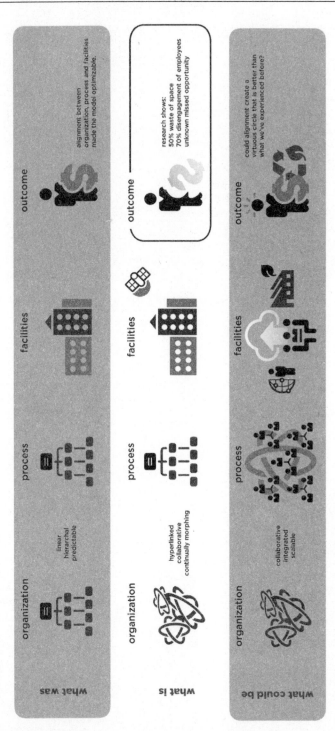

Figure B.7 The Case4Space Big Ideas

Figure B.8   Holland, MI Summit: Book Cover Exercise

Four teams were assigned to distill the research into a book cover

Figure B.9 Holland, MI Summit: Final Version of the Book Cover Exercise

Figure B.10 Chicago Summit: Final Recap of the Movie Trailer Exercise

Five teams were assigned to explain the research in a movie trailer

Figure B.11 Driggs, ID: Initial Story Board to Synthesize the Book Research

NOTES

Chapter 1 Are You Ready to Sail the North Atlantic?

1. Michael Schrage, *No More Teams!* (New York: Random House, 1990).
2. David Wolman, "Facebook, Twitter Help the Arab Spring Blossom," *Wired,* April 16, 2014, http://www.wired.com/2013/04/arabspring/.
3. "Arab Spring." Wikipedia. Wikimedia Foundation, n.d. Web. June 15, 2014. http://en.wikipedia.org/wiki/Arab_Spring.
4. Bob Johansen, *Leaders Make the Future: Ten New Leadership Skills for an Uncertain World* (San Francisco: Berrett-Koehler Publishers, 2009).
5. IBM Corporation, *Leading through Connections: Insights from the Global Chief Executive Officer Study,* 2012, accessed June 9, 2014, http://www-935.ibm.com/services/us/en/c-suite/ceostudy2012/.
6. Alex Sosnowski, "Icebergs Still Threaten Ships 100 Years after Titanic," *AccuWeather,* April 14, 2012, http://www.accuweather.com/en/weather-news/icebergs-still-a-threat-100-ye/63626.
7. Edgar H. Schein, *Organizational Culture and Leadership: A Dynamic View,* 2nd ed. (San Francisco, CA: Jossey-Bass, 1992).

Chapter 2 The $1 Trillion Black Hole

1. Achor, Shawn. *The Happiness Advantage: The Seven Principles of Positive Psychology that Fuel Success and Performance at Work* (New York: Broadway Books, 2010).
2. "State of the Global Workplace 2013." Gallup. N.p., n.d. Web. June 16, 2014. http://www.gallup.com/strategicconsulting/164735/state-global-workplace.aspx. Kirka, Danica. "Employers step in to prevent worker burnout." *Yahoo! Finance.* December 2013. Web. February 11, 2014.

http://finance.yahoo.com/news/employers-step-prevent-worker-burn-out-074239271—finance.html.

3. Winston Churchill, speech in the House of Commons, October 28, 1943.

4. Edward T. Hall, *The Hidden Dimension* (New York: Anchor Books, 1990).

5. American Psychological Association, "Psychologically Healthy Workplace Program: Fact Sheet by the Numbers," 2010, https://www.apa.org/practice/programs/workplace/phwp-fact-sheet.pdf.

6. Partnership to Fight Chronic Disease, "Milken Institute Study: Chronic Disease Costs U.S. Economy More Than $1 Trillion Annually," October 2, 2007, http://www.fightchronicdisease.org/media-center/releases/milken-institute-study-chronic-disease-costs-us-economy-more-1-trillion-annual.

7. Air Quality Sciences, Inc., "Indoor Air Quality and Sick Building Syndrome: Basic Facts," 2001, http://www.greenguard.org/Libraries/GG_Documents/Reformat_IAQ_and_Sock_Building_Syndrome_Basic_Facts_1.sflb.ashx.

8. Andrew Newberg and Mark Walden, "The Most Dangerous Word in the World," *Words Can Change Your Brain* (blog), *Psychology Today*, July 31, 2012, http://www.psychologytoday.com/blog/words-can-change-your-brain/201207/the-most-dangerous-word-in-the-world.

9. "List of countries by GDP (nominal)." Wikipedia. Wikimedia Foundation, n.d. Web. June 15, 2014, http://en.wikipedia.org/wiki/List_of_countries_by_GDP_(nominal).

10. That drain equals about $19,500 per toxic employee.

11. $550 billion is approximate 3 percent of United States $17 trillion GDP.

12. Dennis Jacobe. "Warning: Corporate Scandals May Demoralize Employees." N.p., October 10, 2002. Web. June 23, 2014, http://businessjournal.gallup.com/content/826/warning-corporate-scandals-may-demoralize-employees.aspx.

13. Jeff Maher, "Forbes: 64% of Employees Wasting Time at Work," *News10.net*, September 13, 2013, http://on.news10.net/1eP4XFG.

14. Brian Brim, and Jim Asplund. "Driving Engagement by Focusing on Strengths." *Gallup Business Journal*. N.p., November 12, 2009. Web. June 17, 2014, http://businessjournal.gallup.com/content/124214/driving-engagement-focusing-strengths.aspx.

15. Laurence Weber "Bad at Their Jobs, and Loving It—At Work—WSJ." At Work RSS. N.p., March 27, 2013. Web. June 17, 2014, http://blogs.wsj.com/atwork/2013/03/27/bad-at-their-jobs-and-loving-it/?mod=WSJ_Management_ At_Work.

16. Jason Fried, "Why Work Doesn't Happen at Work," TEDxMidWest video, 15:21, October 2010, http://www.ted.com/talks/jason_fried_why_work_doesn_t_happen_at_work.

17. Marcello Ballve, "How Much Time Do We Really Spend On Our Smartphones Every Day?" *Business Insider*, June 6, 2013. Web. June 17, 2014. http://www.businessinsider.com.au/how-much-time-do-we-spend-on-smartphones-2013–6.

18. Cheryl Conner, "Who Wastes the Most Time at Work?" *Yahoo! Finance*, September 7, 2013, http://finance.yahoo.com/news/wastes-most-time-120700150.html.

19. Maia Szalavitz, "What Does a 400% Increase in Antidepressant Use Really Mean?," *Time*, October 20, 2011, http://healthland.time.com/2011/10/20/what-does-a-400-increase-in-antidepressant-prescribing-really-mean/.

20. Arianna Huffington, "Burnout: The Disease of Our Civilization." *The Huffington Post*. TheHuffingtonPost.com, August 21, 2013. Web. June 17, 2014. http://www.huffingtonpost.com/arianna-huffington/burnout-third-metric_b_3792354.html.

21. "Obesity in the United States," *Wikipedia*, last modified May 28, 2014, http://en.wikipedia.org/wiki/Obesity_in_the_United_States.

22. Lisa DeBruine, "The Truth about 'The Truth about Sitting Down,'" *Research Headlines* (blog), November 13, 2013, http://researchtheheadlines.org/2013/11/13/standing-desks/.

23. U.S. Centers for Disease Control and Prevention, "Vital Signs: Prevalence, Treatment, and Control of Hypertension—United States, 1999–2002 and 2005–2008," *Morbidity and Mortality Weekly Report* 60, no. 4 (February 4, 2011): 103–108, http://www.cdc.gov/mmwr/preview/mmwrhtml/mm6004a4.htm.

24. National Diabetes Information Clearinghouse, "National Diabetes Statistics, 2011: Fast Facts on Diabetes," February 2011, last modified September 9, 2013, http://diabetes.niddk.nih.gov/dm/pubs/statistics/#fast.

25. Tim Springer, President of Hero, Inc. introduced this insight that decisions around space are conditioned by whether we see it as an asset or a liability to limit.

Chapter 3 Something Wicked This Way Comes

1. "Fortune 500 Extinction," *CSInvesting* (blog), January 6, 2012, http://csinvesting.org/2012/01/06/fortune-500-extinction/.

2. Stoddard, Nat. "ChiefExecutive.net." ChiefExecutivenet *Chief Executive Magazine*. The Costs of CEO Failure Comments. N.p., December 1, 2008. Web. June 17, 2014. http://chiefexecutive.net/the-costs-of-ceo-failure.

3. "Employee Tenure Summary." U.S. Bureau of Labor Statistics, September 18, 2012. Web. June 17, 2014, http://www.bls.gov/news.release/tenure .nr0.htm.

4. Bruce Sterling, "Superlinear Cities," *Wired*, July 27, 2011, http://www .wired.com/beyond_the_beyond/2011/07/superlinear-cities/.

5. Allan Engelhardt, "The 3/2 Rule of Employee Productivity," CYBAEA, October 16, 2006, http://www.cybaea.net/Blogs/employee_ productivity.html.

6. Michael Hammer and James Champy, *Reengineering the Corporation: A Manifesto for Business Revolution* (New York: HarperBusiness, 1993).

7. Richard Kadzis, *2013 Workplace Trends Survey* (Richard Kadzis Consulting, 2013).

8. Smaller and shorter leases will significantly reduce fees in the current model. These smaller and smarter new spaces are more complex and will require new services and expertise. High vacancy rates will continue to push lease rates down. Most buildings will require considerable investment to upgrade and adapt to include a wider variety of mixed use. Smaller leases for shorter durations will collide with added costs for more sophisticated services for brokers, and greater capital outlay for renovation for building owners and developers.

9. Jeff Wacker, "Sizing Up the Next Big Thing in Information Technology" (2006 World Future Society presentation).

10. "Cubicle," *Wikipedia*, last modified May 27, 2014, http://en.wikipedia .org/wiki/Cubicle.

11. "The waterfall model is a sequential design process, often used in software development processes, in which progress is seen as flowing steadily downwards (like a waterfall) through the phases of Conception, Initiation, Analysis, Design, Construction, Testing, Production/Implementation, and Maintenance"; "Waterfall Model," *Wikipedia,* last modified May 19, 2014, http://en.wikipedia.org/wiki/Waterfall_model. "Waterfall" and "critical path" have come to define isolated efforts.

12. Clay Shirky, "Healthcare.gov and the Gulf between Planning and Reality," *Clay Shirky* (blog), November 19, 2013, http://www.shirky.com/weblog/ 2013/11/healthcare-gov-and-the-gulf-between-planning-and-reality/.

13. Rex Miller et al., *The Commercial Real Estate Revolution: Nine Transforming Keys to Lowering Costs, Cutting Waste, and Driving Change in a Broken Industry* (Hoboken, NJ: Wiley, 2009).

14. Martin Fischer is the director of Stanford's Center for Integrated Facility Engineering, and Chris Raftery was at the time a Project Executive for Magnusson Klemencic in Seattle.

Chapter 4 What Every Leader Needs to Know about the Future

1. Balfour Beatty used Gallup's StrengthsFinder assessment to identify natural talents in a team, and added the CoreClarity system to the results for a deeper understanding of team dynamic.
2. Rick Levine et al., "95 Theses," *The Cluetrain Manifesto,* 1999, 2001, http://www.cluetrain.com/book/95-theses.html.
3. This information is from April 2014.
4. "Moore's Law is the observation that, over the history of computing hardware, the number of transistors in a dense integrated circuits doubles approximately every two years." "Moore's Law," *Wikipedia,* last modified June 4, 2014, http://en.wikipedia.org/wiki/Moore%27s_Law.
5. Jane McGonigal, *Reality Is Broken: Why Games Make Us Better and How They Can Change the World* (New York: Penguin, 2011).
6. Gabe Zichermann, "Keynote Gabe Zichermann at TNW2012 | The Next Web," *The Next Web,* YouTube video, 35:43, April 27, 2012, http://youtu.be/UdUclLUDxRg.
7. Zicherman, Gabe. "The Six Rules of Gamification—Gamification Co." *Gamification Co.* June 19, 2014, http://www.gamification.co/2011/11/29/the-six-rules-of-gamification.
8. Michael Schley, ed., "Speaker Dr. Susan Stucky, IBM," *Workplace Strategy Summit 2012: Research in Action* (Houston: International Facility Management Association, 2013), www.ifmacfc.org/WorkplaceStrategySummit-2012.pdf, 42.
9. Jason Dorrier, "Is Cisco's Forecast of 50 Billion Internet-Connected Things by 2020 Too Conservative?," *SingularityHub,* July 13, 2013, http://singularityhub.com/2013/07/30/is-ciscos-forecast-of-50-billion-internet-connected-things-by-2020-too-conservative/.

Chapter 5 What Every Executive Needs to Know about Millennials

1. Mutual Responsibility, "The Tragedy of Our Times Defined by Anthropologist Michael Wesch [Pop Tech Video]," YouTube video, 6:00, September 11, 2012, http://www.mutualresponsibility.org/culture/the-tragedy-of-our-times-defined-by-anthropologist-michael-wesch-poptech-video.

2. Bob Johansen, *Leaders Make the Future: Ten New Leadership Skills for an Uncertain World* (San Francisco: Berrett-Koehler Publishers, 2009), 10.

3. Miller, M. Rex. *The Millennium Matrix: Reclaiming the Past, Reframing the Future of the Church* (San Francisco: Jossey-Bass, 2004).

4. Bob Johansen, *Leaders Make the Future: Ten New Leadership Skills for an Uncertain World* (San Francisco: Berrett-Koehler Publishers, 2009), 10.

5. Erica Orange and Jared Wiener, principals at Weiner, Edrich, Brown, Inc., presented research to the World Future Symposium in 2013 into the compressed time frame for defining cohort traits.

6. "The Internet of Things . . . is the network of physical objects accessed through the Internet, as defined by technology analysts and visionaries. These objects contain embedded technology to interact with internal states or the external environment. In other words, when objects can sense and communicate, it changes how and where decisions are made, and who makes them." Cisco Systems, "Internet of Things," accessed June 4, 2014, http://www.cisco.com/web/solutions/trends/iot/overview.html.

7. Dave Davies and Julia Angwin, "If You Think You're Anonymous Online, Think Again." *NPR All Tech Considered*, February 24, 2014, transcript, http://www.npr.org/templates/transcript/transcript.php?storyId=282061990.

8. Edutopia, "Project-Based Learning," accessed June 4, 2014, http://www.edutopia.org/project-based-learning.

9. Karen Quackenbush, "Columbus Signature Academy Funds a Well," The Water Project, accessed June 10, 2014, http://thewaterproject.org/community/2010/06/17/columbus-signature-academy-funds-a-well/.

10. Charles A. O'Reilly III and Michael L. Tushman, "The Ambidextrous Organization," *Harvard Business Review,* April 2004, http://hbr.org/2004/04/the-ambidextrous-organization/ar/1.

11. FamilyByDesign homepage, accessed June 4, 2014, http://www.family-bydesign.com.

12. Scott Keeter and Paul Taylor. "The Millennials." Pew Research Center, December 10, 2009, http://www.pewresearch.org/2009/12/10/the-millennials/.

13. David C. Pollock and Ruth E. Van Reken, *Third Culture Kids: Growing Up among Worlds*, rev. ed. (Boston: Nicholas Brealey, 2009).

14. Lisa Leff, "Fortune 500 Firms Expand Gay Rights Support after DOMA Decision," *Huffington Post,* December 8, 2013, http://www.huffingtonpost.com/2013/12/08/fortune-500-gay-rights_n_4409466.html.

15. U.S. Centers for Disease Control and Prevention, "New Data on Autism Spectrum Disorders," March 29, 2012, http://www.cdc.gov/Features/CountingAutism/.
16. National Institute of Mental Health, "Attention-Deficit/Hyperactivity Disorder among Adults," accessed June 4, 2014, http://www.nimh.nih.gov/statistics/1ADHD_ADULT.shtml.
17. Susan Cain, "Shyness: Evolutionary Tactic?," *New York Times*, June 25, 2011, http://www.nytimes.com/2011/06/26/opinion/sunday/26shyness.html?_r=2&pagewanted=all.
18. Clay Shirky, *Here Comes Everybody: The Power of Organizing* (New York: Penguin, 2009), 105.

Chapter 6 Changing Design from Push to Pull

1. John Hagel III, John Seely Brown, and Lang Davison. *The Power of Pull: How Small Moves, Smartly Made, Can Set Big Things in Motion* (New York: Basic Books, 2010), 2.
2. "Taking the Long View," *Schumpeter* (blog), *The Economist,* November 24, 2012, http://www.economist.com/news/business/21567062-pursuit-shareholder-value-attracting-criticismnot-all-it-foolish-taking-long.
3. There are numerous examples of open information flow networks. Procter & Gamble's Connect + Develop, SAP's NetWeaver community, and Amazon's rating and review platform, along with several software development platforms, are just a few to mention.

Chapter 7 Using Space to Shape Culture

1. Edward T. Hall, *The Hidden Dimension* (New York: Anchor Books, 1990).
2. Monte Burke, "Michael Bloomberg: The Exit Interview," *Forbes*, November 18, 2013, http://www.forbes.com/sites/monteburke/2013/10/30/michael-bloomberg-the-exit-interview/.
3. Martha Johnson, U.S. General Services Administration, remarks at the National Association of Energy Service Companies Federal Market Workshop, Washington, D.C., March 22, 2012.
4. Lawrence W. Cheek, "In New Office Designs, Room to Roam and to Think," *New York Times,* March 17, 2012, http://www.nytimes.com/2012/03/18/business/new-office-designs-offer-room-to-roam-and-to-think.html?pagewanted=all.

5. Warren Berger, "Lost in Space," *Wired* 7, no. 2 (February 1999), http://www.wired.com/wired/archive/7.02/chiat_pr.html.
6. Eric Ransdell, "Work Different," *Fast Company,* May 31, 1999, http://www.fastcompany.com/37259/work-different.

Chapter 8 Social and Engaging Design

1. "Design Thinking," Wikipedia, last modified May 28, 2014, http://en.wikipedia.org/wiki/Design_thinking.
2. Roger Martin, "Rotman Design Challenge 2013—Keynote by Roger Martin," YouTube video, 11:42, April 5, 2013, https://www.youtube.com/watch?v=fNgBRcp0u7w.
3. Assessments have become either tools for external marketing (the best place to work), for internal marketing (see what a wonderful place we're providing), or for aiming at red flags and then attacking those hot-button areas with a round of training and holding the managers liable for poor results. In either case employees understand the game and learn how to game the system and discount the propaganda.
4. William Peña and Steven Parshall, *Problem Seeking: An Architectural Programming Primer,* 4th ed. (New York: Wiley, 2001).
5. Inflection Point, Inc., "You Might Be an Engineer If . . . (Part One)," accessed June 5, 2014, http://www.inflection-point.com/jokes/105.htm.
6. Ray Luchessi, Principal at Regenesis, and Case4Space member.
7. C. J. Hughes, "Newsmaker: David Dillard of Project Sleepover," *Architectural Record,* September 2009, http://archrecord.construction.com/news/newsmakers/0909daviddillard.asp.
8. Ibid.
9. Jon Hamilton, "Scientists Say Neuron Provides Ability to Mimic." *NPR.* July 5, 2005, www.npr.org/templates/story/story.php?storyId=4729505.

Chapter 9 The Untapped Potential of the Workplace

1. BOSTI Associates (the Buffalo Organization for Social and Technological Innovation), founded by Mike Brill, is a Buffalo, NY, based group with a 30+ year history of continuous innovation in workplace planning and design, based on active research in each project, and informed by extensive experience with comparable situations.

2. Michael Brill, and Sue Weidemann. *Disproving Widespread Myths About Workplace Design* (Jasper, IN: Kimball International, 2001).
3. Rex Miller et al., *The Commercial Real Estate Revolution: Nine Transforming Keys to Lowering Costs, Cutting Waste, and Driving Change in a Broken Industry* (Hoboken, NJ: Wiley, 2009).

Chapter 10 They Did It, You Can Too

1. Chip Heath and Dan Heath, *Switch: How to Change Things When Change Is Hard* (New York: Broadway Books, 2010).
2. John Blackstone, "Inside Google Workplaces, from Perks to Nap Pods," *CBS This Morning,* January 22, 2013, http://www.cbsnews.com/news/inside-google-workplaces-from-perks-to-nap-pods/.
3. Malcolm Gladwell, *The Tipping Point* (New York: Little, Brown and Company, 2002).
4. Founders of the Lean Construction Institute.
5. Michael Casten, "The Pursuit of Operational Perfection—Part 1." Construction Executive. N.p., April 30, 2014. Web. June 20, 2014. http://www.constructionexec.com/Articles/tabid/3837/entryid/2355/the-pursuit-of-operational-perfection-part-1.aspx.
6. "As the pioneer of Wellness Real Estate™ and founder of the WELL Building Standard®, Delos is transforming our homes, offices, schools, and other indoor environments by placing health and wellness at the center of design and construction decisions." Delos homepage, accessed June 8, 2014, delosliving.com.
7. Technology is one area of increased investment. The GSK project in Philadelphia, for example, has a similar free-address design and invested $40 per square foot in technology.
8. A broker who secures a 100,000-square-foot contract at $30 a square foot for 10 years will earn a commission of approximately 4 percent of the total value of that transaction, or $1.2 million.
9. Julie Bort, "Management Tips from Red Hat's Crazy Culture Every Company Should Steal," *Business Insider,* February 22, 2012, http://www.businessinsider.com/management-tips-from-red-hats-crazy-culture-every-company-should-steal-2012-2?op=1.
10. Ibid.
11. Frances Frei and Anne Morriss, *Uncommon Service: How to Win by Putting Customers at the Core of Your Business* (Boston: Harvard Business Review Press, 2012).

12. Malcolm Gladwell, *Outliers: The Story of Success* (New York: Little, Brown, 2008).

Chapter 11 Break Out of Insanity

1. Stephen Ambrose, *Undaunted Courage* (New York: Touchstone, 1996), 19.
2. Chip Heath and Dan Heath, *Switch: How to Change Things When Change Is Hard* (New York: Broadway Books, 2010).
3. Ibid.
4. "Sound Business Lessons from Harley's Top Marketer," *The Cayman Islands Journal,* January 6, 2010, http://www.compasscayman.com/journal/2010/01/06/Sound-business-lessons-from-Harley's-top-marketer.

BIBLIOGRAPHY

"Abductive Reasoning." *Wikipedia*. Last modified June 6, 2014. http://en .wikipedia.org/wiki/Abductive_reasoning.

"Adaptable." *The Free Dictionary*. Accessed June 9, 2014. http://www .thefreedictionary.com/adaptable.

Air Quality Sciences, Inc. "Indoor Air Quality and Sick Building Syndrome: Basic Facts." 2001. http://www.greenguard.org/Libraries/GG_Documents/ Reformat_IAQ_and_Sock_Building_Syndrome_Basic_Facts_1.sflb.ashx.

Alberts, David S., and Richard E. Hayes. *Power to the Edge: Command and Control in the Information Age*. Washington, DC: CCRP Publication Series, 2003.

American Psychological Association. "Psychologically Healthy Workplace Program: Fact Sheet by the Numbers." 2010. https://www.apa.org/practice/ programs/workplace/phwp-fact-sheet.

"Anthony Stafford Beer." *Wikipedia*. Last modified January 1, 2014. http://en .wikipedia.org/wiki/Anthony_Stafford_Beer.

"Arab Spring." *Wikipedia*. Wikimedia Foundation, n.d. Web. Last modified June, 15 2014. http://en.wikipedia.org/wiki/Arab_Spring.

"Arbitrage." *Investopedia*. Accessed June 9, 2014. http://www.investopedia .com/terms/a/arbitrage.asp.

"Attention-Deficit/Hyperactivity Disorder among Adults." Accessed June 4, 2014. http://www.nimh.nih.gov/statistics/1ADHD_ADULT.shtml.

Ballve, Marcello. "How Much Time Do We Really Spend On Our Smartphones Every Day?" *Business Insider*. N.p., June 6, 2013. http://www .businessinsider.com.au/how-much-time-do-we-spend-on-smartphones-2013-6.

Baxter, Annie. "Why Companies Are Getting Rid of Cubicle Walls." *Marketplace,* May 21, 2013. http://www.marketplace.org/topics/business/why-companies-are-getting-rid-cubicle-walls.

Beer, Michael, and Nitin Nohria. "Cracking the Code of Change." *Harvard Business Review,* May 2000. http://hbr.org/2000/05/cracking-the-code-of-change/ar/1.

Berger, Warren. "Lost in Space." *Wired* 7, no. 2 (February 1999). http://www.wired.com/wired/archive/7.02/chiat_pr.html.

Berlow, Eric. "Eric Berlow: Simplifying Complexity." YouTube video, 5:42. November 12, 2010. http://www.youtube.com/watch?v=UB2iYzKeej8.

Blackstone, John. "Inside Google Workplaces, from Perks to Nap Pods." *CBS This Morning,* January 22, 2013. http://www.cbsnews.com/news/inside-google-workplaces-from-perks-to-nap-pods/.

Block, Lazlo. "Passion, Not Perks." *Think Quarterly—The People Issue,* September 2011. http://www.google.com/think/articles/passion-not-perks.html.

Bloom, Allan David. *The Closing of the American Mind.* New York: Simon & Schuster, 1987.

Bort, Julie. "Management Tips from Red Hat's Crazy Culture Every Company Should Steal." *Business Insider,* February 22, 2012. http://www.businessinsider.com/management-tips-from-red-hats-.crazy-culture-every-company-should-steal-2012–2?op=1.

Brill, Michael, and Sue Weidemann. *Disproving widespread myths about workplace design.* Jasper, IN: Kimball International, 2001.

Brim, Brian, and Jim Asplund. "Driving Engagement by Focusing on Strengths." *Gallup Business Journal.* N.p., November 12, 2009. http://businessjournal.gallup.com/content/124214/driving-engagement-focusing-strengths.aspx.

Brown, John Seely. "You Play World of Warcraft? You're Hired!" *Wired* 14, no. 4 (April 2006). http://www.wired.com/wired/archive/14.04/learn.html.

Buchanan, Richard. "Wicked Problems in Design Thinking." *The MIT Press* 8, no. 2 (1992): 5–21.

Cain, Susan. "Shyness: Evolutionary Tactic?" *New York Times,* June 25, 2011. http://www.nytimes.com/2011/06/26/opinion/sunday/26shyness.html?_r=2&pagewanted=all.

Casten, Michael. "The Pursuit of Operational Perfection—Part 1." *Construction Executive.* N.p., April 30, 2014. http://www.constructionexec.com/Articles/tabid/3837/entryid/2355/the-pursuit-of-operational-perfection-part-1.aspx.

"Celera: A Unique Approach to Genome Sequencing." *Celera's Approach.* N.p., n.d. Web. March 8, 2014. http://www.ocf.berkeley.edu/~edy/genome/celera.html.

CNET, "Marissa Mayer on Women in Tech—CNET News—YouTube." YouTube video, 6:12. Posted July 16, 2012. http://youtube/prXCrcV-T3M.

"Co-Parenting, Parenting Partnerships Community—FamilyByDesign." N.p., n.d. Web. March 5, 2014. http://www.familybydesign.com.

Conner, Cheryl. "Who Wastes the Most Time at Work?" *Yahoo! Finance,* September 7, 2013. http://finance.yahoo.com/news/wastes-most-time-120700150.html.

Coscarelli, Joe. "All the Mistakenly Identified 'Suspects' in the Boston Bombing Investigation." *Daily Intelligencer* (blog). *New York Magazine,* April 19, 2013. http://nymag.com/daily/intelligencer/2013/04/wrongly-accused-boston-bombing-suspects-sunil-tripathi.html.

"Creative Professional." *Wikipedia.* Last modified January 3, 2014. http://en.wikipedia.org/wiki/Creative_professional.

"Cubicle." *Wikipedia.* Last modified May 27, 2014. http://en.wikipedia.org/wiki/Cubicle.

"Cult." *Merriam-Webster OnLine.* Accessed June 9, 2014. http://www.merriam-webster.com/dictionary/cult.

Davies, Dave, and Julia Angwin. "If You Think You're Anonymous Online, Think Again." *NPR All Tech Considered,* February 24, 2014. Web. March 3, 2014. http://www.npr.org/templates/transcript/transcript.php?storyId=282061990.

Davy, Kyle V., and Susan L. Harris. *Value Redesigned: New Models for Professional Practice.* Atlanta: Greenway Communications, 2005.

de Geus, Arie. *The Living Company.* Boston: Harvard Business Review Press, 1997.

Deutschman, Alan. *Change or Die: The Three Keys to Change at Work and in Life.* New York: Regan, 2007.

Dewey, John. *The Quest for Certainty: A Study of the Relation of Knowledge and Action.* New York: Minton, Balch, 1929.

Dipillis, Lydia. "Amazon Wants to Send Stuff before You Order It. Are Other Retailers Doomed?" *Wonkblog* (blog). *Washington Post,* January 30, 2014. http://www.washingtonpost.com/blogs/wonkblog/wp/2014/01/30/amazon-wants-to-send-stuff-before-you-order-it-are-other-retailers-doomed/.

Dizikes, Peter. "The Office Next Door." *MIT Technology Review,* October 25, 2011. http://www.technologyreview.com/article/425881/the-office-next-door/.

Dorrier, Jason. "Is Cisco's Forecast of 50 Billion Internet-Connected Things by 2020 Too Conservative?" *Singularity Hub,* July 13, 2013. http://singularityhub

.com/2013/07/30/is-ciscos-forecast-of-50-billion-internet-connected-things-by-2020-too-conservative/.

Ellul, Jacques. *The Technological Society*. New York: Knopf, 1964.

Ellul, Jacques. *The Technological System*. New York: Continuum, 1980.

"Emotional Intelligence." *Wikipedia*. Last modified June 4, 2014. http://en.wikipedia.org/wiki/Emotional_intelligence.

"Employee Tenure Summary." *U.S. Bureau of Labor Statistics*. U.S. Bureau of Labor Statistics, September 18, 2012, http://www.bls.gov/news.release/tenure.nr0.htm.

Engelhardt, Allen. "The 3/2 Rule of Employee Productivity." CYBAEA, October 16. 2006. http://www.cybaea.net/Blogs/employee_productivity.html.

Ennefils, Diane. "Number of Personal Computers in the US." In *The Physics Factbook,* edited by Glenn Elert. 2004. http://hypertextbook.com/facts/2004/DianeEnnefils.shtml.

"Epiphany." *Dictionary.com*. Accessed June 9, 2014. http://dictionary.reference.com/browse/epiphany.

"Estuary." *Wikipedia*. May 27, 2014. http://en.wikipedia.org/wiki/Estuary.

FamilyByDesign homepage, accessed June 4, 2014. http://www.familybydesign.com.

Farrell, Peter. "The Real 800-Pound Gorilla of Presenteeism." *HBR Blog Network* (blog), *Harvard Business Review,* May 22, 2013. http://blogs.hbr.org/2013/05/the-worst-kind-of-presenteeism/.

Ford, Kevin, and Ken Tucker. *The Leadership Triangle: The Three Options That Will Make You a Stronger Leader*. New York: Morgan James, 2013.

Foreman, Judy. *A Nation in Pain: Healing Our Biggest Health Problem*. New York: Oxford University Press, 2014.

"Fortune 500 Extinction." *CSInvesting* (blog), January 6, 2012. http://csinvesting.org/2012/01/06/fortune-500-extinction/.

"Free Agent (Business)." *Wikipedia*. Last modified October 16, 2013. http://en.wikipedia.org/wiki/Free_agent_(business).

Freeman, R. Edward. *Strategic Management: A Stakeholder Approach*. Boston: Pitman, 1984.

Frei, Frances, and Anne Morriss. *Uncommon Service: How to Win by Putting Customers at the Core of Your Business*. Boston: Harvard Business Review Press, 2012.

"*Future Shock*." *Wikipedia*. Last modified May 19, 2014. http://en.wikipedia.org/wiki/Future_Shock.

Gates, Bill, and Collins Hemingway. *Business @ the Speed of Thought: Using a Digital Nervous System.* New York: Warner Books, 1999.

Goldstein, Jacob, and Lam Thuy Vo. "22 Million Americans Are Unemployed or Underemployed." *NPR Planet Money,* April 4, 2013. http://www.npr.org/blogs/money/2013/04/04/175697813/23-million-americans-are-unemployed-or-underemployed.

Goleman, Daniel. *Emotional Intelligence.* New York: Bantam Books, 1995.

"Google Reveals Plans for Vast New California Campus: Comments." *Dezeen,* February 26, 2013. http://www.dezeen.com/2013/02/26/google-reveals-plans-for-bay-view-california-campus/.

Gray, Dave, and Thomas Vander Wal. *The Connected Company.* Sebastopol, CA: O'Reilly Media, 2012.

Green, Jeff. "Bluescape, the Touchscreen That Covers a Wall." *BloombergBusinessweek,* May 9, 2013. http://www.businessweek.com/articles/2013–05–09/bluescape-the-touchscreen-that-covers-a-wall.

Hagel, John, III, and Arthur Armstrong. *Net Gain: Expanding Markets through Virtual Communities.* Boston: Harvard Business Review Press, 1997.

Hagel, John, III, John Seely Brown, and Lang Davison. *The Power of Pull: How Small Moves, Smartly Made, Can Set Big Things in Motion.* New York: Basic Books, 2010.

Hall, Edward T. *The Hidden Dimension.* New York: Anchor Books, 1990.

Hamilton, Jon. "Scientists Say Neuron Provides Ability to Mimic." *NPR,* July 5, 2005. http://www.npr.org/templates/story/story.php?storyId=4729505.

Hammer, Michael, and James Champy. *Reengineering the Corporation: A Manifesto for Business Revolution.* New York: HarperBusiness, 1993.

Heath, Chip, and Dan Heath. *Switch: How to Change Things When Change Is Hard.* New York: Broadway Books, 2010.

Hebberd, Laurence. "Why Employee Referrals Are the Best Source of Hire [Infographic]." *Undercover Recruiter,* accessed June 9, 2014. http://theundercoverrecruiter.com/infographic-employee-referrals-hire/.

Hu, Elise. "Inside The 'Bossless' Office, Where the Team Takes Charge." *NPR,* August 26, 2013. http://www.npr.org/blogs/alltechconsidered/2013/08/27/207039346/What-Works-And-Doesnt-About-Bossless-Offices.

Hughes, C. J. "Newsmaker: David Dillard of Project Sleepover." *Architecture Record,* September 2009. http://archrecord.construction.com/news/newsmakers/0909daviddillard.asp.

Huston, Larry, and Nabil Sakkab. "Connect and Develop: Inside Procter & Gamble's New Model for Innovation." *Harvard Business Review,* March 2006.

http://hbr.org/2006/03/connect-and-develop-inside-procter-gambles-new-model-for-innovation/ar/1.

IBM Corporation. *Leading through Connections: Insights from the Global Chief Executive Officer Study.* 2012, accessed June 9, 2014. http://www-935.ibm.com/services/us/en/c-suite/ceostudy2012/.

Inflection Point, Inc. "You Might Be an Engineer If . . . (Part One)." Accessed June 5, 2014. http://www.inflection-point.com/jokes.php.

Jernigan, Finith E. *BIG BIM little bim: The Practical Approach to Building Information Modeling—Integrated Practice Done the Right Way!* 2nd ed. Salisbury, MD: 4Site Press, 2007.

Johansen, Bob. *Leaders Make the Future: Ten New Leadership Skills for an Uncertain World.* San Francisco: Berrett-Koehler Publishers, 2009.

Kaplan, Fred. *The Insurgents: David Petraeus and the Plot to Change the American Way of War.* New York: Simon & Schuster, 2013.

Keene, Douglas, L., and Rita R. Handrich. "Generation X Members Are 'Active, Balanced and Happy.'" *The Jury Expert,* November 29, 2011. http://www.thejuryexpert.com/2011/11/gen-x-members-are-active-balanced-and-happy/.

Keeter, Scott, and Paul Taylor. "The Millennials." *Pew Research Center,* December 10, 2009. http://www.pewresearch.org/2009/12/10/the-millennials/.

Kirka, Danica. "Employers Step In to Prevent Worker Burnout." *Yahoo! Finance,* December 3, 2013. http://finance.yahoo.com/news/employers-step-prevent-worker-burnout-074239271—finance.html.

"Knowledge Worker." *Wikipedia.* Last modified June 4, 2014. http://en.wikipedia.org/wiki/Knowledge_worker.

Korn, Melissa, and Rachel Emma Silverman. "Forget D-School, B-School Is Hot." *Wall Street Journal,* June 7, 2012. http://online.wsj.com/news/articles/SB10001424052702303506404577446832178537716.

Kuper, Simon. "Michael Lewis and Billy Beane Talk *Moneyball.*" *Slate* (from *The Financial Times),* November 13, 2011. http://www.slate.com/articles/sports/ft/2011/11/michael_lewis_and_billy_beane_talk_moneyball_.html.

"Knowledge Worker." *The Business English Dictionary, Cambridge Dictionaries Online.* Accessed June 9, 2014. http://dictionary.cambridge.org/us/dictionary/business-english/knowledge-worker.

La Monica, Paul. "Yahoo: Can This Tech Company Be Saved?" *The Buzz* (blog). *CNNMoney,* September 9, 2010. http://money.cnn.com/2010/09/09/technology/thebuzz/index.htm.

"Latest Bureau of Labor Statistics Employment Turnover Rates." *WebExit Online Exit Interviews improve employee retention.* N.p., n.d. Web. August 8, 2013. http://www.nobscot.com/survey/.

"Leading Through Connections." *IBM 2012 Global CEO Study.* N.p., n.d. Web. November 28, 2013. http://www-935.ibm.com/services/us/en/c-suite/ceostudy2012/.

Lee, Edmund. "*New York Times* Sells *Boston Globe* to John Henry for $70M." *Bloomberg,* August 4, 2013. http://www.bloomberg.com/news/2013–08–03/new-york-times-sells-boston-globe-to-john-henry-for-70m.html.

Leff, Lisa. "Fortune 500 Firms Expand Gay Rights Support after DOMA Decision." *The Huffington Post,* December 8, 2013. http://www.huffington-post.com/2013/12/08/fortune-500-gay-rights_n_4409466.html.

Levine, Rick, Christopher Locke, Doc Searls, and David Weinberger. *The Cluetrain Manifesto.* www.cluetrain.com/book/index.html.

Lewis, Michael. *The Big Short: Inside the Doomsday Machine.* New York: W.W. Norton, 2010.

"List of countries by GDP (nominal)." *Wikipedia.* Wikimedia Foundation, n.d. Web. June 15, 2014, http://en.wikipedia.org/wiki/List_of_countries_by_GDP_(nominal).

Locke, Christopher. *The Cluetrain Manifesto 10th Anniversary Edition.* New York: Basic Books, 2009.

Loftness, Vivian. *Health, Productivity and the Triple Bottom Line.* Center for Building Performance and Diagnostics, Carnegie Mellon University, February 1, 2008. http://www.cmu.edu/iwess/workshops/absic_dec_2007/BIDS%20ABSIC_FINAL%202007.pdf.

Maher, Jeff. "Forbes: 64% of Employees Wasting Time at Work." *News10.net,* September 13, 2013. http://on.news10.net/1eP4XFG.

Mander, Jerry. *Four Arguments for the Elimination of Television.* New York: William Morrow, 1978.

"Marissa Mayer on Women in Tech—CNET News—YouTube." *YouTube.* N.p., July 26, 2012. Web. August 8, 2013. http://youtu.be/prXCrcV-T3M.

"Marketing Myopia." *Wikipedia.* Last modified March 30, 2014. http://en.wikipedia.org/wiki/Marketing_myopia.

Martin, Roger. "Rotman Design Challenge 2013—Keynote by Roger Martin." YouTube video, 11:42. Posted April 5, 2013. https://www.youtube.com/watch?v=fNgBRcp0u7w.

McArdle, Megan. "Your Office Chair Is Killing You." *Bloomberg Business Week.* Bloomberg, April 29 2010. http://www.businessweek.com/magazine/content/10_19/b4177071221162.htm.

Merchant, Nilofer. "Sitting Is the Smoking of Our Generation." *HBR Blog Network* (blog), *Harvard Business Review,* January 14, 2013. http://blogs.hbr.org/2013/01/sitting-is-the-smoking-of-our-generation/.

"Millennials." *Wikipedia.* Last modified June 6, 2014. http://en.wikipedia.org/wiki/Millennials.

"Milken Institute Study: Chronic Disease Costs U.S. Economy More Than $1 Trillion Annually." *Partnership to Fight Chronic Disease.* N.p., n.d. Web. February 12, 2014. http://www.fightchronicdisease.org/media-center/releases/milken-institute-study-chronic-disease-costs-us-economy-more-1-trillion-annual.

Miller, M. Rex. *The Millennium Matrix: Reclaiming the Past, Reframing the Future of the Church.* San Francisco: Jossey-Bass, 2004.

Miller, M. Rex. *The Commercial Real Estate Revolution: Nine Transforming Keys to Lowering Costs, Cutting Waste and Driving Change in a Broken Industry.* Hoboken, NJ: Wiley, 2009.

Miller, Rex, Dean Strombom, Mark Iammarino, and Bill Black. *The Commercial Real Estate Revolution: Nine Transforming Keys to Lowering Costs, Cutting Waste, and Driving Change in a Broken Industry.* Hoboken, NJ: Wiley, 2009.

"Moneyball (2011)—Quotes." *The Internet Movie Database.* Accessed June 10, 2014. http://www.imdb.com/title/tt1210166/quotes.

Monica, Paul R. La. "The Buzz: Is Yahoo still relevant among tech companies?—September 9, 2010." *CNNMoney—Business, financial and personal finance news.* N.p., September 10, 2010. http://money.cnn.com/2010/09/09/technology/thebuzz/index.htm.

National Diabetes Information Clearinghouse. "National Diabetes Statistics, 2011: Fast Facts." Last modified September 9, 2013. http://diabetes.niddk.nih.gov/dm/pubs/statistics/#fast.

"New Data on Autism Spectrum Disorders." *Centers for Disease Control and Prevention.* March 29, 2012. http://www.cdc.gov/Features/CountingAutism/.

Newberg, Andrew, and Mark Walden. "The Most Dangerous Word in the World." *Words Can Change Your Brain* (blog), *Psychology Today,* July 31, 2012. http://www.psychologytoday.com/blog/words-can-change-your-brain/201207/the-most-dangerous-word-in-the-world.

"Number of Personal Computers in the US." *Number of Personal Computers in the US.* N.p., n.d. Web. March 2, 2014. http://hypertextbook.com/facts/2004/DianeEnnefils.shtml.

"Number of TV Households and Percentage of USA Homes with Television—1950 to 1978." *Television History the First 75 Years,* accessed June 9, 2014. http://www.tvhistory.tv/Annual_TV_Households_50-78.JPG.

"Obesity and Overweight." *World Health Organization,* May 2014. http://www.who.int/mediacentre/factsheets/fs311/en/.

"Obesity in the United States." *Wikipedia,* last modified May 28, 2014. http://en.wikipedia.org/wiki/Obesity_in_the_United_States.

O'Reilly, Charles A., III, and Michael L. Tushman. "The Ambidextrous Organization." *Harvard Business Review,* April 2004. http://hbr.org/2004/04/the-ambidextrous-organization.

Palmer, Brian. "Is It Better to See a Younger Doctor or an Older Doctor?" *Slate,* December 11, 2012. http://www.slate.com/articles/health_and_science/explainer/2012/12/are_younger_doctors_better_should_old_doctors_be_tested_for_lack_of_competence.html.

Partnership to Fight Chronic Disease. "Milken Institute Study: Chronic Disease Costs U.S. Economy More Than $1 Trillion Annually." October 2, 2007. http://www.fightchronicdisease.org/media-center/releases/milken-institute-study-chronic-disease-costs-us-economy-more-1-trillion-annual.

Paterson, Tony. "Come Hell or High Water." *The Independent,* July 18, 2009. http://www.independent.co.uk/sport/general/sailing/hell-and-high-water-the-fastnet-disaster-1748093.html.

Peña, William, and Steven Parshall. *Problem Seeking: An Architectural Programming Primer.* 4th ed. New York: Wiley, 2001.

"Peter Drucker." *Wikipedia.* Last modified May 13, 2014. http://en.wikipedia.org/wiki/Peter_Drucker.

Phelan, Karen. *I'm Sorry I Broke Your Company: When Management Consultants Are the Problem, Not the Solution.* San Francisco, CA: Berrett-Koehler Publishers, 2013.

Pine, B. Joseph, II, and James H. Gilmore. *The Experience Economy: Work Is Theatre & Every Business a Stage.* Boston: Harvard Business School Press, 1999.

Pink, Daniel H. "Free Agent Nation." *Fast Company,* December 1997/January 1998. http://www.fastcompany.com/33851/free-agent-nation.

Pollock, David C., and Ruth E. Van Reken. *Third Culture Kids Growing Up among Worlds.* Rev., ed., Boston: Nicholas Brealey Pub., 2009.

"Presenteeism." *Investopedia.* Accessed June 9, 2014. http://www.investopedia.com/terms/p/presenteeism.asp.

Ranii, David. "Red Hat Workers Bring Energy to New Downtown Raleigh Headquarters." NewsObserver.com, June 24, 2013. http://www

.newsobserver.com/2013/06/24/2986664/red-hat-workers-bring-energy-to.html#storylink=cpy.

Ransdell, Eric. "Work Different." *Fast Company,* May 31, 1999. http://www.fastcompany.com/37259/work-different.

Reimer, Jeremy. "Total Share: Personal Computer Market Share 1975–2010." *Jeremy Blog,* December 7, 2012. http://jeremyreimer.com/m-item.lsp?i=137.

Ries, Eric. *The Lean Startup: How Today's Entrepreneurs Use Continuous Innovation to Create Radically Successful Businesses.* New York: Crown Business, 2011.

Rousmaniere, John. *Fastnet, Force 10: The Deadliest Storm in the History of Modern Sailing.* New York: Norton, 1980.

"S&P 500." *Wikipedia.* Last modified June 9, 2014. http://en.wikipedia.org/wiki/S%26P_500.

Savitz, Eric. "Web 2.0: Ballmer Says Microsoft 'Lucky' Yahoo Said No." *Forbes,* October 18, 2011. http://www.forbes.com/sites/ericsavitz/2011/10/18/web-2-0-ballmer-says-microsoft-lucky-yahoo-said-no/.

Shirky, Clay. *Here Comes Everybody: The Power of Organizing without Organizations.* New York: Penguin, 2008.

"Sound Business Lessons from Harley's Top Marketer." *The Cayman Islands Journal.* January 6, 2010. http://www.compasscayman.com/journal/2010/01/06/Sound-business-lessons-from-Harley's-top-marketer/.

Stamberg, Susan. "Columbus, Ind.: A Midwestern Mecca of Architecture." *NPR: Destination Art,* July 31, 2012. http://www.npr.org/2012/08/04/157675872/columbus-ind-a-midwestern-mecca-of-architecture.

"State of the Global Workplace 2013." *Gallup.* N.p., n.d. http://www.gallup.com/strategicconsulting/164735/state-global-workplace.aspx.

Sterling, Bruce. "Superlinear Cities." *Wired,* July 27, 2011. http://www.wired.com/beyond_the_beyond/2011/07/superlinear-cities/.

Stoddard, Nat. *Chief Executive Magazine The Costs of CEO Failure Comments.* N.p., December 1, 2008. http://chiefexecutive.net/the-costs-of-ceo-failure.

Strauss, William, and Neil Howe. *Generations: The History of America's Future, 1584 to 2069.* New York: William Morrow, 1991.

"Taking the Long View." *Schumpeter* (blog). *The Economist,* November 24, 2012. http://www.economist.com/news/business/21567062-pursuit-shareholder-value-attracting-criticismnot-all-it-foolish-taking-long.

"The Marshmallow Challenge." Accessed June 9, 2014. http://marshmallow-challenge.com/Welcome.html.

"Third Place." *Wikipedia.* Last modified May 10, 2014. http://en.wikipedia.org/wiki/Third_place.

Tierny, John. "From Cubicles, Cry for Quiet Pierces Office Buzz." *New York Times,* May 19, 2012. http://www.nytimes.com/2012/05/20/science/when-buzz-at-your-cubicle-is-too-loud-for-work.html?pagewanted=all.

Toffler, Alvin. *Future Shock.* New York: Random House, 1970.

U.S. Centers for Disease Control and Prevention. "New Data on Autism Spectrum Disorders." March 29, 2012. http://www.cdc.gov/Features/CountingAutism/.

"Valve Employee Handbook." http://media.steampowered.com/apps/valve/Valve_NewEmployeeHandbook.pdf.

Vanderkam, Laura. "Stop Checking Your Email, Now." *Fortune,* October 8, 2014. http://management.fortune.cnn.com/2012/10/08/stop-checking-your-email-now/.

"Vertigo in Aviation."*AviationKnowledge.* Accessed June 9, 2014. http://aviationknowledge.wikidot.com/aviation:vertigo-in-aviation.

"Waterfall Model." *Wikipedia.* Last modified June 9, 2014. http://en.wikipedia.org/wiki/Waterfall_model.

Weber, Laurence. "Bad at Their Jobs, and Loving It—At Work—WSJ." *At Work RSS.* N.p., March 27, 2013. http://blogs.wsj.com/atwork/2013/03/27/bad-at-their-jobs-and-loving-it/?mod=WSJ_Management_At_Work.

"White-Collar." *Dictionary.com.* Accessed June 9, 2014. http://dictionary.reference.com/browse/white-collar.

"Wicked Problem." *Wikipedia.* Last modified May 19, 2014. http://en.wikipedia.org/wiki/Wicked_problem.

Wolman, David. "Facebook, Twitter Help the Arab Spring Blossom." *Wired,* May 19, 2014. http://www.wired.com/2013/04/arabspring/.

"Your Office Chair Is Killing You." *BloombergBusinessweek,* April 29, 2010. http://www.businessweek.com/magazine/content/10_19/b4177071221162.htm.

Yung, Ed. "Celera: A Unique Approach to Genome Sequencing." *Bio-computing. Human Genome Project, Act II: Celera's Approach.* 2006. http://www.ocf.berkeley.edu/~edy/genome/celera.html.

Zichermann, Gabe. "The Six Rules of Gamification—Gamification Co." *Gamification Co.* N.p., n.d. http://www.gamification.co/2011/11/29/the-six-rules-of-gamification/.

Zichermann, Gabe. "Keynote Gabe Zichermann at TNW2012 | The Next Web," *The Next Web.* YouTube video, 35:43. Posted April 27, 2012. http://youtu.be/UdUclLUDxRg.

ACKNOWLEDGMENTS

Writing is normally very solitary work. *Change Your Space* was different by design. The Case4Space group of more than 30 leaders took an active role in the research and creation of this book. So, naturally, our first effort to write the story carried several focal themes. But Richard Narramore, Wiley's Senior Editor, guided us to our sweet spot. I am grateful for his willingness to push back and help us to focus on the story that has not been told before.

Case4Space began with Mabel Casey and Mark Konchar. I want to thank them for their willingness to support and coauthor this book. From the beginning they knew that the changes in the marketplace are forcing all of us to rethink and reimagine the workplace.

I thank Dave Radcliffe at Google. His early support for our project created a tipping point that moved us forward and into collaboration with other leaders. He also allowed Chris Coleman to journey with us. Chris often challenged many of our early assumptions about the workplace. Thanks, Chris.

John McColl at Cousins Properties gave strong support to our research. It helped the team, and this book, to have a developer on board. Thank you, John.

Bob Fox and Sabret Flocos with FOX Architects and Phil Bernstein with Autodesk were early and eager supporters. Phil also allowed Erin Rae Hoffer to participate as a core team thought leader. I thank all of you for your early and strong support.

Michael Lagocki came on board as our graphic scribe, but he also helped to design and facilitate our events. Michael, we deeply appreciate your work.

We expanded the MindShift model that we developed for the previous book, *The Commercial Real Estate Revolution*. I thank the original members of MindShift who came on board with Case4‑Space: Craig Janssen, Markku Allison, Ray Lucchesi, and Mabel Casey and her team. In addition to the MindShift associates, our core team for *Change Your Space* comprised Dick Bayer, Paula Bedford, Carrie Meinberg Burke, Kevin Burke, John Coates, Patrick Donnelly, Steven Elliott, Chuck Hardy, Bill Hollett, Cathy Hutchison, Barbara Jackson, Richard Kadzis, Michelle Kleyla, Mark Pleskow, Celeste Tell, and Arol Wolford. I thank all of you for your hard and very creative work.

After our second summit, someone pointed out that no one in the room was under 40! So we recruited several Millennials for the work. Their arrival in Chicago was like a first prom. The Millennials huddled at one end of the room and the rest of us gathered at the other end. Once the "music" started, they began to mix with us. They ended up contributing like true thought leaders. Thank you, Julie De Rosi, Lindsey Etterbeek, Travis Gates, Janet Gonzalez, Daniel Homrich, Katherine Molyson, Trey Ryan, Josh Schierbeek, Haley Smith, Katherine Tracey, and Tim Wakley.

I also thank the experts, advisors, and coaches who helped us meet and interview visionary leaders and visit incredible workplaces. Dean Stanberry, with Jones Lang LaSalle, opened the door for us to meet at the National Renewable Energy Laboratory in Golden, Colorado for our first official summit. Chris Hood, managing director for workplace innovation at CBRE, was very generous with open support and willingness to share.

Jack Hess, executive director for the Institute for Coalition Building in Columbus, Indiana, went to extraordinary lengths to help me capture the story of Cummins Diesel and their partnership with Columbus. He arranged interviews with Mark Gerstel, retired as vice president of community affairs for Cummins, Inc., and with city leaders John Burnett, Tracey Souza, and Sherry Stark. He also introduced me to Will Miller (J. Irwin Miller's son); Mike Reed, principal of the Signature Academy; and David Boatwright, executive director of global facilities and real estate at Cummins, Inc. Thank you, Jack.

I also thank colleagues from TAG Consulting who participated in some of the summits: Jim Osterhaus, Mike Marino, Kurt Andre, David Jurkowski, and Sean Hamon.

Kyle Davy, author of the book *Value Redesigned,* hosted an afternoon on his back patio for Ray Lucchesi, Andreas Phelps, and me to explore the shifting paradigms on value in the workplace. Thanks, Kyle.

Randy Thompson, with Cushman Wakefield and a talented writer, offered to read, edit, and comment on the first draft of the book.

I also thank other experts and advisors for their generosity and assistance: David Dillard, Kate Lister, Roland Openshaw, Bob Johansen, Dave Gray, Richard Hayes, Ed Nolan, Bob Theodore, Laverne Deckert, Jay Gary, Jared Homrich, Darren Smith, Susan Stucky, and Greg Wellman.

We were all helped by, and are grateful for, those who shared their journeys and company stories: Lew Horne, Martha Johnson, David Boatwright, Jay Steimer, Ken Schmidt, Al Manshun, Will Miller, Mike Reed, Shanti Pless, Louise Dixon Chapman, Mason Awtry, Myron Albert, and Jack Yates.

I also thank the Pancake House Roundtable. After 13 years, they still provide a place where I can check in and check my sanity. Thank you, David Dillard, Roy Wilshire, Greg Wilkinson, Jon Herrin, and Coy Talley.

Evernote, LinkedIn, and Google Docs have revolutionized how work and collective efforts can be launched and coordinated. I'm thankful for those fine tools. I also thank Travis Gates and NICHE Creative for developing the website and our social media strategy.

When my original editor had to pull away from the project partway into the book, I turned to an old friend, Ed Chinn at Cool River Pub. Besides his editing work, he became a true partner in the project. Thanks, Ed.

Finally, I thank my wife, Lisa, who thought I was going to be finished in a few months. Once plan B and the rewrite surfaced she saw me routinely get up early and head for Starbucks and then come home after dinner. She occasionally asked, "When do I get my husband back?" I also thank my three children, Michelle, Nathan, and Tyler. They supported the mission and even contributed to a few stories.

The support from Haworth, Balfour Beatty, Google, Cousins Properties, and FOX Architects allowed me to dedicate two years to this vision. I am deeply grateful that you made this work possible.

I am also grateful that social media and the digital revolution have made it surprisingly simple to generate dramatic change in the workplace. I am profoundly grateful for the opportunity to shape the future of something that is vital to everyone—the story and value of work. My son Nathan really summed it all up: "Dad, you really seem like you are having fun."

Thank you to everyone who supported and joined this journey. Yes, it was fun.

INDEX